# WHO WROTE THIS SH*T?!

The Rise and Fall and Rise of a Madison Avenue Lunatic

*by Steve Penchina*

Channel V Books
New York

**V**

Channel V Books
New York

Copyright © 2015 by Channel V Books

Published in the United States by Channel V Books,
a division of Channel V Media, New York, NY.
www.ChannelVBooks.com

Channel V Books and its logo are trademarks of Channel V Media.

ISBN 978-0-9826074-1-1

Library of Congress Control Number: 2014956824

Library of Congress subject headings:
Business & Economics : Advertising & Promotion
Humor : Topic - Business & Professional
Biography & Autobiography : Personal Memoirs

PRINTED IN THE UNITED STATES OF AMERICA

10 9 8 7 6 5 4 3 2 1

First Edition

*for my baby*

*Acknowledgments*

Gretel Going, Ron Louie, Koren Blair, Dr. Evelyn Rappoport,
George Lois, Lew Alpern, Jerry Della Femina, Edit Barry, John Barry,
Doug Wood, Dr. Richard Firestone, Dianne Penchina,
Avery McCarthy, Nicole Taron, Dr. Susan Clarvit, Arty Selkowitz,
Josh Penchina, Randy Shulman, Arik Markus, Daniel Penchina

This is a true story.

Some names have been changed to protect the not-so-innocent.

*"The chief enemy of creativity is good sense."*
— PABLO PICASSO

# CONTENTS

# PROLOGUE

THE FIRST SHOTS of Advertising's Creative Revolution were fired by Bill Bernbach of the agency Doyle Dane Bernbach, marking the beginning of the end of the colorless and condescending advertising of the fifties.

With his transcendent campaigns for Volkswagen ("Lemon" and "Think small."), Avis ("We're number 2. We try harder."), and Levy's rye bread ("You don't have to be Jewish to love Levy's."), this creative visionary single-handedly turned Madison Avenue on its head.

What followed over the next two and a half decades was the perfect storm of creativity: powerful, one-of-a-kind concepts combined with riveting visuals, a fearless determination to avoid traditionalist thinking and the emergence of a new breed of agency owner who didn't blink when confronted with the rigid clients of yesteryear.

**Lemon.**

Vintage Doyle Dane Bernbach ad (c. 1960)

Gone were the stuffy suits depicted in *Mad Men*; and in came scrappy, creative rock stars whose sights were clearly fixed on only one thing: generating the next mind-blowing ad. These relentless upstarts challenged the long-standing agency model, giving birth to a new kind of agency, "the creative boutique," where creative decisions were based on the gut and not on some soulless testing technique.

More inspired advertising came out of this period than any other in history. And I was right there in the thick of it, cutting my teeth, learning copywriting and art direction from the most gifted people to ever hunt and peck on a Royal typewriter or lay out an ad with a black Magic Marker.

Creative departments were crackling with electricity.

We sensed we were part of something special, so it only made sense for us to dedicate every waking moment to the cause. Hell, even sex took a back seat to nailing the perfect headline (well, once anyway).

Of course the work we produced wouldn't have been possible without entrepreneurial clients who had the chutzpah to roll the dice on ideas so compelling they remain etched into our psyches 50 years later. Ads like Alka-Seltzer's "I can't believe I ate the whole thing," Xerox's "The Monk," Rolls-Royce's "At 60 miles an hour the loudest noise in this new Rolls-Royce comes from the electric clock" and FedEx's "When it absolutely, positively has to be there overnight."

*Who wrote this sh*t?!* is not only an advertising story, it's my story. How a young wannabe art director from Great Neck, Long Island, beat the Vietnam War by beating the draft and then devoted the rest of his life to writing ads on Madison Avenue.

I didn't make it easy on myself. I lost count of how many times I was fired, how many people I offended (sometimes unwittingly, usually intentionally) or how many therapists I had to see along the way. But I did make it. And I managed to keep track of the good stuff: winning 19 Clio Awards, being honored by *The New York Times* and *Advertising Age* for creating one of the "50 Best Commercials Ever Made," having my work included in the "Top 10 Super Bowl Commercials of All Time," opening my own shop (and subsequently selling it to advertising giant DMB&B), writing one-liners with Rodney Dangerfield, working with Don Imus, Howard Stern, Joe Pesci and William H. Macy, and helping the number two computer company, Burroughs (now Unysis), declare war on IBM with a single provocative tagline.

I was privileged to have been a part of this "Golden Age of Advertising," when the creative bar rose to heights never before seen. And if, as they say, past is prologue, then the daring, imaginative and innovative thinking that fueled Bernbach's Creative Revolution will return for a killer second act.

# THE 7:39
# FROM GREAT NECK

*I was stranded on a desert island in the middle of nowhere, terrified that I was alone. Suddenly, off in the distance I could make out a female figure running towards me. As she drew closer, I recognized the indelible shape of Raquel Welch in a tattered bikini, swinging a six-pack of Rheingold beer. Excited to see another human being, she threw herself at me. I pulled her firmly against my taut body and gently kissed the window of the Long Island Rail Road train.*

"Gimmeafuckinbreak, ya piece-a-shit train!" I screamed at the piece of shit train.

Yet again, the herky-jerky railroad car had jolted me out of my fourth All-Time-Favorite Dream. (All-Time-Favorite Dreams 1-3: also Raquel Welch.)

But at least it woke me up long enough to catch a glimpse of all the new billboards posted at the stations along the way to Manhattan. I was mesmerized by their stark honesty and wit. They were boldly calling attention to the very thing most ads aimed to cover up—flaws, weaknesses and stigmas about the brand: An American Indian having a sandwich on Jewish rye reassures non-Jews that they, too, can enjoy real Jewish rye bread. An automobile company calling its own car a "lemon" purposefully draws attention to a 1-in-10,000 flaw in the glove

One of the first ads for VW that put Bill Bernbach on the map.
Doyle Dane Bernbach (c.1960)

compartment, of all places, to illustrate its high manufacturing standards. And a major car rental company admitting to the world that they're "second best" instantaneously wins the empathy of, well, everyone else in the world who also isn't number one.

You don't have
to be Jewish

to love Levy's
*real Jewish Rye*

Who'd have thought? Using a Native American to sell Jewish rye bread!
Doyle Dane Bernbach (c.1960)

This was jaw-dropping stuff, fearless and sardonic headlines coupled with unadorned photography and design. It was as if they were speaking specifically to me, "Come hither." But then again, maybe that was Raquel...

These ads were worlds apart from the horrific advertising of the fifties. Advertising may have been in its infancy back then, but ads like Marlboro's "Before you scold me, Mom, make sure you light up a Marlboro." and Kellogg's "The harder a wife works, the cuter she looks!" were vapid and insulting to the very audience they were attempting to reach. It's hard to imagine advertising like that moved the consumer to buy anything.

Vintage Kellogg's cereal ad

It was fall of 1964. I was 20 years old and unfortunately still living at home. I commuted into New York City each day from Great Neck, Long Island, with my dad. He was going to work at his textiles company on the Lower East Side. I was on my way to New York University in Greenwich Village.

I cherished those train rides with my dad. I loved that he always bought me a round-trip ticket despite the fact that the fare had already been calculated into my allowance. He would wait with me on the filthy Eighth Avenue subway platform until I caught the E train downtown to West 4th Street. It was a small thing but to me it was big.

I was in my junior year at NYU majoring in marketing and design. I had taken all of the requisite courses for my bachelor's degree and most were theoretical and often technical in nature. I had learned the ins and outs of sales, marketing, media, research, ad budgets, management and the like, but there was little emphasis placed on the creative side of the business. The artist in me felt shortchanged.

From the time I learned how to fingerpaint in kindergarten, I knew I had a flair for the fine arts. I credited any talent I had to my grandfather, who was a professional wood carver. I remember when I was about six, he would sit with me under my "tent" on my bed, sketching intricate drawings for hours. After that he would carve them in pieces of wood that would soon become legs for a fine dresser or the doors on an armoire. To me, the little kid, those woodcarvings were precious. To me, the adult, they're priceless.

Although I was still in college, I worried (a lot) that I wouldn't be able to translate my artistic talent into a career. But those ingenious, oversized ads I saw whizzing by the train every day showed me the way. I decided then and there that I would be the one creating those ads. *(Yup, I had it all figured out.)*

We clanked and clunked our way into the city early one morning. I was nursing a hangover left from a night of debauchery (starring too many Black Russians, a lot of pot and several relentless attempts to seduce every blonde shiksa in the Village). Like Alexander Portnoy in Philip Roth's *Portnoy's Complaint*, shiksas were my weakness. Or, more accurately, my obsession. The night had started out at The Bitter End on Bleecker and ended up…Christ, I have no idea where. The crowded, bumpy train ride wasn't helping my condition.

Even though my head was pounding like a tympani, I absolutely had to get to class that day. I was already in deep shit with Dr. Drucker, my marketing professor, and I couldn't afford to get in any deeper.

Peter Drucker was a big deal. He was a world-renowned marketing and management guru, who had written more than ten books on the subjects. In his most controversial book, *Concept of the Corporation*, he famously said that General Motors didn't know their ass from third base when it came to running a company or understanding what makes customers tick. (So maybe I paraphrased a bit.) Another important lesson I took away from him was that thick ketchup like Heinz is bogus. "Runny ketchup is the best ketchup in the world," he informed our class. I don't think I could have made it through life without that golden nugget of knowledge.

He and I didn't get on too well. He was so straight-laced, he made Mr. Rogers look like a Hell's Angel. He had already kicked me out of class a million times for wisecracking. But what really pissed him off was when I cast him in the starring role.

"Dr. Drucker," I interrupted him one afternoon. "How much money would you make off your books if they weren't required reading for all of your students?"

The class went nuts.

"I do not appreciate your sense of humor, Mr. Penchina. You can leave now and wait for me in my office."

*So what else is new?* I thought as I sauntered out to the sweet sound of wild cheers. I'd been waiting for teachers and other authority figures in their offices since I was in Hebrew school.

I got to Drucker's class late that day after stopping for a falafel at Mamoun's on MacDougal. He was in the middle of telling the class that we had to write a term paper on a current marketing phenomenon. The paper would account for 50 percent of our grade. Thanks to the advertising department of the Long Island Rail Road, I decided to write my paper on Doyle Dane Bernbach, the agency responsible for most of those great ads. I focused on the founder, Bill Bernbach, who was the driving force behind advertising's "Creative Revolution" in the sixties, seventies and into the eighties.

Before Bernbach burst onto the scene, the big agency approach to advertising had little to do with creativity. Accounts were won mostly on restricted golf courses or over the proverbial three-martini lunch at the 21 Club with the good ol' boys from Princeton and Dartmouth.

Advertising in the fifties was driven by bullshit research and by account executives who thought their job was to simply take orders from the client, then rush back to the agency to dictate their hyper-rational concepts to the creative department. Lacking any creativity or originality, this tired approach only managed to get the point across through repetition: repetition within the ad (painful for the consumer) and repetition through endless and costly media buys (awesome for the agency).

Anacin commercials were famous for this, notably the ones where crudely animated hammers bang against some poor guy's head while the word "headache" flashes on and off the screen. If you didn't have a headache before you saw the commercial, you most certainly had one after. (Now that's strategy!)

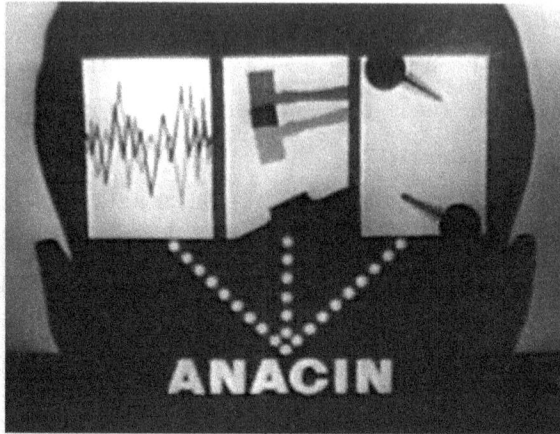

Anacin uses repitition to pound it's point into TV viewers' heads. (c. 1959)

If rules were meant to be broken, then Bernbach was a sledgehammer. Unlike those behind the insipid campaigns of yesteryear, Bernbach believed that advertising could be warm, human and even (God forbid!) humorous. His ads celebrated the imperfection that others sought to conceal. And he credited his audience's intelligence rather than pandering to the lowest common denominator.

Bernbach simply did not subscribe to conventional wisdom which dictated that in order for consumers to get the point, print ads had to have a Godzilla-sized product shot with an equally massive logo and TV commercials had to show the product an obscene number of times.

Art directors and copywriters, he insisted, would have a much bigger role to play in his Creative Revolution. He challenged his own creative staff to come up with original and memorable ways of selling a product or service. His hallmarks were gentle persuasion and wit. He wanted the consumer to relate to the message in a visceral, emotional way, not just a rational one.

I totally identified with Bernbach's philosophy. I was born for his rebellious, break-the-rules approach. I intuitively understood that the key to communicating effectively was to speak to the consumer in a clear, simple, human voice, as if they were, um, human. The idea, I thought, was to get the audience to think, *That's me. That's my problem. That's exactly how I feel. This company gets me–I gotta buy that.* I would sooner have sold encyclopedias door to door than work on those hackneyed campaigns of the fifties.

Thank God for Bill Bernbach!

Returning home late from school one night, I was greeted at the door by my father, who was not wearing his usual happy face. He had just received a letter from the dean of the School of Commerce stating that I had been placed on probation. Despite giving me an "A" on my Bernbach paper, Drucker apparently decided he had taken enough of my crap and gave me an "Incomplete" for my final grade. The sonofabitch simply didn't have a humor chip in his brain.

Together with the rest of my grades, the overall picture wasn't sterling. It also didn't help that the school found out that the NYPD had been called in at five o'clock in the morning to break up a small riot that broke out at my AEPi fraternity house. I had thrown a TGIF party and half of my dorm turned out. Everything was going great until two local hookers wandered in. All hell broke loose when they decided to give away their well-honed talents, gratis. A line of raucous students formed halfway around Tenth Street. When the dean heard about the cops, he also placed the entire fraternity on probation. And despite the blast everyone had, my "all for one, one for all" fraternity brothers turned against me like a Russian spy and booted me out.

My dad was fuming, waving the letter in the air and pacing around the living room deciding what to do with me. It was reminiscent of all the times I'd sat in the principal's office waiting to find out how much detention I was going to get.

"I'm cutting off your allowance," he finally blurted out.

*That's not so bad,* I thought.

"And starting now," he went on, "you're going to make a major contribution to your tuition. I suggest you get a job, pronto.

*Okay, that's bad.*

# 2 FROM THE PRESIDENT OF THE UNITED STATES: "GREETINGS..."

I was honestly less concerned about getting a job than I was about the probation. If I were kicked out of school, I would lose my "2-S" college draft deferment, be immediately re-classified "1-A" and drafted into the Army, which not only meant the world as I knew it would be over but also that I'd be shipped to Vietnam.

*That would be very fucking bad.*

It was now 1966, the height of the Vietnam War. LBJ and his genius Defense Secretary Robert McNamara were drafting up to 40,000 young men a month to fight in a napalm-riddled jungle 8,000 miles from The Bitter End. I was certain that if I were sent to Vietnam, I'd be impaled on a poisoned bamboo stake along the Ho Chi Minh Trail or shot between the eyes by some Viet Cong sniper who'd been hiding in a tunnel his whole life, dining on spiders, just waiting for Private Penchina to waltz by.

"Hi, there. Nice to see you," I could imagine him saying in Vietnamese. Then…

*SSSSPPPPLLLLAAAATTTT!* I'd go to the ground.

Going to Vietnam was simply not an option. I had to do something—and fast.

I, along with the great majority of young kids in this country, didn't want anything to do with the war; it was amoral and unnecessary. Not only were we defending a corrupt South Vietnam regime, the war was based on the "domino theory" of communist expansionism, which I didn't buy. As Muhammad Ali famously said at the time, "I ain't got no quarrel with them Viet Cong."

The controversial war tore a gaping hole in the fabric of our country. Those patriotic young men who believed in it ("America right or wrong.") fought bravely to the end against the savage and relentless Viet Cong and North Vietnamese Army. The Vietnam years were a palpably traumatic time for this nation—and for me personally. The war left a permanent scar on everyone that lived through it and did more than that to the 58,000 men and women who didn't.

The draft card I received before losing my 2-S college deferment in 1967

Watching Walter Cronkite bring the horrors of the war into my living room every night—along with all the political horseshit President Johnson was feeding us so the war could continue—turned me into a major non-believer and president-hater.

Five years later, the Ohio National Guard would be called in to quell an anti-war demonstration on the campus of Kent State University. In a hail of bullets and tear gas, four unarmed students were killed and nine were wounded (one paralyzed for life). It took all of thirteen seconds.

Gunned down? For demonstrating? On a college campus?

Our country had gone mad.


Faced with being drafted against my will into this god-awful conflict, I did what every other red-blooded American boy was doing at the time: I got a passport in case I had to flee to Canada, and spent every waking moment trying to get into the military reserves.

If I voluntarily enlisted in the Reserves or National Guard, I wouldn't be drafted into the regular Army—a much safer bet. Some of my friends took different routes to avoid the war. Two of them became sixth-grade teachers in the South Bronx. My soon-to-be brother-in-law, Bill Blumenthal, got a note from his doctor saying his case of eczema prevented him from serving. And it worked!

Unfortunately, thousands upon thousands of draft-age men had the same idea (about the reserves, not the eczema), which made it nearly impossible to find a Reserve or National Guard unit with an open slot.

But I had an ace card: my brother, Michael.

Two years older than me, he had already enlisted in the Air National Guard and was pulling every string he could to get me into his unit in Roslyn, Long Island. After months of daily panic attacks, I finally got a call from him.

"Where the fuck are you?!"

"Whadaya mean? I'm down in the basement playing ping-pong."

"Ping-pong?! Get your ass down here. Now!"

"Where?" I asked, taken by surprise.

"My guard station, putz. Ya know how to go, right?"

"Uh, yeah, I think so. Am I in?" I asked nervously.

"Just move your ass down here. You gotta take a bunch of tests. They've got one fuckin' slot. One. And I think it's something you can actually do. Type."

"Type. My specialty." I replied.

"See Sgt. Spells when you get here. He's up on the hill in the administration building. He's waiting for you."

"Thanks, man," I said.

"Don't thank me yet. Just get on your horse. We gotta figure out a way for you to pass the damn colorblind test, you blind bastard."

"Hey, seriously. I'm like a week away from getting drafted. You know Danny Weintraub from around the corner? He just received a letter from…"

He hung up. He didn't give a shit about Danny Weintraub.

I jumped into my Chevy Malibu and drove like a lunatic to Roslyn, a couple of towns over, to the Air National Guard Station. I sped up the hill and found Sgt. Spells in his office pushing papers. I started to introduce myself.

"No need for that," he interrupted, chuckling to himself. "There's no mistaking whose brother you are," he said, shaking my hand. "Nice to meet you, Steve." After a few minutes of small talk, he confirmed there was a single opening in the entire guard unit for what he called an Administrative Specialist.

"Can you type?" he asked, bluntly.

"I'm a whiz," I answered.

I stunk.

"Your brother's quite a character around here, but we love him. Not a bad cook either."

"Oh, yeah, he cooks all the time at home. You should try his egg drop soup. Better than Won Ton Garden."

"Okay," Sgt. Spells said. "Let's see if we can reunite you with Mike."

He opened his filing cabinet and pulled out several test booklets.

My heart was pounding. All I'd thought about the past year was how I could avoid getting drafted. Very few of my friends were getting into reserve units. I knew guys who moved to another state in order to have a chance.

If my brother were able to pull this off, I would be paying him back well into the next century. But it would be worth every leaf I had to rake, snowflake I had to shovel or car I would have to loan or bequeath to him.

I got a 65% on the mechanical test. (If I'm representative, no wonder there were no Jews in the motor pool.) I passed the mental exams with flying colors, and I tested at the 99th percentile on the administrative test, which was where the opening was. All that stood between me and a body bag was a quick physical and the damn colorblind test. My brother's reserve unit, the 106th Tactical Control Group, was a radar support unit; being colorblind was unacceptable.

I was told to report to Sgt. Mendoza, the paunchy, jovial, Hispanic base medic who was a good friend of Michael's. He administered the physical and I passed, no sweat. All that remained now was the colorblind test. I looked around. Where the hell is Michael? He said he was going to help me pass this thing.

Just as Mendoza was about to start, Michael burst into the infirmary.

"Hey Sarge," he sing-songed to Mendoza, dangling a bucket of fresh, warm fried chicken in front of his nose. "I've got a little present for you."

As the base chef, my brother was one of the most popular men in the guard station. He would barter food for almost anything: tune-ups, lube jobs, free bridge passes, stamps, cassette tapes, light bulbs, copy paper, you name it.

Mendoza lived for two things: zigzagging his ambulance through traffic at suicidal speeds...and food. Guess what his favorite dish was?

"Oh, what a nice gesture," said Mendoza. "Muchas gracías, amigo." He looked over at me with a thin smile. "Your brother's a saint."

While Mendoza was ogling the chicken, Michael walked over and whispered in my ear.

"Keep your eyes on me. Watch my fingers."

"Huh?"

"Just watch me, don't ask questions," he told me.

Mendoza grabbed the test book and pulled up a metal chair, his potbelly protruding over his GI belt.

"Are you ready, Leetle Penchina?" he asked. "All you have to do is tell me the number you see on the page."

"Can't wait," I replied, needing to go to the bathroom.

My brother stood directly behind Mendoza like an innocent bystander. He held up his hands and wiggled his fingers mouthing, "Watch me."

Mendoza flipped open the book. I couldn't make out a damn thing. Michael held up four fingers.

"What number do you see?" Mendoza queried, his stomach growling.

"Four," I said weakly.

"Good."

He turned the page.

My brother held up ten fingers.

"Now?"

"Ten," I said. "Uh, hmm. How 'bout now?"

Two fingers.

"Two," I answered, gaining confidence.

"Twenty-two. Fifty-five. Seventeen." And so on.

The last page was black and white, and even I could make out those numbers.

"Terminado. You passed." Mendoza declared, slamming down the book. "Congratulations, Leetle Penchina, you're one of us now. Have a chicken wing."

Michael gave me a thumbs-up and quickly headed out the door. "See you guys at mess. Guess what we're havin' today?"

Three weeks later, I was on a chartered jet to the Lackland Air Force Training Center in San Antonio, Texas, or, as everyone referred to it, the armpit of the United States, for basic training.

To say that I wasn't too keen on dealing with authority figures and taking orders all day long was an understatement of national security proportions.

The first week, I got into a fight with my squad leader, a 6'6" gung-ho former Texas Longhorn defensive back. He gave me unrelenting shit over being late for breakfast each morning. Hey, it wasn't my fault. Who can take a shit at 4:30 in the morning with a drill sergeant screaming in your ear, no door on the stall, and no Playboys to read? If that weren't enough, I felt like throwing up from the smell of bacon fat that hung in the air. Alas, the Air Force didn't offer a kosher meal plan.

My entire life, I was always finding trouble. Not just getting into it but actively seeking it out. I can't tell you how many fights I'd been in: fights on the basketball court, the football field, waiting in line at the movies... I even got into a fight for hitting on some jealous motorcycle gang member's fiancée. Man, no sense of humor.

Anyway, this football schmuck had finally lost his patience with me. Standing in the chow line one morning, he shoved his heavy, metal flashlight into my solar plexus. After I caught my breath, I grabbed the flashlight out of his hand and smacked him over the head with it, sending shards of shiny metal flying everywhere.

Naturally, the drill sergeant didn't see the instigation; he only saw me retaliate (foreshadowing perhaps what would become a recurring life theme). My punishment was to march up and down a drill field in full gear with heavy combat boots in the 104-degree, soaking-wet, Texas heat. For hours. The drill sergeant was dear enough to spend the entire time with me.

"Airman Penchina, stop bobbin' and weavin'."

"Airman Penchina, eyes straight."

"Airman Penchina, walk tall."

"Airman Penchina, pick up the pace."

"Airman Penchina, square those corners."

"Airman Penchina… Airman Penchina… Airman Penchina…"

*Christ. Enough with the "Airman Penchina." I'm the only one out here besides you, you dipshit, and I'm pretty fucking sure I know my last name.*

Next, I got into an argument with a short fuck-nuts Italian guy from Brooklyn who, while taking a break from his atrocious Frank Sinatra impersonations, liked to crack jokes about big, Jewish noses. Being in possession of one, I decided to push him through the screen door of our barracks. I paid for that with more demerits and assignment to a special detail.

I was made to carry huge, commercial air conditioners across the base to the officers' club a quarter of a mile away. After one trip I collapsed. I pulled one of the air conditioners from its big cardboard box, crawled in, curled into the fetal position and took a long nap. Could you blame me? I was exhausted from all the damn marching. Not surprisingly, I got caught. More trouble. More demerits. More marching.

I tested my superiors every way I could. I snuck off the base to make phone calls. I feigned illness so I could skip out on my work details. I hung out in the air-conditioned infirmary. I sat on the toilet and wrote letters to my girlfriend. I stole bread from the mess hall and hid it in between the individual window shade panels (next to the big sign that read *No food in barracks*). I slept on the floor underneath my bed so I wouldn't have to make it up in the morning. I paid two Iowa farmers in my squad two bucks each to spit-shine my shoes three times a week…

Needless to say, I absolutely hated the military. It was antithetical to everything I was about. I don't like being bossed around. I hate people yelling at me all the time (it reminds me of my mother). I like taking my sweet damn time. I'm not particularly neat. And I couldn't stand the obnoxious sound of clanging trash bin covers that woke us up at 4:30 every morning.

Finally, after six weeks, one day and three hours, I graduated basic training, demerits and all. They loaded those of us who were going back east on a military bus to the airport. It was the happiest day of my life. As we drove away, I stuck my head out the window and yelled out to all the remaining guys in my squad, who were standing neatly in line under the sweltering sun sweating their balls off.

"Bye-bye, y'all. Love to each and every one of ya! Especially you, you football prick with that nice, new scar on your bald fucking head."

I fulfilled the rest of my military obligation playing Hearts at the Roslyn Air National Guard station twenty minutes from my home.

By law everyone in the National Guard has to go on active duty for two weeks every summer for six years. Preparing for my first trip to Otis Air Force Base in Massachusetts, I was put in charge of loading a 1,000-pound safe onto the back of a truck. I recruited two other weekend warriors to help with the detail.

As we were trying to move the safe back, it began tipping over. I quickly jumped off the truck so I could steady it from the ground. It worked.

"Okay, guys, hold it right there. I'm getting back up. Don't anyone move!"

"AAAHHHHRRRRRRRRGGGGGGGGHHH!!!!!!"

The safe fell squarely on my left foot. I almost passed out from the pain. Lying on the ground with my foot swelling out of my boot, I shouted for Moe and Curly to call for Sgt. Mendoza, "And tell him to bring his ambulance!"

Two minutes later, Mendoza screeched to a halt six inches from my foot.

"Leetle Penchina!" Mendoza shouted, leaping from his ambulance. "What the fuck happened to you? Your hermano's either gonna kill me or estos cabrones."

After packing my foot in ice, Mendoza, Moe and Curly lifted me into the back of the ambulance. Mendoza took off like an Indy driver. His foot never came off the gas pedal. Siren screaming, he blew through every red light for the next 40 miles, all the way to St. Albans Naval Hospital in Queens.

"Don't you worry, Leetle Penchina," he shouted back to me. "I'll have you in hospital muy rapido. You comfortable back there?"

"I'm just great," I moaned. Every piece of equipment in the ambulance had fallen on top of me.

Thanks to the Two Stooges, I eventually got a medical (and honorable) discharge from the Air Force late in 1967. Not only does the u.s. Air Force not accept blind men, it's not wild about airmen with broken toes either.

# 3 HE'S IN THE CONFERENCE ROOM, BANGING YOUR WIFE

After sleeping 48 hours straight (my mom kept shaking me to make sure I wasn't dead), I returned home to complete my senior year at NYU.

I was ecstatic—back to pastrami on rye, good looking Jewish girls in tight mohair sweaters and the best pickup basketball in the city at West 3rd and Sixth Avenue.

Unfortunately, I still had to make good on my dad's tuition punishment. I went over to NYU's Placement Center and scoured the job postings for a part-time job in advertising. I eventually found something at an agency named Cunningham & Walsh. From the research I had done on my Bernbach paper, I knew they weren't a creative shop, but how bad could they be for just a few hours a day?

I had a short interview with the personnel lady, who told me the job was for a night watchman of sorts. They wanted "sturdy young men" to sit at the reception desks from 6:00 until 9:30 at night to accept deliveries, answer phone calls and deal with security issues. Needless to say, this wasn't what I had in mind while daydreaming on the Long Island Rail Road, but it was only a part-time job, and at least it was at an ad agency.

Cunningham & Walsh was not my kind of agency, though. It was right out of *The Man in the Gray Flannel Suit,* a traditional, old-line, backslapping, three-martini lunching, WASPy agency that got its accounts from connections not creativity. It was the polar opposite of Doyle Dane Bernbach, and it soon became very obvious that this kind of shop was not the perfect fit for a scrappy Jewish kid out of Long Island—or from Brooklyn, for that matter. But it turned out they needed two night guards, so a good friend of mine from NYU took the second position.

Streiter and I had met at Camp Tioga in the Poconos, where we were counselors for bratty nine year olds. We hated the kids, hated playing Capture the Flag, hated the crappy food and hated the head counselor, who hated us even more. The only way we kept our sanity was by playing dumb practical jokes on each other, a tradition we continued at Cunningham & Walsh.

I was assigned to the fourth-floor reception desk. Streiter was up on five. It wasn't long before we became bored out of our deranged heads. We weren't supposed to leave our posts, but with my ADD I didn't stand a chance of sitting still at my desk for three and a half hours every night. I would wander the halls looking at all the ads and storyboards. I would hang out in the art studio playing art director with T-squares, magic markers, HB pencils, and rubber cement, and fantasizing about filming commercials in Hollywood with gorgeous six-foot-tall models fighting over me. Despite the fact that Cunningham & Walsh's creative product was out of the dark ages, I still thought that being an art director sitting with my feet up on the desk, dreaming up ideas had to be the coolest job on the planet. I knew right then and there that this was what I wanted to do with my life. I didn't have to think about it. I didn't have to analyze it. Even at my relatively young age, I knew that when something feels right, it usually is. Instincts don't lie.

Every so often my phone would ring, and I'd scramble back to the reception desk to grab it. When not answering the phone, Streiter and I would crack each other up by making prank calls to one another.

"This is Tom Watson, chairman of IBM," Streiter would bark in his best stuffy, middle-aged CEO voice. "I need to speak to Mr. Cunningham, immediately!"

"You see, Mr. Watson," I'd answer. "The thing is, uh, Mr. Cunningham can't take your call right now because he's in the main conference room banging your wife."

One night, while I was down the hall stealing paper clips, I heard the phone ringing and quickly raced back to my desk. I just had an argument with my girlfriend, and I wasn't in a particularly good mood. I picked up the phone. Before he could speak, I blurted out, "Cut the crap, Streiter."

"Excuse me?"

"You heard me. Cut the shit. I don't want to fool around right now."

He paused for a moment and then said, "I don't know what the hell is going on here, but this is Robert Uihlein, president of Old Milwaukee Beer in Wisconsin."

*Streiter won't quit,* I thought. Despite my mood, I played along.

"Oh, Mr. Uihlein? Now I recognize your voice. How are you doing, sir?"

"Just dandy," he said impatiently. "Now, would you please put me through to…"

I interrupted. "You know, Bob. I can call you Bob, can't I? I don't recall ever mentioning this to you before, but you might be interested in knowing what I think of your beer."

Silence.

"I think it's piss-water. What do you say to that, Bobby?"

He cleared his throat. I kept going—I was on a roll.

"And you know what you can do with your piss-water beer, Bobby-boy? You can shove it up your big, fat, Wisconsin ass!"

I slammed the receiver down…just around the time Streiter waltzed in.

Fifteen minutes later, my illustrious career in corporate security came to a crashing end. Following a brief and profane phone call from

WHO WROTE THIS SH*T?!

Cunningham's president explaining that Robert Uihlein, president of Old Milwaukee, was more than a little angry about our phone call Streiter and I were fired on the spot.

Laughing like lunatics, we grabbed our coats and took the elevator down to the lobby. We gave ourselves high-fives. For what reason I have no idea.

Streiter took the subway back to Brooklyn. I lingered on the sidewalk for a while before walking out onto Madison Avenue. I stood alone in the middle of the street, the hot steam from the manhole covers enveloping me. For most people, the acrid smell bellowing up from the subways would be hard to take. For me, it was like perfume.

This was where I belonged.

# 4 PENCHINA'S BASEMENT AD AGENCY

So, my advertising career hadn't gotten off to the meteoric start I had dreamed of. (All-Time-Favorite Dream No. 5: Advertising career that gets off to meteoric start)

I graduated from NYU in January of 1968, a semester late thanks to the war. (A moment of self-awareness reminds me that it could have been worse.) As soon as I was handed my sheepskin, I got in touch with Lew Alpern, one of my old roommates.

During my junior year, Lew and I had shared an old, small, semi-dilapidated, brick-facing apartment with another neurotic soul, Chester Kates. Our apartment was at 55 West 11th Street in the West Village, halfway between Schrafft's on Fifth Avenue and Trudy Heller's, the city's first trendy discothèque, on Sixth. As if God himself was personally looking after my sex life, our apartment was smack-dab next door to Mills College, an upper-crust girls' school.

Gladys, a Clorox-bleach blonde and super-yenta from the Williamsburg section of Brooklyn, sat at an old-fashioned plug-in switchboard in the dimly-lit corner of our 1930s Art Deco lobby. Unapologetically nosy, Gladys carefully monitored everyone going in and out, from a position not dissimilar to my reception job at Cunningham & Walsh. When I walked in with a cute Mills College girl, Gladys would invariably greet me with, "Oh, Stevie, cawl yur motha. She cawlled twice already today." I would cringe.

Despite the burden of having to attend classes once in a while, Lew, Chet and I loved every minute together in that apartment. We each had our responsibilities.

Lew was in charge of teaching us how to bend or break every school rule so that Chet and I could graduate. A year ahead of us, he knew every little trick there was. We actually made it through college without ever seeing the inside of a lecture hall. He was ingenious; I was so proud of him.

Chet was in charge of pot and parties. I really only smoked at parties, and that was only if it would help me get laid. My neuroses and hypochondria had me convinced that smoking grass would be a quick leap to acid and PCP—or even worse, self-reflection.

I was in charge of food. No matter what time of day or night, when any one of us got hungry, my responsibility was to find us something to eat. Not just anything, though. Great, cheap food. (Cooking for ourselves was not an option. Not just because we hated it, but because we used the oven to store our gym stuff.)

John's Brick-Oven Pizza on Bleecker was the gold standard. I searched the city high and low for a restaurant that would compete. I found us a fabulous, greasy lo mein joint in Chinatown, appropriately named Hong Fat. For less than eight bucks, the three of us ate till they had to roll us out onto Mott Street.

Chet was game for anything that gave him an excuse to jump into his baby blue MG and cruise around town with the top down.

Between obsessing over his gorgeous, ball-busting girlfriend and his out-of-control weed habit, Chet was pretty much shot his senior year. I, too, was burnt out, but for a different reason. I had a 24-hour-a-day preoccupation with tall, blonde, Swedish models. Lew was different. He was far more cerebral and responsible than we were. With his elbow-patched, tweed sports jacket, cuffed khakis and Weejun penny loafers, he had the added benefit of appearing normal to the outside world.

But there was a lot more to my friend. He was a gifted writer—truly a writer's writer. He was the sports editor at the *NYU Violet,* the school newspaper. He could write circles around anyone there. The only thing he lacked was confidence. I used to beg him to hang out at Mills Tavern on University Place, drink dark ale with all the published authors and write the perfect novel. He chose advertising instead.

After graduating, he struggled for a while but eventually got a job as a junior copywriter on the Buick account at McCann Erickson. He promised to help me get into an agency when it was my turn up to bat. A month after graduation, I was kicking down his door.

I barged in on him one afternoon while he was absorbed in a big game of darts with two art directors. Apparently, this is how junior copywriters learn their craft. Lew asked me to take a seat for a few minutes while he finished the game. Two hours later, he gave me his undivided attention.

He dragged his dusty portfolio out from behind his office door and began telling me that there was only one way to break into the creative end of the business. That was to put together a speculative portfolio, commonly referred to as a "book." The book needed to contain approximately a dozen make-believe ads on several real products. He explained that I had to invent a new selling strategy for each, write a sharp, Bernbach-style headline, and then come up with a compelling visual idea.

"Sounds like fun," I replied.

"It's not," Lew responded definitively, stroking his red mustache. "It's months and months of hard work—way worse than school. Believe me, Steve, it's fucking torture." These cautionary words would stick in my head throughout the entire process.

"Months?!" I exclaimed. "I don't have months. I gotta get an apartment in the city. If I hear my mother vacuuming outside my door at 7 a.m. or asking me what she should defrost for dinner one more time, I'll shoot her or myself—either way I'm out of my misery."

"Sorry, big guy," Lew said. "I know I've spoiled you with all my shortcuts at school, but there's no getting around this. It's a long, miserable fucking road."

"Gotta be another way," I insisted.

"Nope," he maintained.

"The most important part of the process," he continued, "is thinking conceptually about the product message and writing a powerful, interesting headline, the cornerstone of every great ad."

"Wait a minute. Why do I need to write headlines? I want to be an art director. I can cut out a lot of time right there."

"No you can't," he said firmly. "Because you need to convey the concept of the ad beyond just describing the product. And the best way to accomplish that is to write a terrific headline. Even if you're an art director, you still gotta get the idea down on paper. Then you need to find a photograph or some other visual to round out the ad and bring it to life. Dem's the breaks, kiddo."

"Oy vey," I replied.

"'Oy vey,' doesn't nearly do it justice," he declared, picking up his darts. "That's pretty much the deal. See you in a few months. Call if you need me."

With all this percolating in my head, I took the train back to Great Neck and set up shop on a broken Ping-Pong table in my parents' basement. Difficult as Lew made it sound, I couldn't wait to get started.

The next morning, I drove over to the A&P and bought several sample products: Q-Tips, Colgate toothpaste, Jell-O, Sweet'N Low, Kellogg's Frosted Flakes, Hostess Twinkies and Heinz ketchup. I also picked up a bunch of magazines and newspapers. I sat down and read all the packaging for product information. (You'd be surprised what you can pick up from the side flap of a toothpaste box. For instance, did you know they add seaweed for consistency). Next came the hard part, which was also the fun part—dreaming up a new advertising approach for each product. My goal was to create advertising as compelling as the Doyle Dane Bernbach ads I saw on the Long Island Rail Road.

I scoured old issues of *Life, The Saturday Evening Post, TIME,* and *Sports Illustrated,* searching for visuals that I could use in my ads and anything that would get my mind going. I worked like a maniaic in that cold basement, ten to twelve hours a day, for months. What at first seemed like an easy and enjoyable project soon became a death-like experience. It wasn't easy competing with Bill Bernbach.

I lined up all the products on the Ping-Pong table and tackled each one individually. I researched them, looked at their current ads (which were reliably disappointing) and then sat down at the Ping-Pong table for the difficult creative work.

First, I began thinking about the target audience. How old were they? Were they men, women or both? Casual or serious users? And so forth. Next, I spent days, no weeks, figuring out new ways to uniquely position each product in the marketplace. The last step was to turn all of this information into an interesting and provocative approach to selling the product. More days. More weeks.

I scribbled down a bunch of headline and visual ideas on a yellow legal pad. After a lot of thought and a lot of cross outs, I narrowed down my ideas to one great headline and visual for each product. I hand lettered my best headlines with a thick black Magic Marker (the Sharpie of the 60s), copying the lettering technique from one of Lew's art director friends. I then sketched a rough visual and drew some squiggly lines to indicate body copy. I glued down all the pieces with rubber cement on white oak tag and... *Voilà!* After I-don't-know-how-many months of mind-breaking work, I'd finally finished my first 10 ads.

I laid all of them out on the Ping-Pong table and stood back several feet to get some perspective.

"Holy shit," I shouted to the table, "I think I fuckin' did it!"

*Really?!* The table answered back.

"Would I jerk you around after all we've been through?" I replied with total conviction.

I killed one of the ads, which left me with nine good ones—the beginning of my beginner's portfolio.

"Let's see."

I had three ads for Q-tips:

"OUR JOB IS TO KEEP THE WAX ON THE WANE."

"POTATOES GROW BETTER IN IDAHO THAN THEY DO IN YOUR EARS."

"BETTER THAN A PAPERCLIP."

Three ads for the Long Island Rail Road:

"BUMPER TO BUMPER ON THE LONG ISLAND
RAIL ROAD IS AT 85 MPH."

"'LET'S GET THIS COUNTRY MOVING AGAIN.' —JFK"

"YOU CAN'T TAKE A NAP IN YOUR CAR."

And three for Hertz Rent-a-Car:

"NINE MONTHS A YEAR YOU CAN LIVE IN NEW YORK WITHOUT A CAR.
IN THE SUMMER, YOU CAN DIE WITHOUT ONE."

"AMERICA ON $15 A DAY."

"IF AVIS IS SO GOOD, WHY ARE OUR LINES SO LONG?"

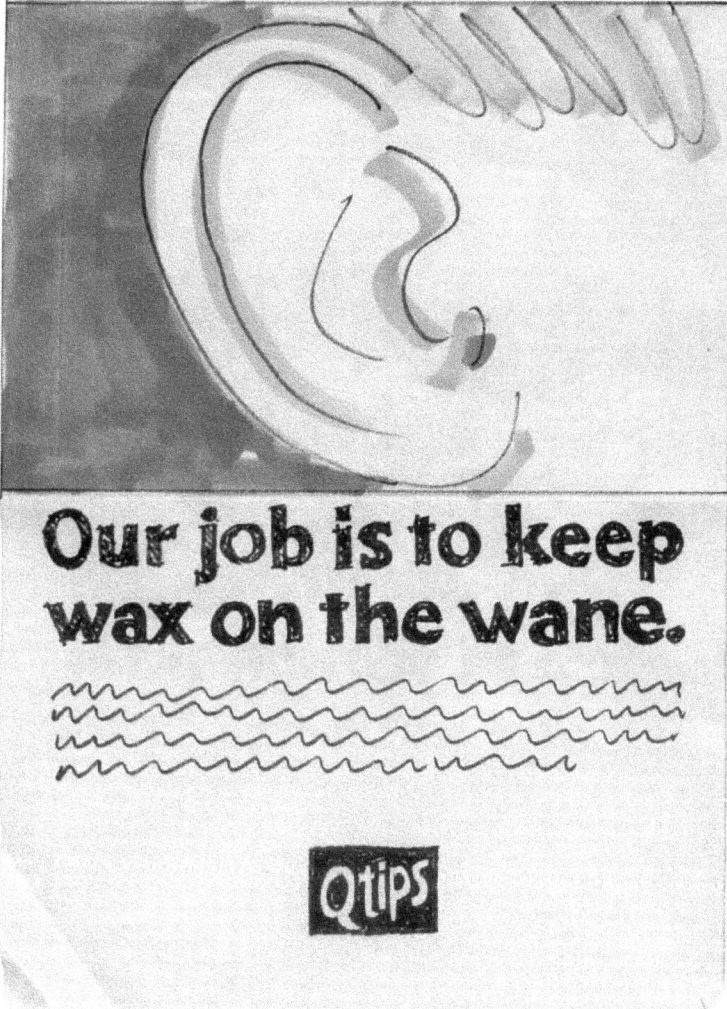

Speculative Q-tips ads for my beginners portfolio.

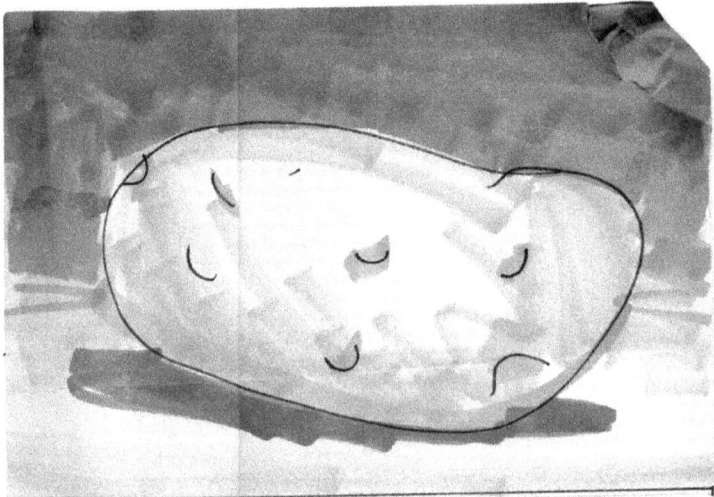

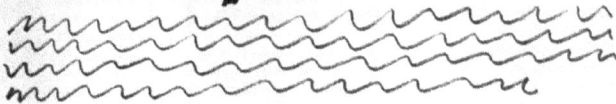

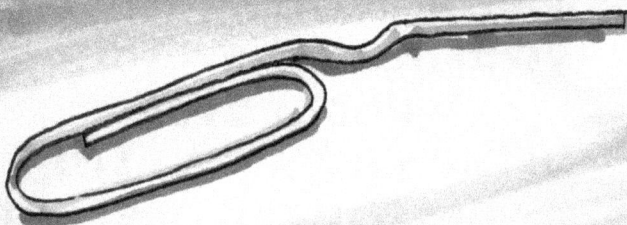

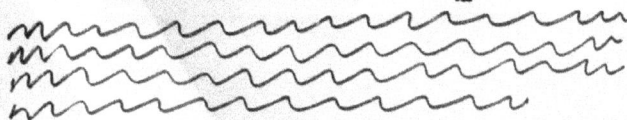

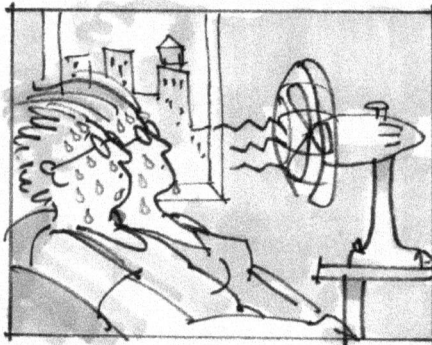

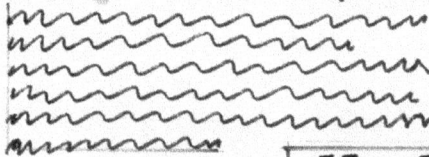

Speculative Hertz ad for my beginners portfolio.

I trimmed all the ads and I was done—at least for now. All I needed was some kind of a portfolio to put them in. I ran up to the attic and dug out an old canvas briefcase.

This would work just fine, I concluded.

I tossed in all the ads and immediately called Lew.

"I'm done. Watch out, I'm comin' over!"

The following day I took the train into the city and headed back to McCann.

Lew was playing darts. Again. And I had to wait. Again.

After he finished up his game, I handed him my book. He carefully placed it on his desk and looked closely at each ad. I waited anxiously for his verdict. He understood what it took to get here. After twenty nail-biting minutes, he looked over at me.

"You're a fucking art director!" He declared. "You've got some really nice stuff here, Steve. Great lines, really solid concepts. And you took less time than I did, you bastard."

"Really?" I said, bursting with relief.

"Honest, I'm not shitting you," he replied. "My only concern is your layouts. They're a little flat, a touch old-fashioned looking. I dunno, maybe you should take some art direction courses at the School of Visual Arts down on 23rd?"

"No way," I said. "I'm finished with school. And school's finished with me. Just give me the Cliff's Notes version, Lew."

"Only trying to help," he responded. "sva is a great…"

"Forget it, Lew," I said seriously.

The only step left was turning my rough layouts into professional-looking ads. Lew told me it was absolutely critical that my book looked like I had some experience. It couldn't look like I was still in school.

To this end I met Lew at his office late one night and we raided McCann's art studio. We took everything we could get our hands on:

Styrofoam boards, spray mount, Magic Markers, press-type, T-squares, rubber cement, pencils, erasers, you name it. I took all the supplies back to Penchina's Basement Ad Agency and assiduously put my nine ads together.

The idea was not to make the ads look real but to make them look smart. I hand lettered the headlines. I sketched out all the pictures so creative directors would understand what the photographs would look like. I wrote body copy for each ad, typed it on McCann stationary (hoping it looked like I had worked there) and glued it on the back side of each ad. Lastly, I copied each brand's logo so it would look reasonably authentic.

I was ready for prime time.

# 5 WHERE'S THE PROMISED LAND ALREADY?

Lew didn't like my canvas bag and kept insisting I buy a proper portfolio. I refused. Not because I couldn't afford one (I couldn't) or because I hated the idea of adopting the same homogenized look of every other creative person in town (I did), it went deeper than that; it went against everything I stood for.

I'm not 100% sure when this whole defiance thing began, but I know it was when I was quite young. It might have started when my first nurse kept pushing warm milk on me as a baby. Or when my mother began dressing me like an Eskimo because *She* was cold. Or when my teachers refused to let me go to the bathroom. Who could live under such tyranny? No wonder I fought back.

Somewhere along the way, I discovered that this feisty, rebellious behavior worked for me. It made me feel powerful and more in control. It probably even masked some latent suspicion that deep down I was, somehow, not good enough. Whatever its origins, I enjoyed giving people shit.

Armed with my scruffy canvas portfolio and an issue of *Advertising Age's* "Top 100 Agencies," which I'd stolen from McCann's reception area, I set out to find my first job.

As Lew had discovered a year earlier, it was simply impossible to get an interview with any of the top creative shops. For starters, there weren't that many. Making matters worse, most of the good shops, with the exception of Doyle Dane Bernbach, were fairly small. And for every available opportunity, there were a thousand starving copywriters and art directors, many of whom had previous experience, already banging down the doors.

I was relentless, though, methodically going down my list and doing everything in my power to get my portfolio seen. By now I knew who all the top creative directors were and I went after every one of them: Roy Grace and John Noble at Doyle Dane Bernbach; Jerry Della Femina; Gene Case at Jack Tinker & Partners, one of the great early creative boutiques; Dick Raboy, who wrote one of my all-time favorite ads ("More fig to the Newton"); David Altschiller, a brilliant writer whom I would later work for at Carl Ally Inc.; and Joel Wayne, who headed up the top creative group at an otherwise dull agency, Grey Advertising. (Years later, he hired me on Kool-Aid and Yuban coffee.)

But hard as I tried, no one would hire me. I was Moses wandering in the ad desert for what certainly felt like forty years. *Where the hell was the Promised Land already? When would the sea part, revealing my path? Where was...* I wasn't even close.

Every night, after pounding the pavement all day, I took the train back home and immediately went down to the basement to continue working on my book. Refining, refining...and more refining.

I would bounce everything I wrote off of anyone I could find.

"Hey, Ma," I shouted over the clanging washing machine. "What do you think of this new Porsche ad?"

"Oh, it's lovely, dear."

"Thanks, Ma."

"What's a Porsche?"

I was demoralized for sure, but I loved the creative process and was determined to break into the business no matter how long it took, how many rejections I got or how many shoe soles I wore down.

Each morning I got back on the train and repeated what I'd done the day before. There was no doubt in my mind that advertising was what I wanted to do for the rest of my life. I felt it in all 206 of my bones. But next to basic training in the armpit of the country and trying to run my first marathon (that didn't end well), this job-hunting thing was the most grueling experience of my life. It was one disappointment after another. As one door shut, another shut after it. But I didn't have any alternatives. This is all I wanted to do. Period. Period. Period.

After a while I conceded that my door-to-door game plan hadn't gotten me far enough, so I decided to change up my strategy. I began writing more letters to personnel departments and headhunters and resolved to make a bigger effort at networking. I began attending seminars, career nights at NYU and the School of Visual Arts (No, I did not take any classes!) and making the rounds at ad clubs and advertising parties with Lew and his dart team from McCann.

Lo and behold, things started turning around.

A lovely and caring in-house creative recruiter at Grey Advertising took a motherly interest in me. Luiza Robinson, all 5'3" and 90 pounds of her, had a reputation on Madison Avenue for discovering and mentoring young talent. Although she worked for Grey, she made it a point to stay in touch with her young "kiddies," eventually finding them a home either there or at some other shop. She was 1/3 recruiter, 1/3 social worker and 1/3 mother.

Luiza fell in love with me—and my book. I'm not sure which happened first, but she said I had the best beginner's book she'd ever seen. Unfortunately, however, there was nothing at Grey at the time, so she told me to keep checking in with her.

"Please do that for me, will you? Something always pops up, my dear." she insisted.

Sure enough, on an icy cold January day in 1969, about a year after I'd graduated college, I called Luiza from a dank, urine-scented phone booth outside of Penn Station.

"Hi, Luiza," I said as cheerfully as I could about to throw up. "It's Steve Penchina. Just checking in."

"Oh, Steve, I'm so glad you called. I just set up an interview for you with a senior group head here. He works on a lot of sleepy packaged goods accounts, but he's a terrific guy and a very talented writer. He's a doll, one of my favorite people in the business. You'll love him. You have a pen? Okay, his name is David Bennett, extension 549. He's expecting your call. Love you. Good luck. Let me know how it goes."

Grey was a giant multi-billion-dollar shop dominated by traditional packaged goods brands like Pledge, Mr. Clean, Kool-Aid, Jell-O, and Yuban coffee. Although Grey wasn't on my list, I was coming to the conclusion that in order to have a shot at the good creative shops, I first had to get some job experience. Somewhere. Anywhere. For now, Grey would suit me just fine.

I was dead tired and feeling a little down the day I headed over there. Turns out winter in New York isn't an ideal time for job hunting (or much else for that matter).

I met Dave at his office after work. Walking back to his desk, I felt the warmth of the agency. It seemed like such a contented environment. I looked out one of the windows. It was snowing. I absolutely loved being in that office environment—typewriters clicking, copiers whirring, the smell of rubber cement remover, cute secretaries ogling over the new face in the office... *Ugh, if I could only land a job.*

As Luiza had described, Dave was a warm, gentle and scholarly man with a wry sense of humor. He was the spitting image of a college professor with his horn-rimmed glasses, Brooks Brothers crew neck sweater, khaki slacks and penny loafers. I handed him my book and he went through my ads quite deliberately. I sat there sweating it out, trying to read his face. He must play a lot of poker. I couldn't get a read. Finally, he leaned back in his chair and crossed his hands behind his head. I held my breath.

"Excellent."

I exhaled. "Oh, really? Thanks."

"For a copywriter, not an art director."

"Excuse me?"

"You've got some terrific stuff here, Steve, but your art direction leaves something to be desired." He paused. "Maybe you should take some courses at the School of Visual Arts? You know, on 23rd Street?"

*He's got to be fucking kidding me.*

"But, damn, your headlines and body copy are wonderful. They're crisp, they're clever, they're thoughtful and they're persuasive. You're really an excellent writer."

On the spot, I made one of the quickest and best decisions of my life.

"OK. I am now a copywriter. You need a writer?"

As it turned out, he didn't, but he told me to keep in touch. I was that close. Bummed, but now a lot more optimistic, I took to the streets again, this time as a copywriter. I used the exact same book and the exact same resume. All I did was Wite-Out "Art Director" and type in "Copywriter." New job description, same old struggle.

I never count on the stuff, but at this point what I really needed was some good old-fashioned luck.

# 6 "UM, WOULD YOU MIND TAKING A LOOK AT MY BOOK?"

After several more months of rejection, my dad, of all people, got me a great lead. Saulie Blau, his best friend from the Lower East Side and now a prominent Park Avenue dermatologist, told him that one of his patients was a big shot in advertising. The big shot turned out to be George Lois, who was, and still is, a legend in the business.

Lois was an immensely talented and successful art director, creative director and graphic designer. He already had his name on two highly-touted creative shops: Papert, Koenig & Lois and Lois, Holland, Calloway. His wild reputation preceded him. He once threatened to jump out his office window if the client didn't buy his ads. (It worked.) I loved him before I even met him.

I looked him up in *Ad Age* and discovered that he was responsible for a legion of groundbreaking campaigns the early work on Volkswagen and Xerox; "I want my Maypo!" for Maypo cereal (which later evolved into "I want my MTV!"); "When you've got it, flaunt it" for Braniff Airlines; and *Redbook* magazine's "Young Mamas" (one of my favorite campaigns of all time). Perhaps his most famous work of all, though, were his many spectacular, award-winning cover designs for *Esquire* magazine.

George Lois drowns Andy Warhole in his own soup on the May 1969 cover of *Esquire*.

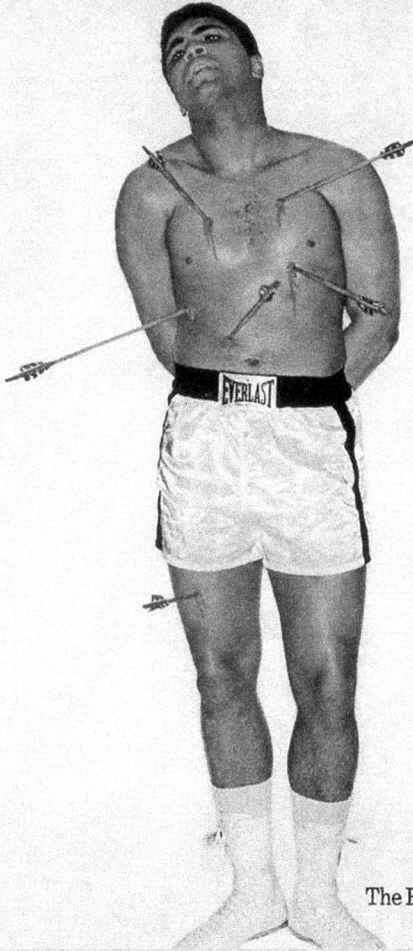

Muhammad Ali poses as a martyr on George Lois's April 1968 Cover of *Esquire*.

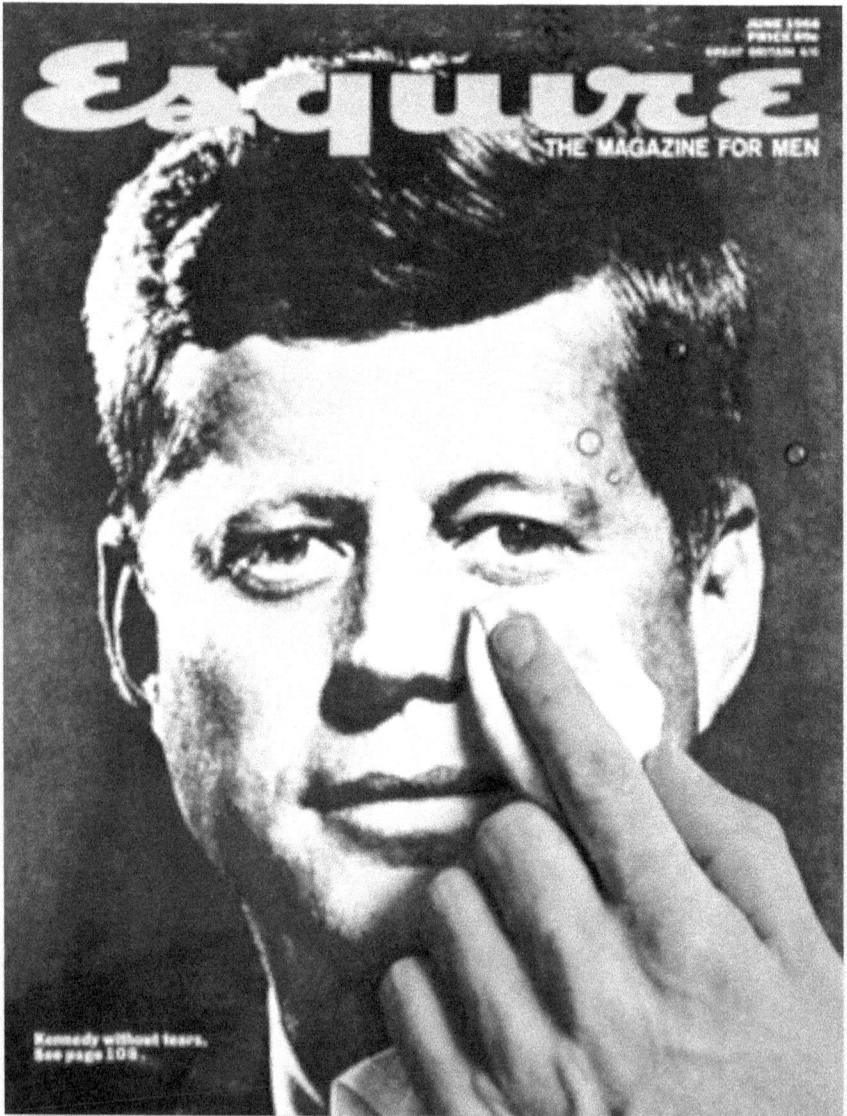

Seven months after JFK's assassination, George Lois portrays Kennedy crying
for his lost destiny on the June 1964 cover of Esquire.

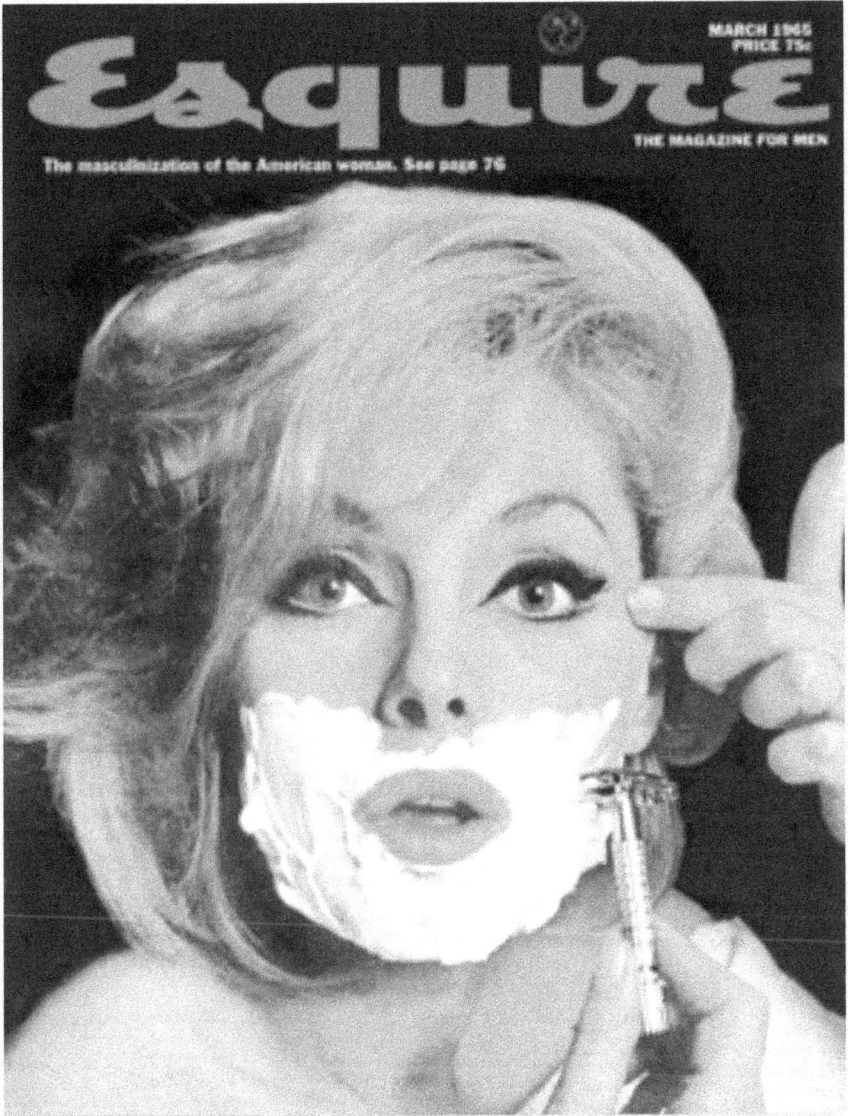

Virna Lisi epitomizes the masculinationization of the
American woman on the May 1965 cover.

Landing a meeting with a giant like George Lois was a coup for a beginner like me, but I confess to not quite realizing the enormity of it at the time.

The morning of my interview, I had planned to play pickup basketball on West 3rd Street with Streiter and some other guys. I had plenty of time to make my four o'clock appointment. ("Sharp!" his snippety secretary had told me.)

I grabbed my canvas bag and stuffed in everything I needed for the day: all my ads (now mounted on Styrofoam boards), clothes for my interview, a half-eaten tuna sandwich and a bottle of cough syrup for the cold I was fighting.

We played for a long time. My team was winning. Streiter kept egging me on to play one more game; I was so into it I totally lost track of the time. It wasn't unusual for me to be late for dates, classes, trains and the like, but when it came to something important like an interview, my head was always screwed on straight. I called a time-out to check my watch. It was 4:00. Four fucking o'clock! And I was still in the Village.

I bolted to the park bench, grabbed my stuff and ran toward the subway entrance. Predicting the subway might take too long, I jumped into a taxi. Wrong. About halfway there, I ran smack into Friday rush-hour traffic. Everything stood still. All I heard was blaring horns. I jumped out of the cab and sprinted the last fifteen blocks to the building.

Huffing, puffing and now coughing my lungs out, I finally made it to Lois's. I quickly dashed into the men's room and, like Superman, zipped out of my basketball clothes and into my Steve Penchina, super-businessman uniform (a sweaty button-down shirt and slightly wrinkled gray suit).

I was an hour late.

An hour late for anyone is unforgivable. An hour late for George Lois is suicidal.

I announced myself to his secretary, who greeted me with a haughty, you're-in-big-shit-kid-and-I'm-going-to-have-a-front-row-seat-when-he-takes-your-head-off look. I have no idea why she took such a liking to me. I took one last swig of my Vicks, and shoved the half-empty bottle back into my bag. She whisked me into his office.

George Lois was an intimidating figure with a great presence. He was big, about 6'5", with a handsome, chiseled Greek face. He was fastidiously dressed in a custom-made navy suit, gleaming white shirt and perfectly knotted tie that he couldn't stop fiddling with. I was surprised that someone as creative as him didn't appear to have a great sense of humor. Instead, he was tense and high-strung with a nervous twitch in his eye like Chief Inspector Dreyfus in the Pink Panther movies. I was soon to become his Clouseau.

"I'm sorry I'm so late," I said. "I got stuck in…"

He interrupted me with a disdainful glance that shot through me like a Masai spear. I stopped talking. He was not a happy man, at least at this moment. I sat there sniffling, coughing and nervously drumming my fingers on my "portfolio" while he finished a layout. He didn't give me so much as a glance. Had the meeting not been set up by Dr. Blau, I'm certain I wouldn't have made it past his lovely receptionist. He made me stew there for about twenty minutes. He finally grunted and stuck out his hand for my portfolio bag.

Still absorbed in his layout, he reached into the bag to take out my ads. He yanked his hand back like a rattlesnake had just bitten him.

"What the fuck?!" he screamed. "What the hell's in here?"

"What?" I said, peering into the bag.

"Are you fucking with me? What the hell is all this crap?" He was rabid.

The cough medicine had opened and was dripping gooey, red syrup all over my ads, but more important—way more important—it had dripped onto his sparkling, white shirt sleeve. And the now limp tuna fish sandwich had come unwrapped and was stinking up his office.

"Gym shorts? Your fucking gym shorts?! Your goddamn, sweaty fucking gym shorts!"

Hesitantly, he stuck his head deeper inside.

"You've got your stinking sneakers in here?"

He took his head out and looked me squarely in the eyes.

"Where. Are. Your. Mother. Fucking. Ads?!"

Man, I thought I cursed a lot.

"Wait. I get it. This is a joke, right?" He looked around. "We're on *Candid Camera,* right?"

"Uh, no, sir. No joke."

I poked my head way down into the portfolio. "I know they're in there somewhere."

As he continued his tirade, he began pulling out my ads one at a time. Growing angrier with each sticky ad, he finally turned the bag upside down and dumped everything onto the floor.

Losing it, he started throwing the components of the pile into the four corners of his office. My size 12 Converse high tops bounced off one of the windows. Ads were whizzing by my head like F-16s on a training mission in New Jersey.

"I've never seen anything like this in my entire fucking life," he went on, adjusting his tie for the billionth time and twitching exponentially more now. "How, in the mother of God, do you know Dr. Blau, anyway?"

"Well, my dad…"

"Forget it. I don't want to know… Because if he's a friend of mine, I'll have to kill him. CARROOLLL!!"

His secretary came rushing in. Her mouth was agape. She stared wide-eyed at her boss, who was covered in what I'm sure she thought was blood. My blood. A flash of relief came over her when she noticed me crawling around the floor picking up ads and sweat socks.

"I need one of those wet-wipe things, Carol. Look what this nut did to my shirt."

As Carol hunted around for wet-wipes, I finished gathering up my ads and sundry sports paraphernalia. There was no doubt in my mind that I was history. As I approached the door, I decided to make what would either be the most genius or delusional move of my young life. I turned around. Lois was staring at his sleeve.

"Um, would you mind taking a look at my book?"

My chutzpah must have caught him off guard because he just sat there in his elegant Herman Miller chair, staring at me with a quizzical look. I'm sure he was trying to decide whether or not I was serious. And whether or not he was going to get up and pummel me into the floor. Instead, he reached out and grabbed my ads from me. He sat down behind his drawing board and began flipping through them. About two thirds through, he paused and looked me right in the eye. Here I started twitching.

"These aren't bad for a beginner," he said.

"Well, uh, that's what I am, a beginner," I said, making a feeble attempt at normal conversation, but sounding stupendously stupid.

"Thanks, I never would have known," he said, monotone.

*He's talking. That's a good sign.*

Going through my ads more carefully, he started talking to me using substantially fewer curse words—his voice about ten decibels lower.

"You know, you have some nice concepts here. Some of them need work but on the whole, they're pretty smart and not at all cutesy. Most beginners' books are cutesy. I hate cutesy."

"Yeah, me too," I chimed in, sounding like a total schmuck again.

*Can't you keep your fucking mouth shut?!*

He ignored me and went on. "But I like these. They're witty without being corny. And you understand how to position a product. Beginners don't know crap about positioning."

For once, I kept quiet. He glanced at his sleeve again, momentarily losing concentration. I winced.

"CARROOLLL! Where are those damn wipe things?" He shot me another dirty look but continued. He was definitely more relaxed now, a totally different person.

"You also have a good sense of humor, which doesn't really surprise me given that fuckin' gym bag you're trying to pass off as a portfolio."

He began to critique my work more explicitly, which was exactly what I had hoped for. This kind of feedback was invaluable.

"I really like your Long Island Rail Road campaign. You got right to the heart of the issue, the benefits of commuting by train versus driving. Nice work. I can relate to that. But a small point. The train doesn't go 85 miles an hour. You gotta fix that."

"Oh? Okay."

He liked the Q-Tips campaign word for word. I actually noticed a thin smile on his face for the first time. He did mention, however, that he thought the visuals could be more sophisticated. "I agree," I said, sounding like a kiss-ass.

"You know, you might consider taking a few courses at SVA."

*Sigh.*

He absolutely loved my Hertz ad. "'Nine months a year you can live in New York without a car. In the summer, you can die without one,'" he said, quoting my line back to me. "Terrific headline."

Then, to my astonishment, he began to get almost fatherly with me, sharing important insights on the business that have stuck with me to this day.

He defined creativity as "a blinding glimpse of the obvious." I ate that up.

"Advertising," he went on, "is about problem solving. Clients have difficult marketing problems. Our job is to help solve them.

"Think simply and conceptually. Remember, concept is king. Execution always comes second. Never the other way around."

"Every ad should be based on a single concept. Never force two ideas into one ad. Clients are always pushing for that. They think they're saving money. But don't let them. It's confusing to the consumer. If a client wants to make two points, make 'em buy another ad.

"And don't forget that this is their entire life. Their whole fucking existence depends on your work."

*Whoa!* I thought. Four years at NYU and I never heard anything close to this.

Suddenly, without uttering another word, he walked back to his drafting board. Taking his cue, I gathered up my things, shook his hand and left.

I was on cloud nine. I could barely contain myself. I might not have totally realized it going in, but after more than an hour with him, I understood why Lois was considered one of the biggest talents in the industry, perhaps the biggest. And that enormous talent really liked my stuff. I almost couldn't process the whole thing, both the good and the bad.

As I passed his secretary, who had just returned with a large carton of spot remover, she gave me one last snide look.

"Great meeting," I said to her.

Several years later, I ran into George playing basketball at McBurney's West Side YMCA. I hesitantly approached him and asked if he remembered me.

"Are you fucking kidding me? That was the worst four hours of my life."

"It was only one," I corrected him.

# 7 HALLEFUCKINLUJAH!

Afraid to piss off any more of the big names in the business, I decided to focus on the smaller ones.

Several of my old NYU classmates who were also struggling to break into the business had told me that big cash-rich, not-very-creative, old-fashioned agencies often took chances on hiring inexperienced creative people. For them, hiring a young art director or copywriter was a minuscule investment in exchange for fresh new thinking for their big conservative clients. Although it would take an 8.0 magnitude earthquake to dislodge these big-budget advertisers from their longstanding campaigns, this approach appeased them in their quest to squeeze every last nickel of "creativity" out of the 15% commission they were paying their agencies. Plus, there was constant pressure on big agencies to do exploratory campaigns and ambitious neophytes were perfect for this kind of dead-end task.

Norman, Craig & Kummel was one of those agencies. Their big claims to fame were two of the corniest advertising campaigns of the time: the Ajax White Knight (a man in a medieval armor suit galloping through suburban neighborhoods on a white stallion shouting, "Stronger than dirt!") and Maidenform's "I dreamed..." print campaign, which featured women getting married/going to work/

shopping/attending the theater and so on, wearing their Maidenform bras outside of their clothing.

This kind of creativity was antithetical to anything I was interested in pursuing, but at this point my goal was to get some experience. It was painfully clear that I wasn't going to get hired by the top creative shops any time soon. So, if gaining experience meant working with a steel-encased germaphobe who galloped around suburban backyards on a gleaming white horse, well, that was the price I was willing to pay.

After writing, calling and otherwise nagging him to death, I finally talked David Upright, the creative director for Norman, Craig & Kummel, into granting me an interview. Dave was a sharp, witty, affable guy who was far too talented to be working there, but, thankfully, there he was. He took a quick look at my book and right then and there said, "I want to hire you."

My heart stopped.

He jumped up. "Be right back. Don't move."

Grabbing my new, super-duper, ultra-professional portfolio, he went next door to the executive creative director's office for what seemed like a month. Twenty minutes later he was back.

"You know what?" he said.

"What?"

"You have a job."

"You're joking, right?"

"Who do I look like, Jerry Lewis?"

Overcome with joy, I leapt off the chair and planted a big, wet smooch on his cheek. Mildly amused, he wiped off my saliva with his silk handkerchief.

"Follow me, young man, I'll show you where you'll live."

I was absolutely giddy. I had worked so hard for so long without success that this moment seemed truly surreal. David was walking down the hallway. I was floating.

We arrived at a tiny, dreary inside office. Dave handed me a stack of personnel papers, a bunch of legal pads, a fistful of yellow #2 pencils and before I could say, "I can't fucking believe this is happening!", he congratulated me on my first real advertising job. As he walked out, I plopped down on my new/old rolling leather chair (which took up half the office), hoisted my feet up in the air and spun around like a centrifuge, screaming silently to myself, "Holy shit! Holy shit! Holy fuckin' shit!"

The junior copywriter position paid $7,200 a year, which was low even by 1969 standards, but given the torturous journey I'd been on, I felt like the CEO of U.S. Steel.

Inexplicably, Dave started me out on a host of women's and household products: Ajax detergent, Sardo bath oil, Cutex nail polish remover, and their big Maidenform bras and girdles account. Having someone like me write ads for bras and girdles was like asking Diane von Furstenberg to do the play-by-play at a Rangers game. The only relevant experience I had with bras was trying to unhook them with one hand. Still, I worked diligently on my accounts despite knowing I didn't have a prayer in hell of doing any award-winning work.

I was told that the owner, Norman B. Norman, was a tight-fisted tyrant who ran his shop with an iron fist. Although he was reputed to be the richest man on Madison Avenue, his office looked like the set of The Honeymooners. He hadn't put a dime into the place since it opened back in the fifties.

At a lanky 6'4" or 6'5" with a buzz cut, a long neck and a stern countenance, he was quite the menacing figure. I never once saw him smile. Occasionally I'd see him walking the halls, scowling, as everyone ducked behind their desks in fear. It was rare that he actually stopped to talk to anyone, but on the few occasions he did, it was to the buttoned-up, ass-kissing account executives. Creative people were like Martians to him.

It was well known in the industry that he had changed his name from a Jewish-sounding last name like Lipshutz to Norman B. Norman, fearful that his Jewish heritage would preclude him from winning big blue-chip clients in the WASP-dominated ad world of the fifties. But I couldn't help thinking that he might have come up with something slightly more original than a second first name. Jack Strauss was another agency owner who felt the need to change the name of his shop (this was not entirely uncommon in the fifties). While trying to come up with a Jewish-proof name for his growing shop, he looked around at the dull, dingy walls of his conference room late one night and decided to call his agency "Grey."

As hackneyed as NCK's advertising was, I still gained valuable experience working there. I got my first opportunity to work alongside an art director as a creative team. I found that I was able to work twice as fast with an art director as I could on my own, and it was definitely a lot more fun.

I was partnered with a wonderful gentleman, Ben McCarthy, who was much older than me. He was a 20-year veteran of the business and had the emotional scars to prove it.

By his own admission his best years were behind him, but I loved to sit with him in his office (he had a window) and listen to all his wonderful advertising war stories. He had been at NCK forever. He was the most patient, interesting and kindest man I had ever met. He taught me the ropes of the business, especially about how to structure a TV commercial, about which I knew very little. As much as I enjoyed working with him, he got a huge kick out of hanging around with me. He loved my cocky, crazy personality and never-good-enough work ethic. He referred to me as his Mad Young Turk.

The poor man had been stuck working on Ajax from the day he walked in the door. He had literally hundreds of storyboards, divided by category and year, leaned neatly against his windowsills. Only a few ever made it to network television. The majority were test commercials that never saw the light of day. The agency essentially used him as canon fodder to pump out client-directed ideas year after year, none of which were taken seriously but which were still good enough to "make a meeting" and demonstrate to the client that the agency was working its tail off on the client's behalf.

I really loved the big fella. He didn't have a mean, unscrupulous bone in his body, which was, unfortunately, at odds with the killer instincts the business requires. I had only worked with him for a year and a half when I learned they were letting him go. I was heartbroken. It was my first brush with the harsh reality of the business world. I cried, but Ben kept his wit right to the end. His parting words to the agency were, "I may not have been good, but I was slow."

I also learned, painful as it was at times, how to work with account executives in the marketing department. Account men and women planned strategy, worked on ad budgets, oversaw media and research, and kept their clients happy by wining and dining them. They were not a pleasant bunch.

NCK, like many of the not-very-creative agencies of the time, was totally marketing- (or business-) driven, which meant there was a distinct hierarchy at the firm. Because the marketing people essentially ran the show, reporting directly to Norman B., who was obviously a serious businessman, the creative people took a back seat to the marketing staff. That meant that many of the important creative decisions were made at the marketing level and not, as it should be, at the creative one. This set up a classic rivalry between the two departments. It's one that still exists to this day at many agencies.

Since the account people alone had the client's ear, they were the ones who went to all the client meetings, often going around the creative director's wishes—or mine, if I did the work. Needless to say, it didn't take long before I had knockdown, drag-out fights with these guys.

(I seemed to do better with the female account execs for some reason.)

I knew from friends who worked at other agencies, as well as from the research I'd done on Doyle Dane Bernbach in school, that this rigid, marketing-dominated philosophy was not the way of all agencies; thankfully, the ad business was changing fast. But for now, this was Norman B. Norman's house and we were playing with his ball.

It had taken me almost a year to land my first copywriter's job. Norman, Craig & Kummel may not have been on my A-list but I will never forget where I got my start or the person who gave it to me: "Jerry Lewis" a.k.a. David Upright. There were many creative directors who had liked my book, but David was the only one with the balls to pull the trigger. There were only a handful of meaningful "firsts" in my life. This one was special.

I learned many lessons from David, sometimes by osmosis. How to use humor and wit to get your way in a big political shop. How to be firm, yet tactful, especially with your creative staff. How to fight hard for great work without losing your cool (even in an impossible environment). Lastly, and perhaps most importantly, David was living proof that you can succeed in this rough and tumble business and still be a decent human being.

I didn't stay at NCK long, less than two years. I was too focused on getting to a creative shop. But NCK put me on the map.

I was finally getting a monthly paycheck. I could rent my own apartment in the city, well out of earshot of my mother and her damn vacuum cleaner.

My dad couldn't have been prouder of me—especially since I succeeded on my own, by good old-fashioned perseverance and determination.

At long last, I was a genuine, bona fide, 100% certified advertising copywriter.

In the eloquent words of George Lois, "Hallefuckinlujah!"

# 8 FUCK 'EM, THEY DON'T DESERVE US

Carl Ally was a genius, a mad genius, but a genius just the same. Running around the office like a lion who missed brunch, Carl was always disheveled. His pot-belly hung out and his shirttails dangled from beneath his suit jacket like a defeated fifth-grader meandering home from private school. Despite his sartorial issues, he built Carl Ally Inc., the premier and most sought-after creative agency of the time, perhaps of all time.

Although David Upright will always have a special place in my heart, underwire bras and laundry detergent didn't cut it for me. I simply had to get into a better shop. But to get hired at an agency like Ally, I knew I had to take my book to another level, possibly three.

Every day after work, I'd rush back to my luxury studio apartment on 81st and 2nd, and while all my buddies were out drinking, playing darts and picking up account assistants, I was home working on my book. I added new products, created new campaigns and continuously refined my headlines, visuals and body copy. Thanks to the time I spent with Ben, my book had finally achieved a professional sheen.

By this time, my buddy Lew had left McCann and with his sensational new book made the giant leap to the award-winning Carl Ally. The white-hot agency was picking up new accounts left

67

and right and the creative directors there were quietly looking to add creative teams to the agency. But only via personal recommendations. No headhunters.

Lew and I had remained in touch during the past year. One day over sushi he asked me how my book was coming along. I told him it had gone from a B to an A. I had added two new spec campaigns, and Ben had put everything together professionally for me. I added a wonderfully warm and clever TV campaign for Ajax called the "The Wanderer," about a little kid wandering the neighborhood all day getting filthy a la Dennis the Menace. My thinking was, *Hey, Mr. Brilliant Ally Creative Director, if I can do something fresh and interesting for a staid brand like Ajax, imagine what I can do for one of your exciting new accounts.*

Once again, Lew came through for me. He was able to arrange an interview with Ally's (and the industry's) top creative directors. It was the longest of long shots—Ally never hired beginners—but Lew and I thought it was worth the try. He told me they'd get a kick out of me and hopefully my book as well.

On the day of my meeting I was terrified. I knew if I could somehow get hired, it would be a life changer. Frankly, I wouldn't have been surprised if they had told me to just leave the book and given me the old "We'll get back to you" crap.

I met with Marty Puris, one of their extraordinary creative directors. At the time his big account was Hertz Rent-a-Car. Soon, he would pick up the prestigious Fiat automobile account. I got up early that morning, dressed as cool as Giorgio Armani and got to the agency a half hour early. I couldn't afford another George Lois fiasco. I waited in the hall outside of Marty's office while he, Lew and Marty's wonderfully eccentric English secretary laughed their way through my book, obviously a good sign. An even better sign was when Marty called in his impeccably tasteful art director partner, Ralph Ammirati, who reacted in the same positive way.

"Who is this guy?" I heard him ask, as Lew pointed me out in the hall. I was wearing my black pleated trousers, black turtleneck and McCreedy & Shreiber Chesterfield boots. (The same ones Ralph was wearing—it was important at Ally to be well dressed and sharp looking,) Ralph took a quick look at my book, and boots, and gave me a nod of approval.

Marty motioned to his secretary and said, "Let's get Durfee in here," referring to Carl's partner and executive creative director of the shop. Within minutes Jim Durfee walked in quickly and skimmed my book.

"Why don't you hire this kid?" I heard him say. My legs began to buckle. "How much is he asking?"

"Peanuts," Marty answered. I tried to hold myself up by grabbing the chair rail, but my arms were going numb too. I was slowly slinking to the floor.

Marty and Ralph called me in and I shook their hands.

"Think you can handle it here?" Marty asked directly. "It's a tough environment."

"I'll work 24 hours a day," I answered. "I won't eat."

"Well, we don't want you to starve. But you may have to give up some of your social life. We work long hours here."

"No problem. I'm in a slump anyway."

They all laughed. Lew was beaming like a proud older brother.

"Ya know, Steve, why don't you give us a few minutes here. You can wait with Lew out in the hall."

I began hyperventilating and biting my nails, and I don't even bite my nails. Lew was confident, obsessively stroking his red mustache. A few minutes went by before Marty's secretary popped her head out and motioned us back into the office.

"Okay, let's see what you're made of, big guy," Ralph said, shaking my hand. "Welcome to the club." Marty's secretary was as gleeful as I was, feeling proud that she played a part. (She had laughed the loudest at my book.) Lew was ecstatic. He had his cheap-food man back.

"Thank you very much," I told everybody. "I won't let you down. I'm so excited, I can't even think of something funny to say."

"Not necessary," Marty answered. "We're glad to have you."

I was the first junior copywriter they'd ever hired. From that day on, I was officially in the "club"—the inner circle of elite creative shops. Ally, in fact, was the inner circle of the inner circle. Indeed, my career, and life, would never be the same.

It wasn't long before I met the man himself. Born in Detroit, Carl Ally was a scrappy, gregarious man with a Zeppelin-sized lust for life. He flew jet planes (he had been a fighter pilot during the Korean War), rode BMW motorcycles, loved big band jazz artists like Count Basie and Duke Ellington and had an insatiable appetite for women or "broads", as he called them. With a sign over his desk that read "Comfort the afflicted. Afflict the comfortable," he held strong opinions on everything from advertising and politics to cars and the New York Mets. He would frequently get into blistering arguments, not only with his own staff, but with his clients, sometimes firing them on the spot. "Fuck 'em," he would say as they walked out. "They don't deserve us." Carl did not suffer fools.

He had a fierce and restless mind and was unyielding in his drive for perfection. There wasn't an ounce of compromise in him. Something was either off-the-charts brilliant or it sucked. And he wasn't shy about telling you. His management philosophy was simple: if you were good enough to get in there, you damn well were expected to meet his stratospheric standards, even if you were relatively inexperienced like I was.

Everyone from the top down lived and died by the quality of their work. No one cared when you came in, when you broke for lunch (if you had time for lunch) or whether, God help you, you were an NRA Republican. If your ads were brilliant, you were golden. If they fell short, you were in deep shit. And if you were in deep shit long enough, say a month tops, you were history. The opportunity to work at such a high profile shop did not come without its price. The intense pressure to perform at award-winning caliber day in and day out was cause for daily panic attacks—and the occasional Valium. Or two. Or three.

The agency was unbelievably hot during the time I was there, from 1968 to 1972. Carl was winning new accounts seemingly daily. You couldn't pick up the *Times, The Wall Street Journal,* or any trade magazine without seeing a story on Carl. He was always out there with some outlandish quote reaming the competition, the industry or an ad campaign he particularly abhorred. He courted controversy like the Jewish lobby. Once, he was quoted about his ongoing battle with Avis (we had Hertz): "We have a competitor who says he's number two. That's hard to argue with."

The ten or so Ally creative directors were chiseled from the same piece of granite, all enormously talented and incredibly demanding. They had neither the time nor inclination to hold your hand. A word or two, a smirk, a thumbs up or down or your copy indignantly crumpled into a ball and thrown back at you was virtually all the feedback you received. What I learned, I learned mostly by just being there—simply by being around that level of talent.

I spent whatever spare time I had walking the hallways observing. Why was that headline broken into two sentences? Why 'would not' instead of 'wouldn't'? Why was that written in the past tense instead of present? Why did he opt to use an illustration instead of photography? I analyzed every minute detail of all the amazing, award-winning ads that the creative people had taped to their office walls, proudly displayed like a soldier's war medals.

Ally was all about words—sculpting powerful, provocative facts into bold, audacious concepts. Every component of an ad or commercial—the copy, photography, headline, music, editing and so on—had to be executed with exacting precision. But the focus was always on the words, and every last one of them was scrutinized to no end.

Carl's creative philosophy took over where Bill Bernbach's had left off. He developed an innovative brand of advertising that has yet to be matched. Where Bernbach's approach was warm and amusing, Carl's was intellectual, brash, and glib. And it always went for the jugular. "At Doyle Dane," Carl used to say, "they tend to goose the customer. At Ally, we punch them in the nose."

Many of Ally's print advertising campaigns are classics.

"DRIVE IT LIKE YOU HATE IT."
(Volvo)

"YOU CAN'T EAT ATMOSPHERE."
(Horn & Hardart Cafeterias)

"MR. FERRARI DRIVES A FIAT."
(Fiat)

Nobody could touch Carl Ally's unique brilliance.
Ads for Volvo and Horn & Hardart Cafeterias by Carl Ally Inc., c.1960s

# MR. FERRARI DRIVES A FIAT.

The Mr. Ferrari we refer to is the very same Mr. Ferrari who makes some of the fastest and most expensive cars in the world.

And for his own personal use, he does drive a Fiat.

It's not that he feels the Fiat is any better than a Ferrari.

He just feels that the car we make is a more sensible car to drive around town in than the car he makes.

However, it is rather enlightening that out of all the small sensible cars sold in Europe—some fifty in all—

he chose a Fiat.

Enlightening, but not astonishing, when you consider that in Europe, where they've been buying small cars for three generations, they buy more Fiats than anything else, Volkswagens included.

Now, if you're thinking about buying your first small car, you might keep all this in mind.

After all, when it comes to cars, you can't fool a Ferrari.

**FIAT**

The biggest selling car in Europe.

Now that's a kick in the nuts.
An early corporate Fiat ad created by Mary Puris and Ralph Ammirati Carl Ally Inc., c. 1960

73

"MACHINES SHOULD WORK. PEOPLE SHOULD THINK."
(IBM)

"YOU CAN'T SEE AMERICA FROM 30,000 FEET IN THE AIR."
(Hertz)

"GOD SAVE CHILDREN FROM THEIR MOTHERS AND FATHERS."
(WCBS NewsRadio 880)

"IF YOU GET A BAD MEAL ON A PLANE, YOU CAN'T WALK OUT."
(Northeast Airlines)

"EAT YOUR BRAINS OUT FOR A BUCK."
(Krystal Fried Chicken)

Can you imagine following those?

My first assignment at Ally was to write a small-space promotion ad for Country Club Malt Liquor. Pearl Brewing Company out of Texas faced a peculiar problem. They had bought thousands of cheapo giveaways in an attempt to entice college students to drink more of their booze. The problem was that the freebies—a silly-looking beach towel, a tacky cigarette lighter made out of a Country Club can, and a dumb night lamp (also made from a can)—were so lame that virtually none of the students claimed them. The client was stuck with a warehouse full of this junk.

Ally, as with most agencies at the time, always paired a writer with an art director to work on an assignment. (Who invented this technique? Yep, Bill Bernbach.) I was paired with a plump, eccentric, fun-loving, yackety-yak art director named Jim Brancaleone. Jim, who was more senior than me, had just joined Ally from Doyle Dane Bernbach. His formidable background intimidated me at first, but my anxiety soon dissipated thanks to his loony, down-to-earth personality. "Stick with me," he would say about some problem we were working through. "I'll have you farting through silk." Right from the get-go we worked famously together, eventually becoming a permanent creative team and close friends.

There was no denying that Jim was a superb art director but he was equally well known around the agency for his rooftop play-dates with his secretary, Heather. The two of them would sneak up to the roof of our building at 437 Madison, spread Jim's sports jacket down on the hard pebble surface, tear each other's clothes off and have rip-roaring sex for hours. The only thing that slowed them down was the onset of winter. "Geez, I'm freezing my nuts off up there," he would complain when he got back to the office, blowing into his cupped hands. "Too much fuckin' wind today."

One afternoon, he returned from the roof agitated.

"What's wrong?" I asked. "You and Heather have a fight?"

"No," he said unfastening his belt and dropping his drawers. "I think my dick is frostbitten."

In between Jim's dalliances with Heather we began working on the Country Club ad. After brainstorming for a few days I became frustrated. "You know, Jim," I said, "Nobody would want any of this shit if it weren't free."

Jim paused for a second and then lept off his chair. "That's it!"

"That's what?" I asked.

"That's the fuckin' headline, schmuck."

He scribbled the line down with a Magic Marker, "Three things you would never want if they weren't free." I changed "you would" to "you'd," and we had it.

The ad had sheer honesty, irony, wit and sarcasm, all of which would come to define my creative style for the rest of my career.

# Three items you'd never want if they weren't free.

My first print ad at Carl Ally Inc. for Country Club Malt Liquor

Although we knew the headline was a winner, we still had to get it approved by our creative directors. Jim was unfazed. I looked like a Chihuahua in a snowstorm. Jim led the way to our bosses, Ralph and Marty, with his macho confidence. Although this was only a one-off, small-space print ad to run in college newspapers, our insatiably demanding creative directors gave it the same scrutiny they'd give a national TV campaign. This was par for the course at Ally. Nothing was too small not to be perfect.

They loved it. The two of us strutted out of their office like a couple of wise guys after a good meeting with the Don. "Yeah, that's right. That's right. We bad!"

It was a defining moment for me. There would only be one first test at Ally and I had aced it. As soon as the ad was produced, the first proof went right up on my office wall like the other hotshot writers and art directors. It was only a promotion ad, but I would sit and gaze at it for hours, proud as a new father, his nose pressed up against the nursery window. Incidentally, the ad was not only a success for me personally, Country Club emptied their entire inventory in just two weeks, which meant they were also selling a lot of malt liquor. Being self-deprecating and admitting their giveaways were junk made the Country Club brand cool.

Good ads work.

Of course, I learned quickly that you had better have more than one good ad taped to your wall. The expression "you're only as good as your last ad" had to have come from Ally. And there was another version of the adage, "You're only as good as your last piece of body copy." Writing copy at Ally went beyond providing information about the product or service. It was an art form. The creative directors would pore over every word like it was going to be etched eternally in marble tablets. I sweated each and every syllable. But as painful as the process was, the end result was that I became a "Carl Ally writer."

Body copy was the battleground where all the writing wars were fought. For the most part I learned everything by trial and excruciating error, going back and forth from my office to the creative director's so often I wore a rut into the floor. The only two words I longed to hear were "It's approved."

Every once in a long while someone at the agency would take the time to offer me some invaluable guidance.

Amil Gargano and Jim Durfee were Carl's partners. Carl brought them along from Detroit in 1963 when the agency was born. I had a good relationship with Amil, but Amil, as an art director, oversaw all the art directors and designers in the shop. He supervised typography, design, photography, layouts etc, so naturally, as a writer, I had less to do with Amil on a day-to-day basis.

Jim, however, I came to know very well. He was a superlative writer and deep thinker. He didn't interact very much with the rest of the firm, mostly keeping to himself, his back to his office door, pensively going about his business. He was a bit older than most of the other creative directors. He stood 6'5", had a shock of white, white hair, was built like a defensive end and had a serious demeanor, all of which made him quite intimidating. And like everyone else in the place, he did not suffer fools very well.

Once, I needed Jim's approval on a piece of Hertz copy I'd been struggling with for weeks. I knew it wasn't right. So I waited anxiously outside his door to talk to him about it. I was really sweating.

*Oh, you don't have time to see me today? No problem. I'll be happy to come back later, Jim.*

*Better yet, maybe I'll run across the street for a cup of coffee and get hit by a bus and die instantly. Meeting canceled. Sorry, Jim.*

Of course, he noticed me standing there.

"What do you have for me, Steve?" he asked politely, pushing back from his desk and motioning me to pull up a chair. Although I was scared as shit of him, I think he liked me. I had built a reputation at the agency of a talented, young, scrappy guy who gave it his all no matter how small the assignment.

"I dunno, Jim," I said, nervously clicking my ballpoint pen so furiously the plastic was about to melt. "I've been working on this damn thing forever. I just can't seem to make it work. There's just too much information I have to get in here. See, I gotta say…"

"Let me take a look," he offered.

He took the copy from me and gave it a quick once over. He then set the paper down on his lap and leaned towards me. I was shaking. I thought I was going to be fired.

"Steve," he said, calmly, taking me by surprise. "Why don't you just tell me, in your own words, exactly what you want to say here."

I looked down at the copy and began to talk.

"No, no, no. Put the paper down and just look at me," he said firmly but compassionately. "Now, just talk to me. Quietly. In your own words. Like we're having a conversation on a Sunday afternoon before the ball game begins. Tell me what you want to say."

So I did.

"Good," he replied. "Now, that's exactly how you should write, like you're talking, personally, one to one, to one of your many girlfriends. You speak beautifully. Write the way you speak. It's as simple as that."

Best piece of advice I ever got.


Marty Puris, my immediate supervisor, was much tougher on me than Jim. He simply didn't have a wealth of patience for anyone. He was a brilliant writer but didn't like to spend a lot of time handholding, as he called it. Once in a long while, however, he did just that, and it just so happens that he was an incredible teacher as well.

I came into his office one morning complaining that I was having trouble writing a very long piece of copy for a two-page spread for Fiat. I needed to explain about a dozen of the new car's features, and I simply couldn't organize my thoughts. The writing was all over the place.

"Give it here, Steve," Marty said, grabbing the copy from me.

"You need structure," he exclaimed. "Writing body copy is like writing a three-act play. Pretend you're Shakespeare."

"In Act I, you need an opening paragraph or two that introduces readers to the issue or problem. Here, you need to set the reader up. In this case, tell them how the new car will make their lives better. And you need to say it in a way they can empathize with."

"Act II is essentially the product sell, all the facts and features about the car that gives the customer permission to believe the ad's promise. In this case, it's the important selling points of the car. But you can't simply tick them off like a menu. You must persuade the reader, romance them. You have to make them fall in love with you (the car)."

"Finally, there's Act III, where you take the nice little story you created to its logical conclusion, usually tying it back to the opening paragraph or the headline. If you've done your job, the reader is now on the hook. Just reel him in."

"Capisce?"

"Yeah, I capisce. Thanks, boss, I appreciate it."

"No problem. Now, don't let the door hit you in the ass on your way out."

Carl, along with the legendary David Ogilvy, swore by long body copy. Intuitively, that didn't make a lot of sense to me. Who in their right mind would want to sit and read an entire freakin' page of body copy in tiny, nine-point type unless of course you were stuck under a hair dryer all afternoon at Sassoon?

A Pan Am ad with long copy written by Jim Durfee.

As it turned out, my instincts were correct. Research eventually proved that 80% of body copy went entirely unread. As years went by (and with the explosion of the MTV generation) even Ally's copy finally got shorter.

Famous for their creativity, Ally often scored big with their clients for shrewd marketing strategies as well. Northeast Airlines and Hertz are two cases that immediately come to mind.

During the recession of the late sixties, Northeast was struggling to fill seats on their Yellowbird jets and came to Ally for help. Carl devised a brilliant strategy. Since the planes were flying out half full, he suggested that the business traveler (70% of total travelers) pull down the empty middle seat and use it as a comfortable desk. Northeast then promoted themselves as the airline for business travelers. It turned a huge negative into a positive. Ally launched their famous Northeast Yellowbird "Seat-and-a-Half" campaign built round this single, unorthodox concept. And it worked. Northeast's sales started flying as high as their planes.

Hertz Rent-A-Car was dealing with a very different problem. Avis, their biggest competitor, had skillfully positioned themselves as the underdog in the business: "We're only No. 2. We try harder." Carl's response was, "Okay, we'll give you second place, and then we're going to tell the whole fucking world why we're number one." Carl, true to form, took the fight directly to Avis, emphasizing Hertz's overwhelming dominance in the industry by telling the customer that when you rent from Hertz, you'll feel safe and confident. And if by chance something goes awry with your rental, you'll have the biggest car rental company in the world behind you.

The tagline: "Hertz. You don't just rent a car. You rent a company."

# For years, Avis has been telling you Hertz is No.1.

# Now we're going to tell you why.

Hertz

Hertz finally gives Avis the finger in Ally's introductory ad for Hertz.

Ally's reputation was clearly that of a brilliant creative shop that solved problems with innovative print and television, but a funny thing happened on the way to becoming a premier Madison Avenue agency: Ally also became known as one of the more innovative strategic agencies. The lesson? Don't let your reputation, no matter how good it is, pigeonhole you. As George Lois taught me years ago, just solve the client's problem.

Great ideas are great ideas.

# 9 SERIAL PSEUDO-INTIMACY

Virtually everything in the ad industry of the '60s and '70s was dramatically different than it is today…and that includes sexual mores. The Sexual Revolution was in full tilt in the late sixties. AIDS hadn't exploded into the public consciousness yet, and condoms were harder to find than a kosher deli in Dubai. Agencies were brimming with the sexual tension of a high school homeroom. It seemed everyone was screwing around with someone and being married didn't enter into the equation. Advertising, like Hollywood, was always considered a glamour industry. There was no shortage of sexy, stylish young women who wanted to be secretaries or assistants, especially at the hot creative shops. (There were a lot of sharp, stylish men as well, but I wasn't interested.)

One of those girls was Tory Baker, a very cute, spirited, 22 year old, fresh out of Miss Porter's School and the Southampton Meadow Club. She was the "shiksa goddess" I had long dreamt about; long, lean and beautiful with straight golden blonde hair. She always put herself together in that understated, alluring, WASPy way. The top three buttons of her tailored blouse were always open juuussst enough. Apparently I was the only male in the office who hadn't noticed her, a major lapse on my part. Fortunately, she noticed me.

She used to walk by my office a little too often, never looking directly at me, but making her presence known nonetheless. I began to recognize the click-clack of her heels and her long stride on the hard slate floors from halfway down the hall.

One day, she came into my office to deliver a memo and I finally got to really see her for the first time. She was undeniably beautiful and after chatting briefly it was clear she was also charming and witty and gentile. What more could a Jewish copywriter want? From that moment on, I couldn't keep away from her, flirting at her desk every chance I got, timing my leaving the office so I'd bump into her at the elevators, "Oh, so there you are?" And using the men's room way down at her end of the hall so often she must have thought I had a urinary infection.

I couldn't get enough of her. Aside from several summer camp romances, Tory was my first real deal. From the moment I met her I had a queasy feeling in my stomach and it was becoming permanent. I couldn't eat, sleep, or concentrate on anything for more than a few minutes. Combine this with my ADD and, needless to say, I wasn't terribly productive during this period.

When I passed her in the hall my heart would thump so loudly, I swore everyone in the office could hear it. They may not have actually heard it but after several weeks they all knew about it.

I finally got up the nerve to ask her out. I decided to take her to Brandy's on 84th, where they had live Carly Simon-type music and the best frozen daiquiris in the city. Brandy's had always been a great first date place for me. And it was with Tory. We quickly got hammered and openly flirted with each other in a way we couldn't do at work. She was young but I was soon to discover that young in those days didn't mean inexperienced.

When I walked her home, I was faced with the proverbial first-date kiss quandary. I figured I had five options.

Option One: No kiss. Act totally cool. Say good night. Leave.

Option Two: Kiss her on the cheek. Act cool. Say good night. Leave.

Option Three: Kiss her on the lips. Act less cool. Say good night. Leave.

Option Four: Kiss her on the lips. Drop the cool thing. Make out. Leave.

Option Five: Ditch the cool thing entirely. Make out like a lunatic. Beg her to let me sleep over.

I went with Option Five. If she hadn't been living with her mother at the time, I would have begged her to let me move in. (Option Six)

Four months later, she moved in with me to my Kips Bay apartment. We were crazy about each other. We spent all day and all night together—and that still wasn't enough. The butterflies continued. I had never experienced real love before and I loved it. We couldn't get enough of each other. Sex felt like the first time every time. I became addicted to it and thankfully so did she. Once, we went out to her mother's house in Southampton. Tory forgot the key and we couldn't get in. No problem. We found a semi-private area of her backyard and made love all afternoon. Her brother eventually let us in. He'd been home for two hours.

We did everything together. We went to Knicks and Jets games, saw rock concerts, played softball, traveled all over the world, hung out at her mom's house with her brothers and older sister on weekends and played tennis on the manicured grass courts at the Meadow Club (subsequently getting kicked out when I refused to wear white).

One afternoon at work, I was abruptly called into the office of one of Tory's bosses. He slammed the door behind me.

"What's up?" I asked.

"Tory is my private stock. So back off!"

"What are you talking about?" I asked incredulously.

"Just stay down at your end of the hall."

I stood there speechless, staring at him in amazement. I was so caught off guard by what he said, I needed time to process it.

"You know, Tory and I have been with each other for months now,"

I finally spoke up. "She just moved in with me."

No reaction.

"A word to the wise," he proffered in a very serious tone. He then walked over to the door to signal that our conversation was through.

In those days sexual harassment cases were virtually non-existent, so Tory and I didn't have a practical option of talking to his boss about the incident or, even further, taking legal action. I decided that regardless of how pissed off I was, the best course of action would be to ignore the whole thing. His infatuation (or whatever it was) would likely pass, especially if he saw me flirting with Tory all day long. One thing was certain, though, I sure as shit wasn't going to back off.

One morning, we both came into the office with our hair still wet from the morning shower. This boss of hers took one look at us and, like a spoiled kid whose parents had just taken away his Erector Set, ran into his office and slammed the door behind him. I didn't know if he was jealous, in love with her, in love with me or what, but he was hugely pissed off and seemed to have no shame about letting us know. I had a sinking feeling that this bizarre game was far from over.

It wasn't. From that moment on, he started killing every piece of copy I wrote. He made me rewrite the same damn body copy on two great Fiat ads a dozen times in a dozen different ways—and all of them were good. He simply refused to approve anything that had my fingerprints on it.

The drama was closing in around a trip to Europe that Tory and I had been planning for months. After literally working through the night on my sixth revision of one of the ads, I went into his office exhausted, sat down and handed him the copy. He scanned it.

"Not right," he said for the seventh time.

"Ya know, I'm leaving on vacation tomorrow. With Tory," I told him as nonchalantly as I could put it.

## IN ROME, WHERE IT'S HARD ENOUGH JUST BEING A CAR, THE FIAT 124 IS USED AS A TAXI.

FIAT. THE BIGGEST SELLING CAR IN EUROPE.

## JUST BECAUSE A CAR IS INEXPENSIVE, DOESN'T MEAN IT HAS TO LOOK LIKE A VOLKSWAGEN.

Two of my early ads for Fiat.

"Rewrite it," he demanded, not looking up.

"There are only so many ways I can write this," I pleaded.

"Look, Steve, I'll make it simple. If you don't have a perfect piece of copy on my desk by the end of the day, you can kiss your vacation goodbye."

I grabbed the copy and left.

There wasn't a chance in hell I was canceling our trip to play, "Let's rewrite more body copy." But I gave it one last shot. Later that night I dropped off my final draft, and the next day Tory and I took off for Europe as planned. I called Jim, my art director, at home.

"Jimmy boy, do me a favor. If you hear rumblings that I'm about to be fired, call me in Rome."

"You sure you want to fuck with him, Steve-o? He's angry as hell."

"No shit. But if he's really going to fire my ass, there's no reason to rush back. Tory and I will stay another week or so."

A week into our trip, the hotel phone rang.

"Take a nice long look at the Sistine Chapel," Jim said.

Tory and I tacked another week onto our vacation. Maybe I should have been more concerned about losing my job—and Tory's. But she was moving on anyway. She had just accepted a job in media sales at NBC to begin after we got back. After all I'd been through I actually felt relieved that I wouldn't have to put up with his crap any longer.

Although her pain-in-the-ass boss would have loved to see me go, fortunately not everyone at Ally felt the same way. When we returned, I learned that one of the other creative directors had come to my rescue. Apparently, my writing talent, the thing that has always saved my ass, saved it again. Dave Altschiller, a more nurturing and supportive creative director (but no less demanding) had requested that I be transferred into his group.

All told, Tory and I had been dating for more than four years, almost as long as we were at the agency. But there comes a time in every long-standing relationship when you have to take the next logical step. While Tory was looking ahead to something more permanent I was looking ahead to the next Knicks game.

Although she never mentioned marriage to me explicitly, I knew she wanted something more. She had even talked about converting to Judaism when we were on a trip to Israel. Obviously, that touched me deeply but I simply couldn't handle the self-inflicted "pressure".

I kept envisioning walking down the aisle of Temple Israel in Great Neck. On one side of the aisle would be my insane Jewish family, on the other Tory's restrained, understated, Locust Valley, lock-jawed, Southampton family. During cocktail hour my 60 aunts, uncles, and cousins would be fist-fighting over blintzes and gefilte fish while Tory's family would be ten deep around the bar guzzling Smirnoff vodka by the jug.

I was paralyzed with fear.

We eventually went through a painful breakup, landing me on a shrink's couch for the first time and beginning what would become a lifelong commitment to psychotherapy.

My therapist told me I had been living in "pseudo-intimacy."

"What's that?" I asked him.

"What do you think it is?" he responded shrinkishly.

It took me weeks of analysis to figure out the answer. During one of our sessions, he asked what my feelings toward Tory were at a particular time in our relationship. I was so emotionally bereft that it took me an entire fifty-minute session of deafening silence to finally ask, "What exactly do you mean by 'feelings'?"

As for pseudo-intimacy, after a gazillion sessions (by now I was on the couch four days a week) I finally understood that I was merely going through the motions with Tory, not really connecting with her on a deeper, more mature and emotional level. Yes, we were living together. Yes, we loved each other. But for me it was kind of a fun game. I had someone to eat, sleep and play catch with, but I never fully gave myself to her and sadly never truly understood what a special soul she was.

My wise Orthodox father, on the other hand, did. Turns out I wasn't the only Penchina man who loved her. Tory was the first shiksa my father ever invited to one of our Passover Seders. Insisting that Tory sit next to him at the head of the table, an honored seat in our family, he led her word by word through the Haggadah, the story of the Jewish exodus from slavery in Egypt, and insisted she drink the requisite four cups of sweet wine (which she did, no problem).

My father understood Tori in a way I didn't.

After we broke up, Tory moved on quickly. Too quickly as far as I was concerned. I was lost for a long time with feelings of regret, sadness, depression and confusion. After hundreds of emotionally taxing sessions with my therapist, I decided I wanted her back. But it wasn't going to happen. She had found a nice gentile guy from Southampton and gotten married. That was that. I blew it.

Despite all my trials and tribulations at Ally—the intense pressure to produce the amazing advertising that was the very essence of Carl's shop day in and day out and the fiercely demanding creative directors who never took their feet off the gas pedal—I accomplished what I had set out to. I learned how to write from the best print agency that ever was, arguably the preeminent ad agency in history. I eventually made peace with all the creative directors there, primarily because I had become a great writer like them. As I said, the moment I walked into the agency, I became a permanent member of the club of elite agencies.

But when I finally left Ally in 1972, I was emotionally spent. I had always considered myself a pretty tough character, someone who could take a punch as well as he could deliver one, but my years at Ally had taught me otherwise. I had a porcelain chin.

In the end I was ambivalent about leaving. After all, I had worked so hard to get where I was. But as much as I loved Carl, his extraordinary agency and all that I achieved there, I was severely lacking in one big piece of the business. I hadn't done a single TV commercial during my time there.

# 10 IT'S A MIRACLE!

While I was figuring out my next move, I halfheartedly committed to a job at a small, weird but creative shop by the name of DKG. Their important clients were Remington shavers, Talon Zippers, and Coty cosmetics. More importantly, to me at least, they made a lot of TV ads.

I hadn't been at DKG long when I returned to my office after a day of filming one of my first spots for Lady Remington with a half-naked, wholly beautiful Lauren Hutton. (I had never worked with anyone so beautiful. Usually I was too busy writing glamorous rental car copy.) While I was standing at my desk replaying the day over and over and over again in my head (All-Time-Favorite Dream #9: Shoot commercial with half-naked Lauren Hutton. Check.), I noticed a pile of phone messages from Allen Kay, the creative director on the Xerox account at Needham, Harper & Steers.

I had never met Allen but I was quite familiar with his work, having recently judged a bunch of Xerox advertising at recent award shows. Needham was right up there with the best agencies in the city. After some hesitation I decided to call him back.

Allen got right to the point and asked if I was interested in coming to Needham. Although I was anything but in love with my current situation, I politely told him I wasn't ready to make a move. Truth be told, I was a full-fledged, card-carrying Ally snob, and Needham was not in the club. Xerox intrigued me though. It was a global, high technology, business-to-business account that was miles away from the kinds of products I was used to working on.

Allen was tenacious. He kept calling and calling until I finally agreed to meet him after work one day. Unexpectedly, Lois Korey, Needham's executive creative director, joined us. I instantly fell in love with both of them. They were warm, funny, quick and seemed to be down-to-earth, decent people. As my mother would say, they were *hamish.* It didn't take 20 minutes to feel like I belonged there. After a couple of hours of laughter and 15 minutes of serious discussion, Lois made me a generous offer on the spot to work alongside Allen on Xerox. I told them I would need a few days to think it over.

I called back the next morning.

Needham was a totally different animal than Ally. For the first time in years I didn't feel like gnats were doing a conga line in my stomach when I stepped off the elevator in the morning. With its midwestern roots (they were headquartered in Chicago), Needham was a much more laid back and friendly environment. I had forgotten what nice people were like. In stark contrast to the ball-busting creative directors at Ally, Allen and Lois were teddy bears. Lois was the nurturing mother to everyone in the creative department. Undeniably, they were both talented, but just as importantly, they ran their department like one big, happy, neurotic, Jewish family. It felt like I was home for the high holidays, but without the noodle pudding.

Allen was a perfectionist, an obsessive-compulsive genius of an art director. He spent most of his day head down in his layout pad, doodling and mumbling to himself about whether to tighten the spacing of his headline a millionth of an inch. The rest of the day he spent bumming cigarettes off anyone who would swear not to tell his wife he still smoked.

In Lois's previous life, she had been a successful comedy writer in Hollywood, working for Joan Rivers among others. She had the quickest, funniest mind I'd ever encountered. She would walk around the agency cracking acerbic one-liners that had the whole department in stitches. But she was also a top-flight creative director. She hired talented art directors and copywriters, paid them fairly and let them do their thing. She was motherly but never hovered. Unlike many creative directors she trusted her hires.

Allen, Lois and their creative teams consistently came up with stellar advertising for Xerox, the best of which was a 90-second commercial entitled "Football." In the spot a frustrated football coach finds himself losing the big game because his lame-brained players couldn't remember the plays. During halftime he sends his quarterback into the locker room to quickly run off copies of the plays on the team's new Xerox portable copier. The coach tapes the copies to the uniforms of his players, enabling them to read the Xs and Os during the game. In the final seconds, a receiver checks the play one last time, takes one step backward and catches the winning touchdown pass.

The bar had been set very high.

The creative troops on the account had been struggling for months to come up with a worthy sequel. My first assignment was to do just that. Write a 90-second commercial introducing the world to the new Xerox 9200 Duplicating System, the first high-speed copier of its kind.

Xerox's future was riding on the innovative new machine. So was mine.

Since I had come from one of the hottest shops in the city, everybody expected me to walk on water. But as confident as I was in my abilities, I was no messiah. Deep down I knew "Football" would be a tough act to follow.

The account team immediately descended on me with a full-blown orientation on the new machine, the key selling point being that this super-sized, super-powerful, super-fast copier made perfect copies at the amazing speed of two pages per second. What's more, it then collated, bound or stapled them into individual bins so you could make booklets of documents amazingly fast. There was nothing even close to it on the market. This new machine was expected to transform the entire copier business.

I ran into trouble almost immediately. The first problem was that unlike every other art director I ever worked with, Allen didn't like teaming up with his copywriter. He preferred for each of us to work alone, something I hadn't done since the days on my parents' Ping-Pong table. Even then, my mother and sister were always around. I tried to cajole him into working collaboratively, hanging around his office, tossing around ideas. But he eventually kicked me out, saying I should give the assignment some thought on my own. Dejected, I dragged myself back to my office and began working. Solo. I leaned back in my chair, put my feet up on the desk and began to think.

And think.

And think.

I stared up at the crinkly white ceiling tiles and ran everything I had learned from the account group through my mind. Since I didn't have anyone to bounce ideas off, I bounced them off myself.

ME: "Boils down to two main product benefits: the machine copies booklets of documents and does it amazingly fast. Right?"

MYSELF: "Right."

ME: "It's about booklets of documents, not individual copies."

MYSELF: "Right again. You're quick."

I glanced down at my desk and began digging through reams of brochures, research documents and stacks of old concepts left over from the last team.

ME: "All right, there's got to be something here I can pick up on. It can't be all bad."

I looked through the old ads.

MYSELF: "Sorry, pal. It's all bad."

ME (*picking up a layout*): "'The Print Shop of the Future.' Is this guy kidding? No wonder they hired me so fast. I should've asked for more money."

MYSELF: "Told you . . ."

ME: "That's piss-water under the bridge. Focus."

Frustrated, I threw a few sharp yellow pencils into the ceiling tiles. They all stuck.

ME: "Cool. Okay, I have to think of something good before they fall down. That's my deadline. Now, who in the hell would need booklets of documents, not individual copies, but booklets? Booklets?"

MYSELF: "I dunno, teachers?"

ME: "Maybe? Rules for students?"

MYSELF: "Wake me when you've got something."

ME: "Some business situation? A big presentation of some kind?"

MYSELF: "Wow, something about business. Now that's a novel approach. Bet they haven't thought of that before?"

ME: "What the hell do I do? What...do...I...do?"

MYSELF: "I'll tell you what to do. You get on the crosstown bus, and march your ass back to that weird little agency, get down on your knees and beg them to take you back. That's what you do."

ME: "It's too late, I've already started here. It would be viewed as a colossal defeat. All right, all right, relax.

Let's see? Politicians? A strategy manual for a Senate race or something?"

MYSELF: "Okay. You're getting warmer."

ME: "Yeah, there may be something there, write that down... Let's see, maybe we can do something about sports?"

MYSELF: "Oh, that's golden. That's what we'll do. A fuckin' sports commercial. Hey, how 'bout a football spot? They haven't done that for six whole months. "

ME: "Give me a break, I'm new here."

MYSELF: "You got that right."

ME: "I'm a raving asshole."

MYSELF: "Your words, not mine."

This went on for nearly a week, with Allen peeking into the office every now and then to see how I was doing. All day, all night, a million concepts ran through my head. Every thought was about the Xerox 9200. I didn't even answer my phone, which was unheard of considering it might have been one of my shrinks. My panic attacks were back with a vengeance.

ME: "God, what the hell do I do with this fuckin' thing? Hmm… God? Hell? Heaven? Wait a minute! Maybe God himself needs the new machine?"

MYSELF: "God created the whole damn universe in six days. You think he needs a copier?"

ME: "Hold it! Something's coming. Something…is…coming. Maybe it is about God…or someone who works for him."

MYSELF: "What? Like his gardener?"

ME: "Not exactly, schmuck, more like a rabbi or priest. Maybe we'll do something that takes place in a church.

I gotta take a leak."

MYSELF: "Now? You have to go to the bathroom *now?*"

Still in deep thought but edging toward cautious optimism, I pushed back from my desk. As I was running out, I noticed a pencil drop from the ceiling. Was this a sign?

Unlike the Almighty, I hadn't taken a day off since I got the assignment. But on this day, standing at a urinal in Needham's 19th floor men's room, the idea hit me like falling concrete.

ME: "A monk!"

MYSELF: "A monk?"

ME: "A fuckin' monk! Copying a manuscript…for years…meticulously…by hand…in the crypts of a monastery, only to find out that his Father Superior wants him to make one hundred more sets. No, let's make that five hundred more sets."

ME AND MYSELF: "Immediately!"

ME: "That's it! A big, fat, living, breathing, celibate, wine-chugging monk!"

I immediately ran down the hall to Allen's office and blurted out the idea. Without lifting his eyes off his layout pad, he smiled to himself, and as nonchalantly as if I was handing him a time sheet, told me, "I like it. Write it up."

Like George Carlin on speed, I wrote the original 90-second spot in under an hour.

ME: "So, after hearing from the Father Superior that he wanted five hundred more sets, our chubby little monk goes downtown to a friend who works at a copy center and asks him to run off the big job. His buddy knocks out five hundred more sets lickety-split.

"Copies in hand, the monk scrambles back to the monastery and gives the completed sets to the Father. Utterly stunned, the Father Superior looks up toward Heaven and says, 'It's a miracle!'

"Our hero monk gazes up, and gives You-Know-Who a knowing glance, as if to communicate, 'You and I both know what just went down, but let's keep this between us, all right?'"

The spot that put me on the map.
The final frame of Xerox's "The Monk" commercial, 1976.

MYSELF: "You nailed it, you brilliant sonofabitch!"

I went back to Allen's office and read him the script. In anticipation he had already drawn up the storyboard with this cute cherubic monk poring over his manuscript in the catacombs, taking a bus into the city, getting the booklets copied and delivering the huge stack of copies to the Father. In the last frame our contented little monk looks up toward Heaven with an innocent smile. Allen's storyboard brought the whole idea to life. We sat there in his office, laughing our asses off.

Suddenly, Allen was out the door. "Let's take it to Lois," he said.

"Now?" I asked, panic-stricken.

"What, you afraid?"

"Me? Afraid? I used to work at Ally, remember?"

We walked down the hall to Lois's office. I had to go to the bathroom again.

Lois was working at her sofa, as usual. Allen took her through the storyboard. She began smiling immediately—she was so quick. Allen then turned to me, "You're on, big guy." I began reading the script.

My heart was thumping out of my rib cage. I hadn't felt like this since presenting my first Country Club malt liquor ad at Ally. *Think about what you're doing*, I told myself. *Read it with energy and pace, big fella.*

Lois didn't hesitate.

"It's wonderful," she said, smiling broadly. "It's really charming, guys. And funny. And you did a very persuasive job of selling the copier, it really is an *incredible* machine. Wally [meaning Wally Olesen, Xerox's corporate Marketing Director] is gonna love this. Very nice work, Steve. Okay, you, too, Allen. I wouldn't change a thing. Just terrific…"

She quickly picked up the phone and summoned the account team.

Two minutes later, three account guys came rushing in, huffing, puffing, rep ties flying, sweating nervously. They'd been waiting for this moment for months. Allen took them through the storyboard. I read the script again.

Silence.

Crap, I thought. True to form, these chicken-shit account guys are going to find some dumbass reason to kill it. But they're not going to hurt me. I'll shoot myself first. I looked around Lois's office. Where's a gun when you need it?

Finally, Michael Kirby, the management supervisor, broke the silence. In his affected British accent he said, "Bloody well, I think we actually did it!"

*We? What we?! We didn't do shit!*

Peter Cooney, second in command, ran over and gave me a high-five. "First time up to bat, Penchina, and you hit a goddamn grand-slam!"

"Mazel tov!" announced Brian Sherwood, my best gentile friend in the office. "This might even be better than 'Football.' Great job, Steve. Well done, Allen. I may even invite the two of you to my Christmas party."

Several days later, we presented to Xerox. They flipped over the commercial. Three big-ass clients stood there in the conference room, howling. There was an audible sigh of relief; they'd all been feeling the same pressure I was. The "It's a miracle!" line was a huge hit. It worked on so many levels: It was a miraculous new copier, had miraculous speed and performed so many miraculous tasks. Indeed, Xerox was a miraculous company.

Surprisingly, selling it up the ranks at Xerox wasn't the slam-dunk we all expected. Yes, the marketing and product guys in Rochester flipped over it, but several corporate executives in Stamford were concerned that the idea might be offensive to the Catholic Church. Thanks to the wily efforts of Wally Olesen, though, we were able to sell our little monk to Xerox's Chairman of the Board. After that, everyone fell into line.

Wally was a very smart man with a great sense of humor. He understood that it was emotion that made his brand tick. He wanted businessmen and women to like Xerox, to feel good about Xerox, to know that Xerox identified with their problems.

"Don't worry about the products. They'll sell themselves," he repeatedly drilled into our heads. "Our job is to sell the Xerox brand." He was way ahead of his time.

Although everyone fell in love with our plump little monk, the spot was so much more than just entertaining. It sold product. The first time it aired, during the 1976 All-Star game, the United States Navy bought two of the thirty $30,000 machines directly over the phone. It was the first verifiable time Xerox had ever sold a copier as a direct result of a television commercial.

All over the world people identified with the monk's plight: working long, tedious hours on an assignment only to be given a major last minute change by their boss and, oh yeah, it had to be done yesterday. Knocking off the job quickly and easily is everyone's fantasy. "The Monk" was a timeless, warm and human way to make the point.

The campaign accomplished another thing clients would give their first born to achieve. It gave them an icon for the brand. Wisely,

Xerox used "Brother Dominic" everywhere and anywhere they could: At conventions, tradeshows, retail events, store openings, sales programs, event parties, copy stores, and new product seminars.

Jack Eagle, a Borscht Belt comic from the Catskills, starred in the commercial as the Monk. Everyone thought I had lost my marbles when I casted him. "There's no way in hell the client will approve him," the account guys warned. "Too Jewish." *Wrong*. The client loved him.

As incredibly successful as "The Monk" was, Xerox felt they still needed to add a second commercial to the mix. Talk about a tough act to follow. For this new spot I worked with a very funny and talented guy named Tony Angotti. After several long weeks, we created a funny commercial dubbed "The Binkley Brothers".

You try finding eight redheads.

In preparing for a critical meeting with the Binkley brothers, the information technology chief of the firm runs off four copies of the presentation—one for himself, one for his boss and one each for the brothers. His hysterical boss notices the copies and cries out, "You know how many Binkley brothers there are?!"

Cut to: eight Binkley brothers, soon to be joined by their mother, all with red hair.

If you want to make a splash in this world, you've got to take risks. In this case, creative risks. My dad pounded into my head from an early age not to be a conformist. "Stick out from the crowd," he used to tell me. The Monk, or as Jack Eagle used to say, the "Schmonk," became a larger-than-life personality, bigger than anyone could have imagined. It launched a multi-billion-dollar business for Xerox in a very short time, and there was little doubt that the television introduction was a critical part of the success.

"The Monk" campaign ran for more than 20 years. You can count on one hand the number of advertising campaigns that have had that much staying power.

Indeed, I hit a resounding, base-clearing homerun my first time up to bat at Needham. This one 90-second spot would turn my entire world upside down.

Christ, maybe I *could* walk on water?

# 11 THE MONK MADE ME DO IT

The success of "The Monk" was a career, and life altering event. While I'll never let Allen off the hook for making me sweat out the writing by my lonesome, he more than came through in taking the spot from storyboard to America's (and the world's) living rooms. Not only did he help refine the idea, he virtually single-handedly produced it.

The night "The Monk" won The One Show Gold Pencil for "Best in Show"—the advertising equivalent of the Oscars "Best Picture" award—Allen turned to me in the sold-out auditorium at Lincoln Center and whispered, "If we win, you go up and pick up the Clio."

"What are you talking about?" I said. "We should both go up."

"No, you go alone. You deserve it. Besides, I've got a lot at home already."

With the exception of Lois Kory, I didn't know of anyone in the business who would have given away such an honor. Most industry people would trample their grandmothers to death just to grab the spotlight for a couple of seconds.

Moments later, the master of ceremonies opened the envelope and announced, "And the one you've all been waiting for. The winner of Best in Show for Television issssssssss… 'The Monk,' from Xerox Corporation. Agency: Needham, Harper & Steers, New York." Production Company: Lovinger, Tardio, Melsky."

"We won?" I asked Allen, like I'd suddenly developed a hearing problem.

"Duh, yeah?!" he answered. "Get goin'!"

I couldn't. My legs had turned to Jell-O. Allen slapped me on the back and pushed me out of my seat. The 15 or so people in the Needham contingent were going wild. As I began making my way down the aisle I was blinded by the glare of the spotlight. The entire scene was surreal. My friends and colleagues were applauding and whistling, kissing me, slapping me, giving me high-fives.

I caught a glimpse of myself on one of the two giant TV monitors at either end of the stage. I must confess I looked sharp in the new Armani suit I had bought for the occasion. Very sharp.

Everything was moving in slow motion. I felt like it had taken me an hour to finally reach the stage. Every sound was muffled like I was underwater. *Could all this really be for me?* I began to sweat. *What if I get to the stage and find out this was all a huge mistake? Then what the fuck do I do?*

For so many years people had given me tons of shit about my wild behavior. Hell, I had given me shit. I constantly put myself down, was sarcastic and cynical, and acted like I didn't have a care in the world. Looking back, that was all bullshit. I cared a lot. About everything. Certainly everything about my work. Indeed, I was a perfectionist. To the outside world I looked like nobody could hurt me. Inside, I was banged up and bruised.

But on this night I was awash in self-confidence. I noticed Dave Altschiller, one of my old creative directors and mentors from Ally, the one who saved me from being fired over the Tory episode. He was standing there applauding, beaming like a proud father watching his son graduate with honors. I began tearing up.

As I was walking up to the stage, I heard a loud burst of laughter. Still blinded by the spotlight, another wave of anxiety shot through me:

*Was my fly open? Had my new Armani pants split? Shit, I shouldn't have rushed the tailor.* I squinted up at one of the big monitors. Unbeknownst to me, the commercial had been playing. I looked up in time to see the final scene where Brother Dominic glances up with his coy grin. The Xerox logo faded up and the Father Superior, dumbfounded, announced, "It's a miracle!" The crowd erupted.

Possibly for the first time in my life, I felt like everyone in the world was pulling for me, lifting me up and carrying me onto the stage in a jeweled litter like the male Cleopatra. All I could hear were the shouts and applause, not only from those who knew me, but also from those who didn't, which made it that much more special.

A ten-foot-tall model in a slinky evening gown handed me my Clio, interrupting my ruminations. I tried to act appropriately nonchalant, but she must have noticed my hand shaking because she held on to the statue just a few extra seconds until she saw I had a firm grasp on it. Mercifully, we had been told not to make acceptance speeches, so I just hoisted the Clio overhead and waved it to the 1,500 or so people standing in the audience.

"Thank you," I said. "Thanks very much."

They were still applauding as I left the stage. By this time my knees had congealed and I was finally beginning to enjoy the moment. I had come a long way since getting thrown out into the cold from the night reception job at *Cunningham & Stuffy*.

After the show a bunch of us from the agency went out celebrating at Elaine's, Woody Allen's favorite haunt, on the Upper East Side. I plopped down my Clio in the center of the table so everyone in the restaurant could see. I'm not really sure why I did this. My usual custom was to act as though winning wasn't such a big deal. I guess, on this night, even I believed it was. Strangers came up and congratulated me. I was high as a kite and I hadn't even ordered a drink yet.

By 1978, my stock at Needham had really shot up. I got a big raise and received reams of press coverage from *The New York Times, The Wall Street Journal,* and all the trade publications.

Allen and I went on to win the Andy Awards' first-ever $10,000 cash prize for Best in Show, more One Show Gold and Silver Pencils, a bunch of Addy's, awards from The International Film Festival and many others.

Industry people recognized me everywhere. When I showed up at award shows reporters were always after me for interviews. Up-and-coming art directors and copywriters would push their way through the crowd to talk with me or let me know they were in the market for a new job. I would inevitably find myself standing at a crowded bar trying to answer all their questions.

When I traveled to Xerox offices around the country, employees would often ask for my autograph or for me to sign an 8" x 10" glossy of Brother Dominic. Indeed, the monk and I would become inextricably linked for the rest of our lives.

However, I didn't have the luxury of riding with the "Monk" off into the sunset. I also did a lot of award winning print advertising for Xerox.

Here are just a few:

At Xerox you need a master's.
The first ad for Xerox's Training Center in Leesburg, Virginia.

Guaranteed not to shrink.
A trade ad for the manufacturing sector.

About as funny as corporate ads get.
An ad illustrating Xerox's line of 22 copiers.

At Ally I was derided for my wise-ass ways and rebellious behavior. Now, the product of that very same behavior was being rewarded and admired. Receiving that much acclaim had a profound impact on my life, like getting out of the Vietnam War or finally losing my virginity at an old age home in Queens (long story).

For the first time ever I felt invincible, like bullets would simply bounce off me.

I was Superman with a #2 pencil.

# 12 NOW THAT'S AN OFFICE PARTY!

The year we did "The Monk", Needham's management decided to go all out for their annual Christmas party. Many agencies in those years elected to throw their holiday parties in the office, eschewing some expensive chichi club.

Needham's creative floor was transformed into a convincing replica of Studio 54. They hired a DJ, installed a parquet dance floor, dimmed the lights and hung a spinning crystal disco ball with colorful spotlights from the ceiling. The bartenders served up so much champagne they could have flooded out Third Avenue. It wasn't long before everyone was hammered. People I had never seen before were dancing half-naked on desks and chairs. Two drunken research assistants insisted on showing everyone their holiday bras. And guys were puking in the men's room like they did at their Delta Chi fraternity house.

Allen, unfortunately, was limited to how much partying he was able to do, he'd brought his wife. I, on the other hand, was a swingin' single and intended to party my ass off.

A few hours into the bedlam, I exceeded my own expectations. I found myself lying on my back on the floor of my office with not one, not two, but three delightful female employees. I was so plastered I could barely make out who was who. I knew two of them worked on another floor and the third was a nutcake producer I'd had my eye on for a year.

Before I could say, "What's your name again?", Lisa, the producer, was standing over me stark naked. It happened so fast I didn't even see her get undressed. Let me say this unequivocally: there is nothing in the world as erotic as seeing one of your fellow staff members standing buck naked next to your IBM Selectric typewriter.

As if on cue, the other two—who I finally recognized as Amy and Christina, two secretaries who worked down the hall from me—were stripping down. There I lay, flat on my back about to throw up, with three beautiful naked women on top of me, having a fourgy, less than ten feet from the dance floor. I had just one thought: *How in the hell am I going to handle this?*

I'd certainly had my share of sexual forays in my life, but nothing quite like this!

The girls answered my question for me.

Lisa tore off her party clothes and took a swan dive on top of me. Then all hell broke loose. Naked bodies were flying everywhere.

"Lisa, is that you?" I whispered.

"No, it's me, Christina."

I reached out in the dark office, illuminated only by the lights from the Third Avenue.

"Amy?"

"No. Lisa."

"Oh my god, that was great, Christina!"

"It's Amy, Steve. Better make sure I get the credit."

"My goodness, Steve," Christina declared about twenty minutes in.

"What?" I asked.

"You're pretty good at that. I never knew you were so, uh, talented. I mean, over and above your copywriting, I'm seeing a whole different side of you."

"Well, thank you, Christina," I said proudly.

"I'm Lisa. And you're very welcome."

An hour later when things began to calm down, the three girls gathered up their belongings, quickly got dressed and, as matter-of-factly as they might step out for lunch at Bloomies, they walked out of the office.

"Good night, Steve," Amy said, kissing me on the cheek.

"Have a good weekend, my talented new friend."

"Nice party, don't you think?" Christina purred. "You should come visit us more often."

The next morning, I awoke with a colossal hangover. I couldn't believe what had happened the night before. It was like winning the lottery, the Kentucky Derby and the Publisher's Clearinghouse Sweepstakes all on the same day.

I was 29 years old, on top of my career, on top of three colleagues and on top of the world.

# 13 DOING TIME AT SING-SING

As much as we all loved the perks of the ad business, the bottom line in this industry is that your ads must translate into business success. According to Xerox and some post-testing they conducted, our print ads sold a lot of machines. They also always made *Forbes* magazine's "Best Read" list, which was based on *Forbes'* own testing of the awareness produced by and effectiveness of every ad they ran. Xerox put a lot of stock in this market research.

Along with the successful introduction of the 9200, Xerox launched a succession of high-tech machines. One of these was the Xerox Large Document Copier that was able to take oversized documents or drawings and reduce them to an easy-to-handle smaller size. My art director on this assignment was also Tony Angotti, and we came up with an unusual way of demonstrating the new machine.

The 60-second spot, entitled "Sing-Sing Prison," starred the celebrated middleweight boxing champ Jake LaMotta (made famous by De Niro's Oscar-winning performance in Martin Scorcese's masterpiece, *Raging Bull*).

In our commercial LaMotta plays a tough prisoner (not a stretch) planning a prison break. The plan didn't hatch the first time around because Louie, his numbskull accomplice, couldn't slip the large

"Laundry Chute [Louie spells it "Shoot"] Escape Plan" through the narrow slot in the prison visiting area. Louie then leaves the prison, gets hold of the new Xerox Portable Copier, wheels it into his sleazy, blinking, neon-lit, 42nd Street hotel room and reduces the plans to smaller, 8½" x 11" copies that now easily fit through the slot. Despite their best laid plans, the would-be escapees get busted at the end as Jake passes copies of the plans around to his buddies in the prison exercise yard:

"All right, boys.

"Here's one for you, Mugsy.

"One for you, Fingers.

"One for you, Spike.

"And one for you, Warden. Warden??!!"

Shooting television is always a challenge. You essentially have one chance to get it right, especially when you're on location (reshoots are virtually impossible). But shooting in a real-life, maximum-security prison was truly frightening. Before anyone could set foot inside, everybody had to go through a high-level security clearance, as if we were actually visiting a prisoner. We were given those large Day-Glo orange passes to wear conspicuously around our necks, differentiating the make-believe inmates from the real ones.

It was a chilling experience, literally and figuratively. The wind chill that February day on the banks of the Hudson was 40 below zero. Actors hate the cold. Everything is more difficult: memorizing lines, taking direction, shooting retakes and standing around for long periods of time trying to keep warm. Not to mention the inmates gave everyone the creeps, shuffling around the prison yard in their drab gray prison garb, dead ringers for Edward G. Robinson and James Cagney in the old black-and-white prison movies of the '30s and '40s.

Most of our filming took place in the exercise yard, where the only thing that separated us from murderers and rapists was thin yellow plastic caution tape and a couple of guards, who frankly looked as dangerous as the prisoners.

We had been shooting in the prison for 12 hours straight and were beginning to run out of daylight in the shortened days of winter. Everyone was on edge and freezing to death.

We finally got to the last scene where Jake and his buddies were gathered in the exercise yard. We choreographed all the actors, shot a few takes, got what we wanted and wrapped the set just before dark.

As the crew began breaking down the equipment, the client bounded out of his snuggly warm rental car and began racing toward me.

"Wait! Wait!" he yelled.

I turned to face him. "What's the matter?"

"I don't like what Jake is doing."

"What's he doing?" I asked, smelling a problem.

"He's sucking on a toothpick."

"So?"

"So I don't like it."

"What's wrong with it? He's been doing that all day."

"I don't like it. It's too downscale."

"Downscale?! He's a freakin' prisoner for God's sake!"

"I don't care. It's gotta go. It's not in our image."

*This yo-yo has got to be shittin' me,* I thought. *It's 40 fucking degrees below zero, pitch dark, and he's busting my balls over a fucking toothpick?* Clients never disappoint, even the good ones.

I ran over to Paul Herriot, our director, and told him to stop packing up. "We have to shoot the last scene again. The client doesn't like Jake's toothpick."

"You're putting me on?"

"Sorry, big fella, we gotta shoot the last scene again. I tried to talk him out of it. He wouldn't budge."

"Well, I'm sure as shit not going to take his toothpick away from him," Paul said emphatically, squelching my plan to have him do the dirty work. "He's a fucking middleweight boxing champion. Did you see *Raging Bull?* He's nuutttttsss!"

I asked a couple of crew members to go over and take out Jake's toothpick. Nobody budged. I went over to the assistant director. Technically, it was his job.

"No fuckin' way. He'll punch my lights out."

I looked over at the client for some sympathy.

"The toothpick's gotta go. Sorry, Steve."

*Yeah, right,* I thought.

After this long, miserable day I had no choice but to take matters into my own hands. I took a few deep breaths, pumping myself up in the frigid damp air. Having convinced myself that I was making a much bigger deal of the situation than necessary, I approached the grizzled boxer. With Paul yelling that we had about three minutes of light left, I decided that rather than go into a long song and dance with Jake, my best course of action was swift resolution. I reached out and yanked the toothpick out of Jake's mouth, dropping it on the frozen ground. He glared at me for a long second, which was long enough for me to realize the colossal mistake I had just made. This guy made a living out of beating the crap out of people. He was known for stalking his opponent around the ring, enduring brutal punishment, so that he could land one good shot.

He reached out and with one massive hand grabbed me by my coat collar, jerking my 180-pound frame to within an inch of his angry face.

"If you ever touch me again, I'll kill you."

I believed him. I tried to say, "I understand," but no sound emanated from my mouth.

If you look carefully at the last scene of the final cut of the commercial, you'll notice that Jake (on the far right) has something dangling from his lips. Guess who won the toothpick battle?

The toothpick I almost died for.
The last frame of the Xerox "Sing-Sing Prison" comercial, starring Jake Lamotta (far right).

I knew I'd had it good, maybe too good, in the Needham years, from 1976-1980. There had been no tantrums, no rebellions, no projectile telephones or fistfights (well, one). My inner child felt safe and unthreatened. And thanks to the environment or karma or feng shui or Zen phenomenon, my creativity soared like a pigeon circling the New York Public Library, ready to make its descent.

The moral of my Needham story was twofold:

1.   Support me and nurture me but don't boss me, and I will climb Mount Everest for you. Barefoot. In shorts. Without oxygen. No sunscreen.

2.   Comfort and success, paired with a lack of familiar chaos, distracts me from what's important to me. In this case, it was my dream of one day having my own shop. (All-Time Favorite Daydream #8: Don't work for anyone. Ever again.)

But before I could make that happen, I had to move on to a bigger stage, a stage where all the money and glamour were...

# 14 WHAT BECOMES A LEGEND MOST?

Shrewd. Sexy. Ruthless. Charismatic. You didn't have to be in her presence very long to be utterly captivated by her.

Mary Wells was a larger-than-life figure, the perfect blend of Grace Kelly and Jack Welch. She was a stunning woman but if that's all you saw, you'd be entirely missing the point. She was razor sharp, a creative visionary and a hard-nosed businesswoman.

I joined Wells, Rich, Greene shortly after leaving Needham. Wells' billings then were an amazing $200 million, about four times the size of Carl Ally Inc. Carl and Mary started at roughly the same time. Although both agencies had strong creative reputations, they went about growing their shops quite differently. Carl lived and died for breakthrough creative; if he made money along the way, great. Mary believed in cutting-edge creativity too, but making big bucks was strategically important to her. She needed to be big.

Their individual creative philosophies were subtly different. Whereas Carl's advertising was in-your-face and cerebral, Wells was largely about image and style, taking monolithic corporate brands and injecting them with an incandescent glow. (Humor was also very important there.) They had an impressive roster of national, big-name television accounts that represented a huge opportunity for me.

Every pore of Wells, Rich, Greene reeked with style. The first time I set foot in their offices, in the white marble GM Building directly across the street from the Plaza Hotel, I was totally star-struck.

(Here's an interesting anecdote: My dad's best friend, Sol Blau, the doctor who introduced me to George Lois, once showed me the building plans for the new GM Building on Fifth Avenue. His close friend was the architect. He asked me which marble I preferred, white or gray? I told him white. And that's what the color they went with. So, I picked out the marble for the building that I was now working in).

The agency looked more like a rich Park Avenue apartment than an office; it was as upscale as its owner. It was formal and sophisticated with a distinct woman's touch. With the staple aromas of perfume and Minwax on the antique furniture, the office even smelled rich.

Mary did everything first class. Each executive's office had its own unique personality, furnished with real antiques, artwork, and oriental rugs. Original oil paintings worth tens of thousands of dollars dotted the hallways. TV commercials were viewed not in the conference room, as in most agencies, but on a big 35mm motion picture projector in a lush, private movie theater. Vice presidents (myself included) were served catered lunches on linen tablecloths at our desks by white-jacketed butlers. At Ally, we didn't even eat lunch. If someone did an exceptional job on one of Mary's pet projects, a bottle of Dom Pérignon and a handwritten note would greet them at their desk the following morning. And if they really knocked her stockings off, plane tickets to the Caribbean or, even better, to her chalet in the south of France would be sitting next to the Dom.

It was an intoxicating atmosphere, but there were no illusions when it came to the work. Everyone was expected to produce—big time and often. The inexorable pressure of delivering original, breakthrough advertising wasn't quietly smoldering beneath the surface. It *was* the surface.

Mary and her colorful, hall-of-fame creative director, Charlie Moss, together with a handful of creative superstars carried the whole agency. Like Carl, Mary didn't hire a lot of juniors. She had a unique staffing philosophy: overpay and overwork. She created an environment where her tremendously talented, restive and neurotic superstars were free, or rather expected, to push the borders of conventional thinking.

She was often the driving force behind bold, innovative ideas, like convincing Braniff Airlines to change their dull stewardess outfits to custom-made Pucci designs. She topped that by getting them to paint their entire fleet of planes in beautiful pastel colors so they'd stand out on the runways. These were ideas that went far beyond just advertising.

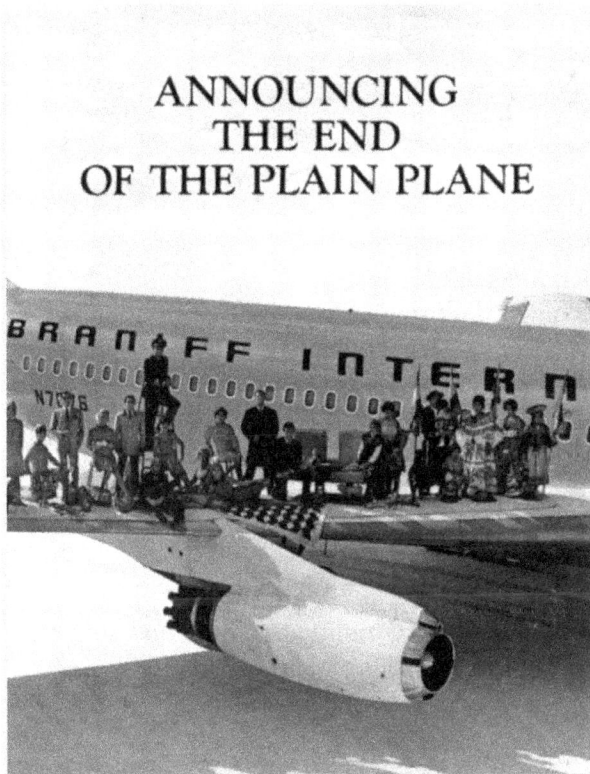

Mary Wells does away with boring planes and equally boring stewardess outfits for Braniff.

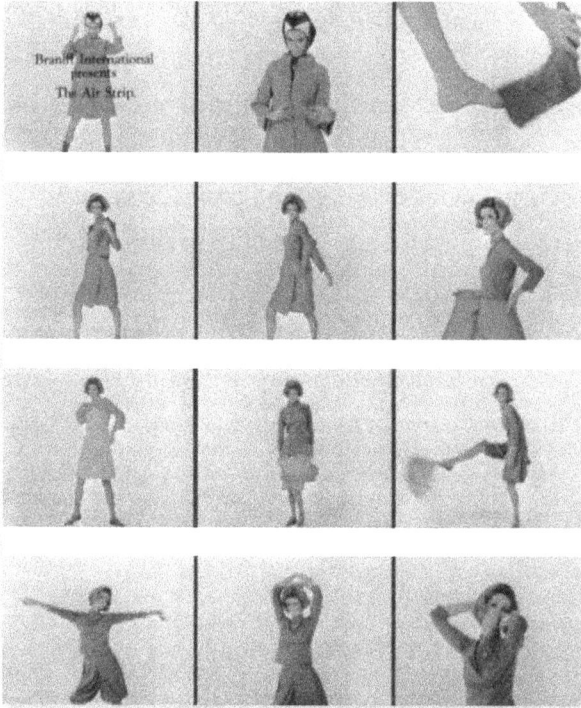

For the first time, stewardesses hit the runway.
Wells turns stewardess apparrel into high fashion in a commercial for Braniff.

Charlie's magical writing and personality brought every TV spot and print ad to life. He was the day-to-day engine that drove the shop. His stamp was on everything that went out the door. Of course, Mary's stamp was on Charlie. Their loyalty to each other was unshakable. They had worked intimately together since the early days of the agency in a room at the old Gotham Hotel on Park Avenue. She would call him at all hours of the day and night, from every corner of the world, with hunches and ideas. Charlie, ever the good soldier, always came through for her. He was the one person in a 300-strong shop who she could always count on.

Charlie had a special comedic gift, similar to the wry wit of Bob Newhart. Humor was very important at Wells. Many of their clients had a preference for funny, entertaining advertising. For example, Alka-Seltzer's witty, award-winning TV spots—"I can't believe I ate the whole thing" and "Try it, you'll like it," to name just two—were a Wells, Rich, Greene hallmark. Their humorous approach to selling stomach remedies had not only proven to be highly effective, but had became part of the public consciousness; late-night comedians and news programs often incorporated their famous slogans.

Charlie could take a storyboard and make it funnier or more effective by simply changing a word or two or by shifting a couple of TV frames. When it came to television, no one on Madison Avenue had better instincts.

Presenting to Charlie wasn't nearly the ordeal it had been with the creative directors at Ally. And when Charlie had an audience he carried on more like a stand-up comic than a creative director. But make no mistake, when it came to the nuts and bolts of selling a product, he was remarkably insightful. As with the heads at Ally, he would settle for nothing less than perfection. Yes, he had a preference for comedy, but funny or not the advertising had better be on strategy. Before he would even comment on your execution, he determined whether your concept was delivering on the marketing objectives. If it wasn't your meeting was over.

Charlie demanded that a commercial be "tight": well written and well structured without any extraneous words (the average commercial had about 75 words). If your concept was on the mark, he'd light up like a four-year old on Christmas morning. And when he laughed at your writing, it carried weight. Affirmation is underrated.

But when it came to selling a campaign to the client, there was no better salesperson on the planet than Mary. She was a lion tamer in a Chanel suit. If you gave her something that was even remotely presentable, it was as good as sold. In a nanosecond she would have the toughest, meanest clients eating out of the palm of her Bergdorf

Goodman-manicured hands.

When it came to selling something big, she would do whatever it took to make the sale. If that meant bending the truth here or there, so be it.

A short time after I joined Wells, the agency encountered a major crisis on the client I was hired for, their highly-visible, $50-million-plus Alka-Seltzer account. The problem was public advocate Ralph Nader's blistering criticism of Alka-Seltzer's advertising.

Nader complained that Alka-Seltzer contained aspirin, a stomach irritant, in addition to its antacid. He protested virulently that our advertising made no mention of aspirin and accused Miles Laboratories of intentionally withholding that information. The FDA agreed. Indeed, our advertising only depicted Alka-Seltzer's effect on an upset stomach.

The people from Miles stormed into the agency prepared to fire us. They were livid over the public humiliation and placed the blame squarely on the agency. Why hadn't Wells, Rich, Greene and their public relations resources controlled the situation? Why hadn't they modified their commercials in light of Nader's attacks? Someone at the agency had seriously fucked up.

Mary summoned everyone who worked on the account to her private conference room. The group consisted of Charlie (naturally) the entire account team, the creative staff including Howie Cohen and Bob Pasqualina (my bosses and the creators of the original campaign), Stan Schofield (my art director) and me.

Howie and Bob's initial campaign included both the famous "Try it, you'll like it" spot and "I can't believe I ate the whole thing." It was an iconic piece of advertising. Stan (my new Jim Brancaleone) and I had recently been hired to carry the torch on the account, as Howie and Bob moved on to other accounts. Our mission was to add fresh new thinking to the highly successful campaign. Despite a warped affinity for Yasser Arafat, Stan was a tremendous art director and working partner, and he soon became one of my close crackpot friends. Give him a blank storyboard, a six-pack of Heineken and a plate of lasagna (crispy on the sides) and he could work for days without a break.

Stan and I were in the middle of writing our first pool of commercials when we were called down to Mary's office. The client unleashed their Nader-fed fury directly at Mary, demanding to know how the agency could have ignored such a significant problem and who was to blame. "Someone's going to pay," the top client said, threatening to pull the account.

Mary waited patiently until his tirade was over. She then got up and stood calmly in the center of the room, the client's words still reverberating in the air. She paused a moment for effect, inhaling deeply what little oxygen was left in the room. She then looked the lead client directly in the eyes. As always, she thought quickly on her feet, methodically dissecting the problem and mapping out a plan to assuage his anger.

"First, I take full responsibility for the agency's mishandling of Nader's complaints. I should have been on top of it. Second, from this moment on, all Alka-Seltzer advertising will address dual symptoms—upset stomach and headache—in each and every commercial. Period. No discussion. Third, I will personally take over the day-to-day management of your business, and I will make immediate changes to the account team. I will add, at the very least, two additional senior account directors by the end of the week. I will call you to discuss their resumes. And fourth," she continued, "I will fire and replace the entire creative team on your business. There will be no more juniors working on Alka-Seltzer."

I almost passed out. If Stan hadn't grabbed me, I would have hit the floor. Alka-Seltzer was probably the premier television account on Madison Avenue, and Stan and I had beaten out the best young creative teams in the city. We had gotten off to a fast start, coming up with six new commercials that everyone, especially Charlie, loved.

Nader was single-handedly blowing up my career.

I turned to see the client's reaction to Mary's soliloquy. He seemed pleased. Mary had pushed all the right buttons. Suddenly, she turned to Howie and Bob and announced, "You two are fired. Your whole team is fired." I sat there, staring at her, numb. I had no feeling in my legs. I wanted to throw up. They would need to put me on suicide watch. Stan stood up and nudged me towards the door. Howie and Bob were already filing out. As the four of us shuffled out of the conference room, Mary turned toward Howie and Bob, her back to the client and mouthed, "I. Love. You."

I didn't understand. Hadn't she just fired all of us? As soon as we got upstairs to Howie's office, he explained. Mary had no intention of firing anyone. It was all done for effect.

"How do you know that?" I pleaded.

"Not to worry, young man, nobody's going anywhere."

That, in a nutshell, was Mary.

# 15 THE LATVIAN SCHOOL OF ADVERTISING — DOWNTOWN CAMPUS

With our new marching orders, Stan and I quickly went back to work. We labored day and night for two months on a new pool of commercials. Generally speaking, Alka-Seltzer spots were a blast to write. Coming up with ridiculous situations where people get acid indigestion was almost as much fun as full-court basketball. Under Nader's new guidelines, it became a lot more challenging.

We eventually came up with a half-dozen or so new storyboards and felt confident that we had nailed the new direction. We presented to Bob and Howie. They bought everything. "Take 'em down to Charlie," Howie said, still laughing. "He'll really like those."

Excited, the two of us raced downstairs to the management floor and took Charlie through the new boards, making sure that he knew Howie and Bob had signed off on them. He made a couple of small suggestions but was otherwise pleased. "This should go a long way toward putting a smile back on Miles' face. Good job, men. Let me know what the account team says. They're a nervous wreck right now."

Stan and I soon had the pleasure of presenting the boards to one of Mary's "new senior account directors."

We took the new guy through the first board and waited for his reaction.

"No, not right," he said, dismissively. "Wrong tone."

"What do you mean, wrong tone?" I questioned, instantly feeling my blood pressure rise.

"Just wrong tone, wrong tone."

*Okay. He's new. I'll cut him some slack.*

Stan and I showed him two more storyboards.

Board number three: "Nope, too controversial."

Board number four: "Don't really like that approach. Got any more?" he asked, like he was buying pies at a roadside stand.

I seriously hated this guy and he hadn't been in my office more than two minutes.

We took him through three more spots.

Board five: "No."

Board six: "Nope."

Board seven: "No go, fellas," he declared, waving his hand over the boards like the Pope.

I was beyond angry. I knew this feeling well. My rage was beginning to well up. It started down at my knees, went into my stomach and all too often it ended up in my fists.

If he were a decent guy or if he had offered some valid criticism, I might have backed off, but he was just a pompous prick.

"What, pray tell, is wrong with all of these?" I asked.

He pointed to each in succession:

"Don't get it. Not funny. Not what we want to say there. Off-strategy. Not clear. Humor is lost on me. Weak."

"Sorry, gents, back to the coal mines."

Every muscle in my body was aching to punch this guy out but thinking about Charlie, I got a grip on myself. I was still relatively new and didn't want to blow my reputation so early.

"Tell me, Dr. No," I said. "Who died and left you with the keys to the creative department? You realize that Charlie blessed all these?"

He ignored me.

"Incidentally, I'm curious. Where did you pick up all your creative acumen? It's really quite impressive." I crossed my arms in front of my chest. I couldn't wait for his answer. "Don't tell me. The Latvian School of Advertising, downtown campus, right?"

"Steve guessed it." Stan added, proudly. "Or was it the uptown campus?"

"Listen, buddy," he said to Stan. "I know more about advertising than you and your girlfriend here put together. I spent many years doing focus groups."

"Welllll, that's a *to*tally different story then!" I exclaimed.

I paused for dramatic effect.

"You know what you can do with your focus groups? Bend down, I'll show you."

"Why don't you go fuck yourself," he snorted, lurching toward me.

"You know what?" I announced.

"What?" the douchebag inquired, as he stuck his face an inch from mine.

"I think I've had enough of you." I yelled.

I spun around my desk, ripped the telephone off the wall and threw it at him from point blank range. He made a feeble attempt to duck, but I nailed him flush behind his ear. He screamed out in pain.

"Christ, I'm bleeding!" he shouted, reaching for his J.C. Penney, faux-silk pocket handkerchief.

"I'm crying for you," Stan said. "Now, get the fuck outta here or we'll hang you with the phone cord."

I think he actually believed him because he shot out of there like Evel Knievel going over the Snake River Canyon.

Douchebag needed three stitches. And my actions, although entirely justified, landed me first in the president's office, and then in Charlie's. (Stan missed out for some reason.)

"Steve," Charlie said with the look of a parent stifling a smile because his child had done something wrong but nevertheless amusing. "What happened up there?"

"The guy's a world-class douchebag, Charlie."

"He may be, but you really can't do that, Steve. Did you really throw a phone at him?"

"He deserved it."

"Maybe so," he laughed to himself. "But when, uh, Douchebag gets back from the emergency room, I want you to go up there and apologize to him."

"If you say so, Charlie, but this guy doesn't know his ass from his pock-marked face when it comes to advertising. What was Mary thinking?"

He didn't answer.

Later, I mentioned the incident to my shrink. To my surprise, he wasn't at all surprised. But he did schedule a few extra sessions, telling me I needed to learn "more suitable alternatives for handling frustration."

Several days later, sans Douchebag, we presented the new pool of spots to the Miles client. They approved all but one.

"Nice work, fellas. And you pulled it off very quickly," they said. "That last spot, though, the one called 'Pork and Beans', is really about flatulence, and we're not a flatulence product. Let's hold onto that and see if we can use it sometime down the road."

Translation: *It's absolutely 100% fucking dead, but we don't want to disappoint you on the eve of the new production.*

# 16 JOE HOLLYWOOD

Shortly after our presentation I was on a 747 to sunny California with Stan and fellow lunatic Jim Spillane, our TV producer. We were going to shoot the first of our new spots, "Travel Agent."

Filming "on the coast" was about as cool as it got for someone like me, especially in the dead of winter. It was one part work, three parts spring break. Everyone from Wells, Rich, Greene stayed at the venerable Beverly Hills Hotel or "The Hills", as everyone called it. On any given day during the winter months, there were so many people from Wells, Rich, Greene shooting in LA and staying at The Hills that it became known as "Wells, Rich, Greene West."

Walking into that vintage Hollywood atmosphere for the first time, I was mesmerized. It was even grander than I had imagined with 1930s palm fern wallpaper and carpeting and shiny Art Deco brass signs on the walls in a vintage typeface that read "Coffee Shop" and "Polo Lounge". I saw a tiny bellhop racing across the lobby wearing a monkey hat, holding up a sign and shouting, "Phone call for Mr. Johnny Carson. Call for Johnny Carson." I remember thinking, *Shit, Johnny Carson and I are staying at the same hotel? Man, I've really come a long way.* Later in the week, I played tennis on the court adjacent to him. I can tell you with authority that his comedy was a whole lot better than his tennis.

It didn't matter that my room was so tiny I could almost touch the walls just by stretching out my thirty-five-inch arms. It also didn't matter that my room was directly over the clanging basement boiler or that the view from my veranda was off the service entrance and that a huge air-conditioning unit blocked even that. The fact that I could order up an $8 glass of fresh-squeezed orange juice and a bagel with lox ($43, without the tip) from room service at 3 a.m. more than made up for all the shortcomings.

I didn't stay in my tiny room for very long. I went down to the lobby and rented a cool red Mustang convertible and cruised all over Beverly Hills until nightfall, gawking at all the mansions with their manicured lawns and kidney-shaped pools. I played tennis the next day with US Open champ Alex Olmedo and ate steak tartare for the first time at a trendy, celebrity-packed restaurant with George Gomes, advertising's premier comedy director, and his gorgeous script girl Anne, whom Stan and I fell so madly in love with we stammered around like high school idiots in front of her.

Between Anne, George, The Hills, the trendy restaurants (and the attendant stomach aches), the celebs in bikinis lying out by the pool, the tennis, the cool clubs we never would have gotten into without the pull of the production company and the star maps on Sunset Drive, I had died and gone to advertising heaven.

George had directed the first pool of Alka-Seltzer spots, creating a distinctive comedic style that viewers would instantly recognize as an Alka-Seltzer commercial. We spent weeks casting our actors—the most critical part of any TV production. We began casting in New York on videotape and then finished with live casting calls at our Hollywood casting studio, which was incidentally the former home of Broderick Crawford, the star of the popular TV series *Highway Patrol*.

When filming comedy, as compared to drama, it's even more imperative to get the talent right. With comedy there's no latitude for error. You can't split the difference. Something's either funny or it's not. It's like that old tale of Groucho Marx on his deathbed. As he lay with medical tubes connected everywhere, someone purportedly asked him, "Is this hard for you?" "No," he answers. "Dying is easy. Comedy is hard."

We were looking for funny actors with a lot of character. They had to walk the thin line between too goofy and too straight. We typically looked at hundreds of actors for the lead roles, ending up with just one or two viable candidates to present to the client. We were very fortunate. Our Alka-Seltzer clients had excellent creative judgment, and when they couldn't make up their minds they deferred to the agency and/or director.

The day before our shoot, we held a comprehensive pre-production meeting where we went over casting selections, locations, wardrobe, props, the director's shooting board and the final scripts. (Tough luck: I had to work very closely with Anne on this.) After several hours the client approved everything. We were all set. I couldn't wait until morning.

After a restless night's sleep, I jumped out of bed at 6 a.m. I pulled the curtains back and couldn't believe my eyes. It was pouring. Not just rain, but a freakin' monsoon. Despondent, I sat at the end of my bed waiting for the official cancellation call from Spillane. The phone rang. The shoot was off until the weather cleared. So with nothing to do except wait out the storm, Stan and I found an indoor tennis court. After a few sets we decided to kill the rest of the day at a local bar near Rodeo Drive. We hopped up on the bar stools, lit cigars and ordered two beers.

"I'll have a Heineken. It's the best beer in the world. Ya know, President Kennedy used to drink it," Stan obnoxiously told the bartender, quoting Jack Nicholson in *The Last Detail.*

Puffing away on our cigars, we were interrupted by someone shouting from the back of the room.

"Hey, fellas, come on ova here. Join me for a drink. I'm buyin'," the gravelly voice commanded.

We turned to see who it was. It couldn't be. He had to be talking to someone else. But Stan and I were the only ones in the bar, literally. The bartender motioned us to the man sitting at the table. It was none other than George Burns, chomping on a giant stogie. "Come on ova here boys," he repeated, as we hesitantly approached his table.

We wound up spending half the afternoon with the iconic comedian as he regaled us with jokes and fascinating tales about his famous career. Yesterday, I was just a guy shooting a killer commercial in LA; now I was the guy hanging out with George Burns. I was dying to tell someone.

Since I didn't have a girlfriend at the time, I decided to call my parents in New York. Soaking wet, standing on a pile of limp Yellow Pages, I called them from a rapidly flooding telephone booth across the street from the bar.

"Hey, Ma," I shouted into the receiver.

"Hi, dear, everything all right? I hear it's stormy out there."

"Yeah, everything's fine. Guess who I spent the afternoon with?"

"Umm, let me think. Marilyn Monroe?"

"Ma, she's dead."

"Oh, really? Who then?"

"George Burns."

"George Burns!" she echoed. "Hey, Meyer," I could hear her yell out to my father in his Yiddish name. "Guess who Stevie spent the last week with?"

"I dunno, Marilyn Monroe?"

"Come on, Meyer, even your six-year-old granddaughter knows Marilyn Monroe is dead."

(In the background: *Ana one, ana two…*)

"I'm in the middle of Lawrence Welk. Tell him to call back."

It rained for two long days. I was miserable. Los Angeles in the rain is a dismal place. I sat in my tiny room and did little else but watch *Concentration* and old black-and-white movies on TV. As the weatherman predicted, the storm finally blew out two days later and the skies brightened (along with my disposition).

"Travel Agent" featured a middle-aged married couple that needed to get away for a little peace and quiet. Their travel agent booked them into a lovely spot in the heart of the "Mellow Mountains." On their first day, while enjoying lunch by the pool, major construction begins wreaking havoc at the resort. The grounds are shaking, overrun with deafening jackhammers, bulldozers, giant cranes, earthmovers and screaming construction workers on megaphones, giving the startled couple upset stomachs *and* headaches. (Happy, Nader?)

At the end of the thirty-second spot the husband, now feeling better, looks to the camera and begins to extol the virtues of Alka-Seltzer. As he begins to talk, an ear-splitting jackhammer drowns him out.

"Alka-Seltzer . . . It's the grea–DA-DA-DA–est

"DA-DA-DA-DA-DA-DA-DA-DA-DA

"stomach–TA-TA-TA-TA-TA-TA-TA–medicine–in the–"

"RAT-TA-TA-TA-TA-DA-TA-TA-TA-TA-TA-TA-TAT-A-TAT-TAT TAT-A-TAT-TAT-TAT–world."

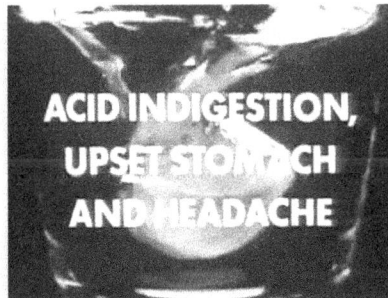

The first spot after Ralph Nader's criticism of Miles Laboratories.
Alka-Seltzer "Travel Agent" 1972 (Director: George Gomes)

Several months later, I collected another Clio Award. Not only did "Travel Agent" turn out to be very funny (not always a sure bet) but network tracking studies showed that Alka-Seltzer sales jumped significantly during the period that "Travel Agent" was on the air.

I was becoming a regular in L.A., not only shooting for Alka-Seltzer but also for Diet Rite Cola, Chex cereal, Sure deodorant and others. The doorman at The Hills greeted me personally, "Welcome back, Mr. Penchina," "Good afternoon, Mr. P.," "How was your day, Sir?" "Can I pull up your convertible now?"

The Hollywood scene boosted my sensitive ego. To be seen by all my peers sitting poolside, eating avocado and cucumber sandwiches on toast points (a far cry from my usual pastrami on rye) sipping margaritas, talking on a phone that had to be specially plugged in at my table meant that I had truly arrived.

Television elevated me to the next level. I was no longer just a feisty young copywriter from Long Island.

I was Joe Hollywood.

# 17 MAN WITH A VAN

I was sitting alone at a booth in Beverly Hills' notorious Polo Lounge. The bar was teeming with big-shot producers, directors and actors, talking deals or just out being seen. As I was thumbing through the latest issue of *Variety*, waiting for a beer in my new Fred Segal tennis outfit, a beautiful girl approached me.

"Is this seat taken?" she asked.

I gulped. *This is the most UN-taken seat in the entire universe.*

She was right out of a Beach Boys record. She had short-ish, sun-bleached hair, a centerfold body, perfect skin and cleavage I hadn't seen since my Aunt Gloria tried to fit into her wedding dress on her fiftieth anniversary.

"No, please sit down," I answered quickly, before some movie producer could try to get his grubby hands on her. "What's your name?" I asked nonchalantly, yet caring more than anything I ever cared about in the last ten years of my life.

"Peaches."

"Uh, Peaches. Really? I like fruit."

"Well, my name is really Florence but everyone calls me Peaches."

"Are you an actress... Peaches?" I asked, transfixed by her short shorts.

WHO WROTE THIS SH*T?!

"I'm trying to be... I also dance. Are you an actor or a producer person?"

"No, no," I said, most humbly. "I'm a writer. I'm out here on a commercial."

"Well, maybe you can find a place for me in your commercial, um——?"

"Steve," I filled in. "Maybe I can," I answered, lying like a congressman.

"What's your commercial about?"

"It's for Alka-Seltzer."

"Really? I can use some right now. I just had a black bean, seaweed and jalapeño shake, and it's not going down well."

"That's quite a combination," I said.

We talked for a while, but I wasn't really listening. I was daydreaming about taking all her clothes off. We started drinking Bloody Marys and after an hour or so were both pretty sloshed. I eventually worked up enough alcohol-assisted chutzpah to ask her up to my room. (I had by now been moved to a mini-suite on the third floor, far, far away from the boiler room).

"Oh, I'm sorry. I can't do that."

"Why not?" I asked, crestfallen. "I have a beautiful room with a view of Bela Lugosi's bungalow. We can order up room service. They have the best fresh-squeezed orange juice. We can have anything we want out of the mini bar. I have a key."

"I'm really sorry, Steve... I just feel a little uncomfortable." She paused for a second. "But I do have my van parked outside."

"A van?"

"Come, I'll show you."

She took my hand and led me out to an old Volkswagen van, parked smack dab in front of the hotel entrance. "Don't be bashful," she said, opening the door for me. "Climb in."

I hesitated for a second then jumped in, bumping my head on the roof. What irony: I had finally made it to the world-renowned Beverly Hills, met my fantasy blonde California shiksa, and I wind up squished into a damp sleeping bag on the rock-hard floor of a psychedelic VW van. How could I tell my buddies back home?

I spent the night with Peaches, who, I might add, introduced me to some highly acrobatic, West Coast sexual artistry. I was amazed by what she could do in such a confined space. I loved California.

I was worried about missing my shooting call, so I asked the parking attendants to make sure I was up in time.

The following morning I heard a polite knock on the steamed-up back window. "Mr. P., it's your 6 a.m. wakeup call." I was exhausted, not having slept the entire night.

As I was pulling myself together, I asked Peaches for her phone number. I couldn't wait to see her again, van or not.

"Oh, I don't think so," she answered.

"Why not?"

"Because my husband, who's a Master Sergeant in the Marine Corps, is coming home tonight, and if he knew about you, he would come over here and break your neck. I've seen him do that with chickens."

"Pleasure meeting you, Peaches," I said, jumping out of the van.

The car jockeys were howling watching me trying to hold my pants up as I ran/shuffled/limped/back to the hotel. From that night on they all affectionately called me "Van Man."

Sitting at my desk a couple of weeks after I got back from LA, I received a call from Mary's assistant who wanted to know if I would sit in on an urgent TWA meeting. TWA wasn't one of my accounts but I had worked on Northeast Airlines at Ally, and Mary thought I might be useful in the meeting. I later learned that TWA was having big-time second thoughts about their relationship with the agency. There were staffing problems, among other issues. When I got down to the conference room, I quickly figured out Mary's play. She packed the room with staff with prior airline experience to show TWA the depth of resources at the agency.

Mary took center stage and gave a virtuoso performance. She'd done her homework (as always), and knew every detail about both TWA specifically and the airline industry in general. Point by point she allayed their concerns. Two and a half hours later these six tough, irate airline people not only didn't fire the agency, they extended their contract. Mary, who was dressed to the nines with her blond hair neatly tied back in a ribbon, was, frankly, sharper than any of the clients, and likely had them the moment they walked through the door. When the meeting ended, she wined and dined them with an elegant lunch, her best Bordeaux adding a nice exclamation point to the meeting. Nobody entertained with more panache.

Mary knew how to keep her accounts, and she was even more passionate about going after new ones. Nothing gave her more pleasure than showing prospective clients the Wells, Rich, Greene "star quality" reel. If for some reason it didn't knock their socks off, she felt they shouldn't be there in the first place.

In the '70s, her reel looked roughly like this:

"OH, THE DISADVANTAGES OF BENSON AND HEDGES CIGARETTES."
(Benson and Hedges 100 millimeter long cigarettes)

"I'M BUD."
(TWA Bonus campaign)

"LOOK OUT FOR THAT TRUCK! WHAT TRUCK?
BEHIND THE BUS! WHAT BUS?"
(American Motors)

"THE END OF THE PLAIN PLANE."
(Braniff Airlines)

"FLICK YOUR BIC."
(Bic Lighters)

"I LOVE NEW YORK."
(New York State Department of Commerce)

"TRY IT, YOU'LL LIKE IT."
(Alka-Seltzer)

"I CAN'T BELIEVE I ATE THE WHOLE THING. PLOP–PLOP, FIZZ–FIZZ"
(Alka-Seltzer)

"EVERYBODY LIKES IT."
(Diet Rite Cola)

"RAISE YOUR HAND IF YOU'RE SURE."
(Sure deodorant)

This ad bites.
Frank Langella in an ad for the New York State Department of Commerce.
Wells, Rich, Greene

It was one of the best reels in the business.

With Wells, Rich, Greene's uncontested reputation, Mary's sheer magnetism, Charlie's enormous talent and all the creative heavyweights she'd amassed, Mary built an iconic brand. I only wish my chauvinistic father could have seen her in action. She was one of the two or three most successful businesswomen in the country.

There was no getting around the fact that Wells, Rich, Greene was Mary's baby. It was her vision, her creation, her creative philosophy and her success. From her not-very-humble beginnings at the Gotham Hotel on Park Avenue in 1966, the agency would grow to well over $2 billion in billings by the late '80s, climbing to one of the top 10 full-service shops in the industry. She used to proclaim, "I want to see how big I can get before I get bad." Indeed, she got big but she maintained Well's creative integrity to the end.

The end came in 1990 when Mary sold the agency to a French holding company, Euro RSCG. But without her leadership, Wells, Rich, Greene lost its cachet and ultimately many of its noted clients. Most agencies continue to grow after they're sold, but Mary was the heart and soul of the agency. Without her one of Madison Avenue's legendary shops eventually shuttered its doors. Mary moved to her chateau in the south of France. Charlie went on to open a successful creative boutique and eventually got into acting, his true passion.

Several years after the sale of the agency, I was riding on a bus heading down Fifth Avenue. Way in the back, I spotted Charlie sitting contentedly reading the paper. I pushed my way through all the straphangers.

"Hey, Charlie?" I said affectionately as I approached him. It had been a few years. "I remember the days when you and Mary took chauffeured limos everywhere."

"This is chauffeured," he said, not missing a beat.

He always liked a tight line.

# 18 GIRLS JUST WANT TO HAVE FUN

I bounced around a bit after leaving Wells, not really interested in going to another agency and essentially biding my time until I could figure out how to open my own shop. I had finally reached the point in my career where I simply did not want to work for anyone anymore.

I had also reached the point where I was getting fed up with dating and thought that maybe it was time to settle down. I got close a few times—with one girl really doing a job on my head—before meeting *the* one. Well, the first *the* one, anyway.

## Lena

Lena fulfilled every erotic dream I ever had about women. She was a stunningly gorgeous Danish girl I had met on a trip to Majorca, Spain, with some old buddies from Great Neck. She had everything I obsessed about in a woman to the 10th power: tall, thin, beautiful, long Scandinavian-white/blonde hair and a funny, brainy personality. We spent day and night together on the beaches of Majorca. The days were great. The nights were greater.

After we left Majorca, we met again under the Eiffel Tower in Paris for another romantic few weeks. I had the mother of all crushes. I was so insanely in love with her, I completely ignored it when all my friends said they couldn't stand her.

Months later, after many letters back and forth, I invited her to New York over Christmas. I counted the days 'til she arrived. I was so nervous when I picked her up, I actually drove to the wrong airport.

By now, she was a very successful model in Paris which bought me some bragging rights with my friends but not much else. Obviously, they all thought she was a knockout but they weren't into the snobby model thing. I didn't care, though. I really thought this was it. But as the weeks wore on, I began to think my buddies were right. The trip and our romance turned out to be a disaster on the scale of Elizabeth Taylor and any one of her husbands. We fought nonstop, about everything.

The lesson: Like the Temptations' Motown classic, "Beauty's only skin deep, yeah, yeah, yeah. Beauty's only skin deep. Yeah-h-h-h-h-h."

## Jane

My friend Barry owned an employment agency that doubled as my personal dating service. Thirty years ahead of his time, he was the precursor to J-Date and I was his target audience. He arranged for me to meet cute girls almost weekly. Once, he set me up with a terrific Jewish girl named Jane, who was anything but plain. The majority of the women I had dated were shiksas, so a Jewish girl like Jane was pleasantly out of the ordinary for me. (I recognize the name Jane doesn't sound particularly Jewish, but I can assure you she was. Proof: She only shopped at Bergdorf's.)

One thing I'll always remember about her was a weekend trip to upstate New York to see the colorful fall foliage with a bunch of friends. Suddenly, Jane began crying in the back seat of the car. "What's wrong, Jane?" I turned to ask her. "Why are you crying?"

"I'm just so sad that you can't see all the beautiful colors," she replied, pitying me for being colorblind.

"No, no, Jane, I said, don't feel bad for me. I can see the colors okay—I just don't know their names."

We dated for a long time, and I was really in to her, but somehow she just wasn't "it." (Although when she wore those leather pants and ultra tight t-shirts, she came very close.) She was one of the most beautiful women I'd ever met. Once, when we were about to leave to visit her parents in Beacon, New York, on Thanksgiving Day, she threw me on my bed at my Kips Bay apartment and pinned me to the mattress for three hours. We never made it to Beacon. But I was torn. As much as I loved sleeping with her, I might have loved Thanksgiving stuffing even more.

## Gunella

In the 1970s, the village of King's Point in Great Neck was awash with Swedish au pairs. My friend Barry and I first discovered this phenomenon while playing in a softball league behind the fire department in the old side of town. We were known as Acme Steel, and our softball games were a big deal. Many of the team's family members, and other locals, would show up to watch the games. I have to say, it was awfully cool to belt a four-bagger while everyone looked on and went wild.

Sitting in the stands one evening were two pretty, young blondes who appeared to be looking after the children of two of our teammates.

"Hey, Barr, who are those girls?" I shouted from center field to my friend at second base.

"No freakin' idea," he answered. "But I'm sure as shit gonna find out."

What we found out was that most of the older family guys on our team were hiring inexpensive au pairs from Sweden to take care of their children.

The minute the game was over (we won), Barry and I made a B-line to the stands to talk to the au pairs. They were perfect for us: young, attractive, spoke good enough English, had a giggly sense of humor, were close friends and, best of all, they were bored as hell in Great Neck. They were looking for a good time after they put their kids to sleep at night and they couldn't wait to get into the city on their days off. Oh, and all they wanted to do was to have sex.

"You've come to the right place!" Barry declared.

So, we started going out. First in Great Neck, and then in the city. We had struck gold. Gunella (my girl) was insatiable. When I visited her at her King's Point house, we barely talked. She would take me by the hand and lead me into the kids' room. She slept there on a small cot. When I was with her, she placed the cot on the floor to give us more room. We would have sex, great sex, half the night, being careful that my baseball buddy didn't hear us. We learned a whole new method of volume control.

By this time I was sleeping with Gunella easily four times a week. She didn't say very much; she just wanted sex. *Fine with me,* I thought. On her day off she'd come to my apartment in the city. "Hi, Steve. Let's fuck." It was wild.

"Gunella," I finally said to her one day. "You know, we never really talk to one another. That's a little weird, don't you think?"

"No, das goot," she said in her broken English.

"Why's that?" I asked her.

"Interferes with fucking."

After months of all this "fucking," I found myself utterly exhausted, and told Gunella that I needed a break. I never thought I'd say these words, especially as it involved sex, but sometimes you can have too much of a good thing.

## Su Jin

I'm not totally sure, but I think I met Su on a subway on my way home from work. She was Korean, a sweet girl and quite stunning. We went out a few times and really enjoyed ourselves. On the third date I finally took her to my apartment. (I can't believe I waited so long.)

I opened a bottle of wine and we soon made it over to my bed. I got on top of her and my gold Star of David necklace dangled over her face. She froze with fear.

"What's that?" She asked me.

"Oh, it's my Jewish star."

"Let me see." She requested. "You Jewish?"

"Yes, I am. Why do you ask?"

"I didn't know you were Jewish."

"Is that a problem for you?" I asked incredulously, immediately becoming peeved.

"Uh, no. Yes. I'm not sure." She paused. "Where are your horns?" She asked, deadly serious.

"What?!"

"Your horns. Where are they?"

"What do you mean?"

"My father told me that all Jews have horns, and I should keep away from them."

For the first (and only) time in my life, I was speechless.

That was the end of that.

## Debbie

Barry and I had just hit our infamous "February Slump," which meant that neither of us was going out with anyone and we were both miserable. Being one of my more resourceful friends, Barry decided to hold a fundraiser for young members of the New York UJA-Federation at a popular New York disco, Hippopotamus. This would shake them out of their winter slumber.

Everything Barry touched, girls-wise at least, turned to gold. I would say nearly 200 people showed up for his party, more than half of them of the female species. About an hour in, sloshed out of my head on Barry's cheap champagne cocktail, I noticed out of my peripheral vision that someone was watching me walk across the dance floor. (My teammates on Acme Steel called me "Hawkeye" for good reason.) She was quite attractive with short, reddish blonde hair, a slim body and blue eyes that twinkled like the disco ball.

Those eyes followed me across the parquet and started dancing with me before I even met her. I noticed that she was already jabbering to some guy. A big guy. I walked over to the bar where they were standing and interrupted their conversation.

"I can assure you you're not gonna like this guy," I said to my own amazement, as I took her hand and pulled her out onto the dance floor. I couldn't believe I had the balls to actually say that. He was a very big fella.

I knew right then and there that there was a connection...at least for me.

As we were dancing, I noticed she was wearing what appeared to be two military dog tags, each with a name and date on it. "Whose names are those on the dog tags?" I asked.

"Oh, those are my two children."

*Gulp.*

After a dozen replays of Chubby Checker's "Let's Twist Again" and an equal amount of Barry's champagne cocktail, I drove her back to her apartment on 74th Street. There was no way I was going to start anything with her two little children at home (Arik, she told me was three; Ditty, was one), but I told myself that if I found a spot in front of her apartment in the pouring rain on a Saturday night, this would be bersherit (meant to be). Just then, a big Buick pulled out and left me a spot the size of Yankee Stadium. We went upstairs and talked for a while. At the end of the evening I promised I'd call her from a photo shoot I was about to leave for in San Francisco.

A week later, I stepped out of the shower of the Mark Hopkins Hotel on top of Nob Hill, put on a white, terrycloth robe, ordered up a Heineken and called Debbie. I could hear a kid bawling in the background. We talked for a long while. She was a bit introverted, but very sharp and interesting. She had lived in Holland and Israel (which explained her children's Hebrew names), was fluent in five languages, had a good sense of humor, and lived a fascinating, if not crazy, life. I liked her.

As for her children, they didn't frighten me away at all, contrary to my initial reaction and how most of my friends and family felt about the situation. When I met them for the first time, Arik was wearing those pajamas with the button-down door in the back, and Ditty was crawling around with her soft blonde hair like one year olds do. Both were cute as can be. It was love at first sight.

We got serious quickly. I began to stop over at her apartment on the way home from my shrink on the Upper East Side. We would discuss all of my current emotional problems (which I think bored her to death) but she was very polite and acted keenly interested. It wasn't long before I was sleeping over. Was it awkward to be living in the same home of someone with two young children? Well, let's see. At 6 a.m. Arik would run into the bedroom, jump up on the bed, and start bouncing. "Is Steve here?" He would ask.

Ditty was confined to her crib, but as soon as Debbie took her out she'd join us in the overcrowded bed. I would lift her up with my legs, balance her on my feet and play Superman while she giggled her cute head off. I had as much fun as they did. On Saturday mornings, Arik and I would hold hands on our walk to the bagel store around the corner and buy bagels, cream cheese, nova and herring.

"This is a Penchina tradition that we must continue!" I emphatically announced, hoisting Arik up high in the air.

A couple of years later, Debbie and I got married. A couple of years after that, we added one, Daniel, and then a second child, Joshua, to the mix. We were now a tight, manic family of six. Arik and Ditty, spontaneously, began calling me Daddy, which made me feel very special. I wanted to adopt them, but their biological father in Israel blocked our efforts. So, we did something even more meaningful. We adopted each other—emotionally. We were all very close and led a fabulous, exciting, expansive life together. I took them everywhere: Europe, Israel, the u.s. Open. I taught them all to ride bikes in Central Park, play tennis, baseball and basketball. I took them to summer camp in Maine, and trick or treating on the Upper East Side. We all had a blast together.

Over the years Debbie and I bonded over our strong interest in Zionism, travel, the motion-picture business that took us to the Cannes Film Festival most years, our respective parents, to whom we were both very close, and, of course, the kids, who would become the glue that held us together for years to come.

# 19

## 14 YEARS, 6 AGENCIES, 21 BOSSES AND 4 SHRINKS LATER

Entrepreneurship is in my blood. I remember the first time my father took me to Penchina Textile on Eldridge Street in the Lower East Side. I was eight and I walked-ran-skipped next to him the whole way there. I can still smell the wool blankets and plastic shower curtains on display in the large, dusty storefront windows, and the noxious scent of the formaldehyde used to pack the sheets and towels as we walked in.

My dad had a commanding presence, especially in his store. Despite working in the gritty, wholesale dry goods district (south of Houston and north of Canal), he went to work snappily dressed in a dark Brooks Brothers suit and tie with expensive, always-polished, sturdy wingtip shoes (the same ones he used to throw at me with shoe trees in them when he wanted me to get out of his room so he could nap). He would summarily take up his position in the back of the store, calmly but firmly telling my three uncles and other salesmen what to do.

Max Penchina already seemed bigger than life in the role of my father, so he was beyond terrifying in the role of tough-minded entrepreneur. He never stopped working. He was constantly giving orders to all the salesmen and his bookkeeper. He signed off on deliveries twice as big as me. He sold to (or haggled with) four customers at a time. And he wrapped giant bundles of merchandise with brown paper and heavy twine at speeds that could break the sound barrier.

During all of this I remember making friends with Rudy, a kind man who was probably about my dad's age, with speckles of snow in his short, cropped hair. Rudy was responsible for stocking the inventory. He'd been with my father from the beginning and they loved each other like brothers.

While my dad and uncles were busy with customers, Rudy would take me down to the basement and teach me how to build a fort out of the big, heavy cartons of sheets and towels. The two of us would eat lunch together, crouched in a huge carton I had designated my private dining room. He always had a bottle of beer, which he respectfully drank out of a brown paper bag while entertaining me with vivid accounts of racing the hundred-yard dash at YMCA track meets on Randall's Island. All of his trophies and medals, he told me, were displayed on his fireplace mantle at home. I was so proud of him. I would sit nestled in the cardboard visualizing him blazing down the track, throwing his arms up as he broke the tape crossing the finish line.

Many years later, while I was working at Needham, I opened the sports section of *The New York Times* and saw a headline that read "The World's Fastest Sixty-Year-Old Human." The article went into detail about this unusual man with a passion for track and field and who, at the age of sixty, was still competing and winning in state track meets.

"Holy shit," I screamed out. "That's my Rudy!"

Over the years my father had given me invaluable advice, business and otherwise. That advice eventually gave birth to Penchina Textile's offspring, Steve Penchina Inc., which wasn't at all a textiles shop, but an advertising one instead.

"The first thing you need to do is find a partner to run the business end of things. This way you can devote all your time to being my genius."

(It wasn't *the* genius or *a* genius; but always *my* genius, possessive. It was my father's way of telling me he was proud of me in Max-speak.)

"Your business partner should be in charge of turning a profit. Holding onto money isn't your strong suit," he used to say. "I know you. Money flies out of your pocket as fast as it comes in. Remember the time I found $500 in your suitcase in the attic? You didn't even remember you had it."

He never told me directly, doling out compliments wasn't his strong suit, but I knew he was quite proud of me. When I was growing up, I longed for more vocal approval from him but it wasn't to be. Later in life I figured out that it wasn't a personal thing. He just wasn't a warm and fuzzy man. But still, over the years, he taught me a tremendous amount. Not necessarily by sitting me down and having a formal conversation, but with a comment here, an observation there, or something he would say to me as we were walking home from synagogue or on our way to pick up lox and bagels in the old village of Great Neck.

He absolutely hated the yes-man mentality, and instilled in me a strong appreciation for individualism. "Don't be a conformist. Be your own person," he would tell me time and time again. "Don't follow your classmates. You're smarter and more creative than they are."

I don't remember consciously taking his advice but it clearly sank in. He had an enormous impact on my career. Thinking back, I can see that the advice he gave me all those years ago was probably the driving force behind my creativity and success, not to mention, my life in general.

"You've got to land an account before you announce your agency," he said to me. "This way, you'll have instant credibility. Nobody will think you're just screwing around.

"Funny thing is that once you get an account, it's much easier to get a second one. It's a quirk of nature that nobody wants to be the first sucker, but everyone will line up to be the second. Oh, and having a little cash in your pocket wouldn't hurt either."

But hard as I tried, I just couldn't pull it off. Clients, especially the bigger ones, simply would not commit their business to an agency that didn't yet exist. It's true that in the past, several well-known creative stars were lucky enough to reel in a client before announcing their new shop: Backer & Spielvogel, for one, locked in the giant Miller Lite Beer account before officially opening. But that kind of good fortune comes along only once in a great while.

As much as I trusted my father, I decided to seek out some council from my old mentor, Carl Ally. We had talked years earlier about starting my own shop, and I could think of no one in the industry who could offer me more valuable insight than Carl.

I called him a number of times to set up a meeting, but he was even more frenetic than when I had worked there, having just won the $50 million Saab account.

Late one summer Friday evening, he finally got back to me. He apologized for taking so long and said that his time was tight, but if I were willing to sit with him in his car while driving up the West Side Highway to the George Washington Bridge, I could ask him "any fuckin' thing" I wanted. It was unorthodox, to say the least, but that was Carl. I went…but that was me.

We sped up the highway, zipping in and out of traffic in Carl's hot, red Saab convertible. (It's customary for agency owners to use the products they're advertising. Can you imagine what the chairman of Saab would do if he saw Carl zipping around town in a Ford Mustang? Legend has it, actually, that Mary Wells once served a fine French wine for lunch in the LA office, despite the fact she had the Gallo Wine account. The Gallo brothers, a difficult client to begin with, apparently took away their multi-million dollar account after getting wind of it.)

All the way up the East River, I peppered Carl with questions about the best way to start an agency. As always, he cut right to the chase:

"No matter what anyone tells you, Steverino, the only way to start a shop is to just fucking start it. If you wait to land an account first or to find the perfect account person to partner with, I can assure you, you'll be fuckin' around with this your whole life. And knowing you, your next life will be sweltering fucking hot. You won't be able to do shit down there."

"Jews don't believe in hell, you know."

"Well, you better be fuckin' prepared, just in case," he said, laughing. "Hey, you! Get the fuck outta my lane!" he screamed out to someone, and then gunned past him.

"But if you must have an account guy to help you with the business end, you need to know that there are basically two kinds of account executives in this world: ones with brains and ones with balls. You need to find someone with both, which by the way, is a fucking impossibility."

I was trying to take notes but gave up. He was swerving too much.

"Listen to me, Steve-o." (That's what Tory called me at the agency—evidently it had stuck.) "The one thing you need to do, above all else, is surround yourself with great talent. Hey, grandma, get over to the slow lane!" he barked at a twenty-something-year-old guy in a BMW.

"Where was I?"

"Great talent," I answered.

"Oh, yeah. You gotta hire people who are better than you, those who will produce. If you feel threatened by them, then you shouldn't be doing this in the first place. Get a job shoveling ice cream at a Baskin-Robbins somewhere.

"Look, I'm just a farmer," he went on. "All I do each day is milk my creative cows. Some give me more milk; some give me less. But at the end of the day, they all have to produce. If they don't, they're off my fuckin' farm."

My ride with Carl lasted only about twenty-five minutes, but his advice would stay with me my entire career. As promised, he dropped me off at the entrance to the George Washington Bridge. I didn't have a clue how to get back to the city, so I ended up walking about a million blocks home.

As Carl sped away, he shouted back, "Knock 'em dead, Steve-o!"

As if sorting out all of this advice weren't hard enough, trying to find a good business partner was through-the-roof difficult. I had breakfasts, lunches, dinners, drinks, chats, long phone calls, short phone calls, notes, letters, meetings in the park, and thousands of cups of coffee at Greek coffee shops from Wall Street to Yankee Stadium.

Carl Ally's words were prescient. I met maybe 60 account people of all sizes, shapes, colors and genders, all without success. I met people with brains but no balls, and those with balls but no brains. But as Carl rightly predicted, I couldn't find a single person with both.

Then there was a third kind of candidate I came across—the kind with tiny accounts, usually retail business, who were looking for a creative partner for their little shop. After investing a lot of time with these characters, I eventually learned to dismiss them out of hand. As promising as their deals appeared at the outset, somehow they just weren't kosher. Every one of them had some quirky/slippery/shaky relationship with their client, were making next to no money and were essentially trying to get me to buy into their troubled agency.

I found myself replaying Carl's advice in my head: "If you can't find the right partner, you're better off going it alone. If you fuck up, at least it's on your head and not some schmuck you married and now can't get rid of."

So, in 1980, at the ripe old age of 35, I started my business. Solo mio.

I immediately got a lawyer and incorporated myself. I hired an accountant and recruited a terrific art director named Bob Needleman to design a logo and stationery for me. *Voilà!* I was in business.

Debbie wasn't happy about my decision. Mostly becasue I had simply walked away from a high-paying job at Wells, Rich to start an agency where my paycheck contained a lot of (and only) zeros. I didn't give her the opportunity to quash my lifelong dream, although in hindsight I see that our differing points of views on the subject were the first few nails in our marriage coffin.

Next up: finding office space for my new enterprise. After traipsing all over the city for days, I concluded that I couldn't afford even the cheapest and crappiest of offices. I thought for a moment about sharing space with someone, but that added another personality to the mix that I didn't need. My personality was complicated enough.

I had no choice but to set up shop in the living room of my apartment. Obviously, working from home didn't cost anything but that didn't mean it wasn't costly. My two older kids, Arik and Ditty, were in school, but that left the little ones, Daniel and Joshua, to wreak havoc all day long. Oh, and did I mention the dog, Hoover?

For the three of them, my presence at home translated to: "Hooray, Daddy's home during the day. Now we can play 'Destroy Daddy's Important Papers'!" They got into everything—all my documents, correspondence, storyboards, print ads, anything they could rip or eat. They even figured out how to pull the tape out of my videocassettes and tie up the dog.

I borrowed one of Arik's school notebooks and began compiling a target list of potential clients. I concentrated on what I knew best— copiers, computers, financial services, food and over-the-counter pharmaceuticals. I called or wrote to every person I knew and many I didn't. After literally hundreds of calls and letters, I sat back and waited nervously for the phone to ring. Zip. Nada. Nothing. It eventually dawned on me that the business world was not waiting with bated breath for Steve Penchina's new ad agency.

One afternoon, while making peanut butter and jelly sandwiches in the kitchen, I heard what sounded suspiciously like a ringing telephone. I launched myself over a pile of blocks and a Lionel train set to grab it, almost breaking my neck.

"This is Steve Penchina," I blurted out.

"Steve, this is Tim Matthews returning your call."

"Oh, hi, Tim. Thanks for getting back to me," I answered, huffing and puffing and shuffling madly through my papers, trying to figure out what company he was with.

"You all right? You sound out of breath."

"Oh, I just scooted down the hall from the copy center."

"So, what can I do for you?" he asked pointedly.

"Well, as I told your secretary, I just started my own agency and thought I could take you to lunch and tell you more about it."

"Whaaaaaaahh!" Joshua was crying from another room.

"What's that?" Tim asked.

"What's what?" I answered innocently.

"Sounds like a child crying."

"Oh, that? It must be coming up from the street. I'm across the street from a private school. I think it just let out. Lemme shut the window."

I peered into the playroom to see what sort of disaster had befallen one of my sons.

"Whaaaaaaaahh!"

"Sure everything's all right, there?" Tim asked again.

"We're—uh, I'm fine, thanks," I said, separating the kids and shutting the door to the room. "So, how about P. J. Clarke's on 55th, say, next Tuesday?"

"Yup, that'll work."

"Great. I'll see you 12:30, June 10th, at P…"

"Hi, Daddy! Who are you talking to?" Daniel blurted into the kitchen phone.

"…J. Clarke's. See you…" I quickly ran to the kitchen phone before Joshua could turn the three-way conversation into a full-blown conference call.

"…then."

It might have seemed like a prudent idea at first, but working from home was not going to work. Fortunately, my in-laws, or rather my father-in-law, came up with a solution to my office problem. Born and raised in Berlin, he and my mother in-law had slipped out of Nazi Germany just before the Holocaust and come by ship to New York in 1938. Zealous Zionists, they had also bought a small apartment in Israel and were about to leave on a six-month sabbatical to Jerusalem.

"Veeel make ut New York apartment available vit you," my father-in-law told me in his thick German accent. "But betta keep it cccclean or your mutter-in-laaw veell sent us both onst to da ssstreet—anst she's not that ccccrazy about you to begin vit."

My mother-in-law was the only mother of any girl I'd ever dated who didn't like me. More precisely, she despised me. I was from Mars, Long Island; she was from Venus, Germany. We couldn't have been more different. She did, however, have an interesting background. She was one of the first Jewish women to be accepted to Smith College, her father was a prestigious doctor at Yale, and her uncle was the world-renowned symphony conductor, Otto Klemperer. Her nephew, Werner, had the dubious distinction of playing Colonel Klink in the TV series Hogan's Heroes. Naturally, she would have preferred he played Hamlet, but apparently he was less concerned with her opinion than I was.

Her problem with me, aside from the fact that I was way too happy for her Teutonic tastes, was that I did not come from an intellectual, excessively cultured and utterly humorless German Jewish family. She viewed me as substantially bourgeois, which was both accurate and an accusation. I was the scrappy, cocky, wisecracking jock son of a Lower East Side schmata merchant. (*Imagine, a merchant?!*)

Despite our deep mutual affection, I set up shop in the living room of their apartment on 72nd Street. It was exactly the quiet I longed for. The only sound I heard was the tick-tock of her antique Bavarian cuckoo clock and the whirring noise the tiny little Austrians in lederhosen made when they poked their heads out of their mini Nazi hut every goddamn half-hour.

I came to realize that getting new accounts was a numbers game, not dissimilar to when I sold Fuller brushes door-to-door on Long Island during summers in college.

"All you have to do is knock on enough doors, son," my district manager taught me. "If you knock on a lot of doors, you'll generate sales. But the key is you have to put in the hours. If you ring doorbells eight hours a day, five days a week, you'll make your numbers—sure as I'm sitting here in this diner taking one of my six coffee breaks today."

He taught me that a bad morning did not mean a bad afternoon. And a bad day didn't guarantee a bad week. But, admittedly, chasing after business all day long could be quite disheartening. When I got down on myself, I remembered one other thing he had taught me: "When you're feeling down, whistle. Whistling a tune while you're working is guaranteed to raise your spirits."

Turns out, it does work. The only problem was the only song that came to mind was Disney's "Whistle while you work, ta-ta-ta-da-da-da-da." It wasn't long before that drove me nuts.

When you're starting a business from scratch, your life feels like it passes in dog years. I can't tell you how much determination it takes. Just as I had discovered 15 years earlier in my parent's basement, the more challenging things got, the more tenacious I became.

After several long months I hadn't even slightly cracked the new business code with my letters and phone calls. So I did what I'd advised my clients to do over the years; I created a brochure and sent out a mass mailing. The promotion piece would showcase my work, but just as important the piece itself would make a statement about my creativity.

After 14 years of doing
award-winning advertising
for the best agencies in
New York, I've decided to
work for the toughest,
smartest, most demanding
creative person I know:

Me.

Steve Penchina Inc. 870 Fifth Avenue, New York, N.Y. 10021 (212) 734-8974

The first two pages of my promotional brochure for Steve Penchina Inc. (1980)

The last page of my first promotional brochure for Steve Penchina Inc. (1980)

It succeeded. I received a slew of phone calls and letters asking to meet with me or wanting more information about my agency. Immediately, my disposition picked up. I had an undeniably strong feeling that I was on my way.

# 20 THERE'S STRENGTH IN NUMBERS

One of the first calls to my new agency was from Mike Garlick, a close childhood friend of mine from Great Neck. He had left our neighborhood for the booming economy of South Florida, where he became a successful attorney. His family owned and operated 35 International House of Pancakes restaurants throughout the state, and being an expert in franchise law, he was eventually lured into the family business as in-house counsel.

Mike and I had been friends since we were in diapers. He was an avid fan of my work and had followed my career every inch of the way, beginning with my first real copywriting job at Norman, Craig & Kummel. He was so proud that his next-door neighbor had made it big in the bright lights of Madison Avenue. Only my mother had given me such unconditional love.

Mike called to tell me that he had created an exciting new business venture called Attorneys Professional Association, an association of lawyers that would benefit from being part of a larger group, similar to any franchise operation like McDonalds. For a small fee, each law firm in the group would refer one another, share cases and give specialized legal advice to the other franchisees, creating a synergistic relationship among the firms. The laws had recently changed to allow lawyers to advertise directly to the public. The key part of his strategy—and this was where I came in—was that the participating law firms would be able to pool their money so they could afford to advertise. It wasn't just the first association of its type, it was also my very first account.

I wrote my first ad for him overnight. It ran full page in the *Miami Herald* a week later.

The first ad for my friend Garlick's new company.
Attorneys Professional Association (1981)

I didn't think the ad was particularly groundbreaking from a creative standpoint, but it was very successful from a business one—especially considering our small media budget. The first day the ad ran, Attorneys Professional received more than 200 phone calls from prospective clients and other attorneys throughout Florida.

I didn't make much money on the business. In fact, I think I may have even lost some. My accounting, bookkeeping and invoicing were so fucked up at that point (I was in charge of them, after all) that I truly didn't have a clue what my financial situation was. My dad was so right. Most creative people don't know shit about running a business. Well, at least this creative person didn't.

Be that as it may, Steve Penchina Inc. was off and running.

# 21 THE BIG BOYS UPSTAIRS

"Is this Steve Penchina?" he growled into the phone.

"Yes it is," I answered politely. "Who may I ask…"

"This is Phil Dougherty of *The New York Times*," he interrupted.

"Oh, yes. Hello, Mr. Dougherty. This is Steve Penchina."

"I know. I called you."

It didn't take long before he was annoyed with me. I had never spoken to him before and didn't have any idea why he was calling. What I did know was that he was both the most feared and revered man covering the industry. He could make or break any agency in town with a couple of keystrokes. My knees were knocking. I was simultaneously excited and scared to death. Concentrate. Concentrate.

"Oh, I'm sorry, Mr. Dougherty."

"It's Phil or Philip," he ordered.

"Okay," I conceded, "Phil." I was a wreck.

"I hear you hung out your own shingle? When did this happen?"

"Oh, about—"

"Not about," he interrupted again. "I need the exact date."

I shuffled through the pile of papers on my desk and couldn't find anything official. I made up a date.

"How old are you?" he barked.

"I'm 35."

"You're a puppy. I have ties older than you. So, what business did you open your shop with, Mr. Penchina?"

"Well, I—"

"Penchina? What kind of a name is that?"

"Uh, I'm Jewish. My father told me our family is from the north of Italy."

"Milan?" He asked.

"Yeah, somewhere up there, maybe Turin."

"They make a lot of cars there," he said.

"Yeah, I know."

"I'm Irish."

"Yes, I thought so." I answered respectfully.

"So, what's this new account of yours, Mr. Penchina from northern Italy?"

I told him all about Attorneys Professional Association—how I got it, what kind of a business it was, how much it billed, and where the media was running. He seemed moderately impressed. He paused for a second.

"Aren't you the guy who did those terrific merry monk commercials for Xerox?"

"Yes," I said proudly, "That is me."

"That is 'I'," he corrected.

"Of course, 'I'."

"Fascinating." He said. "Okay, young fella. Good luck with your agency. Next time call me first with news. I don't like press releases."

"Oh, sure, Phil. I'll call you first," I said before realizing he had already hung up.

As we were talking, I couldn't figure out how he'd heard about my new account. But after the press release comment, I figured it out. Garlick must have sent him a press release on his new company and bragged about his hot new New York ad agency.

Dougherty was an acerbic, hard-nosed reporter, but beneath his tough, leathery personality, I sensed something endearing about him. I liked him. I was scared shitless of him, but I liked him.

**The New York Times**

**Media & Advertising**                    November 19, 1981

A New Account for a New Agency

By Philip H. Dougherty

Steven Penchina, who used to write those engaging monk commercials for the Xerox Corporation while at Needham, Harper & Steers, six months ago, left Wells, Rich, Greene, where he was a senior vice president and creative group head, to open Steve Penchina Inc., up to now a struggling, one-man agency.

But thanks to a reference from a friend of a friend, he has got a client who is talking about spending $2 million next year and $18 million in four years: It is Attorneys Professional Association, the legal profession's answer to the Century 21 real estate franchises, and, according to Mr. Penchina, an upscale version of Jacoby & Meyers.

The Miami-based client has 22 offices in Florida and plans to go national. Michael Garlick is the chairman. The first ad will run within a week as a full page in The Miami Herald. The picture will show a hand holding the card under the headline, "This is all you need to buy real estate in Palm Beach, start a business in Hollywood and get a divorce in Miami."

The first of many articles to appear in *The New York Times* featuring Steve Penchina Inc. (1981)

From Dougherty's small story I received more attention and inquiries than I had from any brochure or letter I ever wrote. Everyone who had anything to do with advertising, marketing or media read his column religiously. It was the bible, the single most powerful public-relations venue in the business. Immediately, my phone began ringing from friends, colleagues and clients who hadn't known I'd started an agency. Dougherty's story had created an instant buzz. And it gave me something a lot of agencies work a very long time to achieve: credibility.

For weeks, I had been following up on a letter I had written to Digital Equipment Corporation (DEC) in Maynard, Massachusetts. I had researched the innovative computer giant; they were the perfect account for me: a cutting-edge, high-tech company with lackluster branding and advertising. They needed someone with imagination and business-to-business experience. And I most definitely needed them.

I called their director of marketing relentlessly for weeks on end until one day he actually picked up the phone. I was speechless when he expressed interest in meeting me. He actually apologized for not getting back to me sooner. He asked if I wouldn't mind flying up for a meeting. All I could think was how I was going to pay for the plane flight and taxis. But before I could drive myself too crazy, he volunteered that he would send "the company chopper" to shuttle me from Logan to DEC headquarters, a 25-minute flight. Christ, what a change. I couldn't even get Garlick to pick up my cab fares.

The chopper came precisely on time, and we flew directly into a thunderstorm. The helicopter shook and dipped and rattled like pocket change in a clothes dryer. Despite the pilot's assurances that there was nothing to worry about, I was certain I'd wind up like Amelia Earhart, never to be seen or heard from again. I could see the headline: "Famous adman lost in thunderstorm over Maynard, Massachusetts." When we finally touched down at DEC, I exited the helicopter and proceeded to throw up all over the landing pad. After some time cleaning myself up in the men's room, I finally made it upstairs to the conference room.

I was met by about a dozen marketing, public relations and advertising execs. Giving off a slight aroma from what had transpired half an hour earlier, I made a succinct credentials presentation that highlighted my Xerox and other b-to-b experience. I took them through my reel and print samples and shared several top-line observations about their company and what I could do to help them transform their terribly conservative image. After my presentation they asked me to leave the room for a few minutes. Twenty-five minutes later I landed my first big-name client. I also got an open retainer of $5,000 a month, plus expenses. The first chance I had to go to the bathroom I looked into the mirror and screamed out a silent "FFFFFFUUUUUCCCCCCKKKKK MEEEEEEEEEEEE!!!!!!"

I had absolutely nailed my assessment of their company. They were quite impressed with my thinking and that I was able to draw an accurate impression of DEC without any help from them. They agreed that what they sorely needed was a corporate image campaign (what is now called branding) that accurately communicated DEC's strengths and forward-thinking business philosophy. Their current agency had struck out on the assignment. Their positioning for DEC was terribly outmoded and their advertising was clichéd.

The marketing director set up a series of meetings for me with senior DEC executives, giving me reams of company information and research data, along with ten years of annual reports, and off I went back to Logan Airport in the damn chopper, praying every single mile for clear weather.

Back in New York, I got a hold of my ace art director, Bob Needleman, and we went to work on the account over lunches at the Brasserie in the Seagram's building. They had the best onion soup in the world and they never pressured me to leave, which made it the perfect venue for Steve Penchina Inc.'s conference room.

DEC was a very successful pioneering computer giant. Unfortunately, most business people weren't even aware that they were a Fortune 500 company. They needed fresh new brand awareness in the worst way. To communicate their considerable relationships with corporate America, they suggested I develop a testimonial campaign. Generally speaking, I disliked this approach. It was overused and not very creative. But for $5,000 a month I could work with it.

Bob and I always worked fast and efficiently. No matter what I said, he would complete my sentences and vice versa. We had this amazing, shorthand way of working together, which was great by me. I was paying him by the hour.

Before we even got to the chocolate mousse cake, we came up with a novel testimonial campaign: to use the CEOs of companies that work with DEC in a straightforward endorsement. But the interesting angle was that we wanted real CEOs with personalities in all our commercials.

The idea would be a win-win for everybody. The CEOs would be able to showcase their company for free, and DEC would get the halo effect of being the computer company of choice for these big, blue-chip corporations. In addition, we would execute the campaign in an unusual way: if we used L.L. Bean, for instance, we'd have the CEO fly-fishing in his waist-high boots, talking about the virtues of working with DEC, and how they helped L.L. Bean with their business problems. It wouldn't be easy to pull off, but if we could get a bunch of CEOs to agree, it would make for a compelling piece of advertising. Bob roughed out the storyboards while I wrote the scripts. He polished everything off at his agency, Scali, McCabe and Sloves, over the next week. A short time later, I was back on the Flying Vomit Machine to make my presentation.

After a brief overview of the idea, I took the clients through all the storyboards. They were happy as Ipswich clams. They made several modifications, but overall they couldn't have been more pleased.

"Now comes the hard part," the marketing director announced. "We've got to get the advertising campaign sold into all of our divisions. After that, of course, we have to take it to the big boys upstairs." (I've always wondered why the "big boys" are always upstairs. And why aren't they ever women?)

DEC was a giant bureaucratic company with hundreds of people in management all over Massachusetts and other northeastern states. I had to go back and forth on that nauseating helicopter more times than I want to remember, presenting to all their major divisions. After a month or so, there was unanimous support for the campaign. I could smell success. Or so I thought.

We finally got in front of the big boys upstairs. They liked the campaign, saying it was a lot better than what their current agency was doing. But as is often the case, when the big boys realized how much it was going to cost to run an impactful television campaign, they checked out.

But I didn't give up. The marketing director and I went back several more times, making considerable progress by paring down the media budget, but in the end they said the advertising was just too costly at this time. Bottom line, the big boys upstairs had no balls. The consolation prize was their approval of a series of print ads that provided me with steady income for a long time.

DEC was a turning point for my young agency. With the first national, blue-chip account officially on my roster, I was beginning to feel like one of the big boys myself.

In a few short months, Steve Penchina Inc. had secured five new accounts and, despite myself, I was making money. With my agency's rapid growth I realized I was running out of space in my in-laws' apartment. I also needed a secretary, a copier, stamp machine, typewriter, travel agent and a messenger service. In short, I needed an office. Even more, I needed someone to help me with all the business stuff. There simply weren't enough hours in the day for me to do everything and, more so, I didn't want to.

# 22

# I DON'T GET NO RESPECT I TELL YA, NO RESPECT AT ALL

Getting a new piece of business generally boils down to four ingredients: perseverance, chemistry, creativity and plain, old good luck.

KIMN, a crazy AM rock radio station in Denver, Colorado, fell into the last category. As part of my new business efforts, I sent my brochure to all the film production houses I had worked with over the years. After all, I was largely responsible for many of the Porsches these guys were driving out to the Hamptons every weekend.

Not long after the mailings went out, I received a call from the president of Jefferson-Pilot Productions, a company I had given a lot of business to while at Wells, Rich, Greene. Its parent company, Jefferson-Pilot Corporation, also owned a bunch of TV and radio stations across the country. My friend over there told me that one of their Denver radio stations was looking for a small creative shop to help them on a new campaign. The station's general manager, a warm, very sharp, but high-strung man named Steve Keeney, was pulling his proverbial hair out trying to find a hip agency in the Denver area. I jumped right on it and followed up with Steve. After several good phone conversations, he flew me out to Denver for more serious talks (no vomiting this time).

The two of us couldn't have hit it off any better. I screened my reel and that's all he needed. He immediately began filling me in on the trials

WHO WROTE THIS SH*T?!

and tribulations of his radio station, the competition and his out-of-control DJs. He also took me through some of the embarrassingly poor advertising the local agencies had developed.

The first thing I told him was that he was breaking a golden rule taught to me by George Lois: "Don't try to say too much in your advertising." I explained to him that he could make one, possibly two points in a 30-second spot, but no more; otherwise, the audience gets confused. Since he had already purchased a large amount of airtime, I proposed that he run a bunch of 30- and 10-second spots, each making a different point.

Up against a tight deadline, he gave me a crash course in the radio business, cramming 20 years of experience into two long 12-hour days. I found the marketing of a radio station to be fascinating, obviously quite different from stomach remedies and copiers. It's a wild, fast-paced, shoot-from-the-hip industry where almost everything plays out live on air. Considering all the whacked-out personalities he'd worked with over the years, he was quite comfortable working with me.

I was born for an account like this.

Steve immediately drew up a simple contract, and I was thrilled to have my first real TV account. Armed with videocassettes, live station tapes, promotional materials and reams of notes, I flew back to New York and got a hold of Needleman. As we were drawing up the new storyboards, I got a call from Keeney.

"What do you think of Rodney Dangerfield?" he asked bluntly.

"I think he's probably the funniest person on earth. I love him."

"You sure?"

"Yeah. Caddyshack is one of my favorite movies. Why?"

"Because I think I can get a deal with him to do our commercials."

"Oh, really?" I asked, somewhat nonplussed.

"How far along are you with our campaign?"

"Almost finished, actually."

"Uh huh," he mused. "Sooooo, what would you think if I asked you to do something with Rodney, provided I could sign him?"

"Well, I'd have to toss out all the work I just completed. But if you can really get Dangerfield, I think it would be a big win for the station."

"The bigger question," he continued, "is whether you think Rodney would be the right image for us?"

"Do bears shit in the woods?" I answered.

"So, if I can sign him, you're confident you can work with him?"

"Uh, who in their right mind would turn down the opportunity to work with Dangerfield? Of course I can. When will you know?"

"I have a meeting with Estelle Endler, his manager, on Thursday. She really wants to do this and assures me I'll be able to afford him."

"You know, he just did a Miller Lite commercial—which, by the way, is hilarious."

"Yeah. She sent me a tape. She told me he had a close call with his heart and now that he's better he just wants to keep busy. He's doing several shows here in Denver soon and he could shoot our stuff while he's out here."

"Great," I said, warming to the idea even more. "Go get 'em, tiger."

A couple of days later, Steve called to say he'd signed Rodney. I was excited but I knew that writing these spots wouldn't be a cakewalk. Getting inside Rodney's deranged mind, and picking up his style and humor would be tricky. I went straight to the video store and grabbed everything I could find on the man, including, of course, Caddyshack. I studied his manner and style and began writing some scripts in Rodney-speak. Two weeks later, I presented to Steve and his marketing people over speakerphone, doing my best Rodney impersonation. They laughed like hyenas, but I honestly thought they were laughing more at my impression than at the new spots.

I had cleared the first hurdle. The second hurdle would be more difficult: I needed Rodney's approval on the scripts. I met Estelle at a coffee shop in New York and took her through the scripts.

"You really captured his persona," she told me excitedly. "Did you write all these jokes?"

"Yeah, I've been a fan forever. I just hope he likes them. When can I present to him?" I asked.

"You know, Steve, Rodney gets a little self-conscious about meeting writers. He gets intimidated."

"Rodney?! Intimidated?!"

"You'd be surprised. Deep down comedians are incredibly insecure. Let me take these to him. Besides, he's gonna love 'em. He's in the city now. I'll get them right over to his apartment. He's not too far from here."

Three days passed and I had bitten my fingernails down to the quick. Finally, I got a call from Steve. "Rodney approved the scripts. Estelle told me he even laughed out loud, which she said he never does. It's full speed ahead, my friend. Congrats."

I couldn't imagine what I would have done if Rodney had hated them; Steve had already signed him to contract. I immediately called Jefferson-Pilot and set the production in motion. We had to start casting, location-scouting, pulling a crew together and working out the logistics of shooting around Rodney's performances. Most important of all, I had to find a good West Coast director.

After looking at dozens of sample reels, I came across a guy named Bill Dear. His sample reel made me laugh so hard my jaw hurt for a day. He had also directed several award-winning music videos with a number of Hollywood celebrities. (He later went on to direct the movies *Harry and the Hendersons* and *Angels in the Outfield*.) I was totally confident he could handle Rodney. And me.

I flew back to Denver for the film shoot and was picked up at the airport by a beautiful blonde production assistant. She told me she'd check me into the hotel, wait for me to freshen up and then drive me to the production office. Great. I'd missed this kind of royal treatment. I was officially back in the game.

Bill Dear had agreed to direct my spots, so we decided to grab a quick dinner that night in downtown Denver. Feeling more relaxed now that Bill was on board, and even more so after meeting him, I felt totally confident about the production.

Between several pitchers of Coors, he took me through the shooting board, frame by frame. Keeney had put us on a tight budget, so we had to coordinate precisely how we would shoot five commercials in just two days. (Normally, a production like this would take three, maybe four days.) Of course, Rodney was the X-factor. Even if he didn't turn out to be too much of a prima donna, we'd still only just make it.

Rodney had been scheduled to give two live performances at the Denver Auditorium the night before our shoot. Bill, Steve and I had to go over some last-minute details with him, so Estelle had arranged for us to meet Rodney in his dressing room after his midnight show.

Waiting backstage as he closed the show, we heard the roars from the mostly college-aged audience. They kept screaming for an encore until Rodney finally threw them a few bones:

"My wife is so ugly, when she goes to the beach, the waves go out."

"Ya know, Bob Hope entertained the troops every year. So did my wife."

"The other night my wife met me at the front door. She was wearing a negligee. Only trouble was she was coming home."

The audience went wild. This guy was in a league by himself. I couldn't believe I was going to be working with him in a few hours.

Rodney finally materialized from behind the curtain in his black suit, white shirt and famous red tie (one of which now hangs in the Smithsonian Institution). An assistant threw him a towel to wipe off his perspiration. His shirt was soaked through. It was his second show of the night and he looked exhausted. I thought of his heart condition.

He walked right by me to his dressing room. Estelle instructed us to wait a few minutes so he could cool down. We stood outside his door, feeling like a bunch of teenage groupies waiting backstage for autographs. Finally, she waved us in.

Rodney was standing in the middle of this large dressing room in a white terry cloth robe imprinted with tacky Las Vegas dice. His shirt was off but the red tie was still around his neck, and his long black garter socks and boxer shorts peeked out from underneath his robe. He was holding a can of Miller Lite in one hand and shoveling a French's mustard sandwich on Wonder Bread into his mouth with the other. The room was packed with a smorgasbord of people: a half-dozen pretty young autograph hounds; another half-dozen good-looking, teenage boys; two buff, mean-looking body guards; Estelle; several photographers; some press people; and the ad team.

Estelle introduced our whole crew to Rodney, beginning with Steve Keeney. "Yeah, uh, nice ta meet ya," Rodney said respectfully, to the man who signed his check.

"And these are the agency people," she continued, introducing Bill and me.

"Yeah, yeah. Good," he said coarsely, preoccupied with slathering another mustard sandwich.

It was late, so Steve got right to the point, asking Rodney to take one last look at the scripts and sign off on a couple of legal nitpicks. "Uh, yeah. Let me take a look," he mumbled, pulling up a folding metal chair. Some ten pairs of eyes were riveted on him as he went over the scripts.

"Who wrote this shit?!" he bellowed.

Everyone froze. I stared down at the floor like everyone else, wishing I were invisible, or even better, dead.

I glanced over at Steve. All the blood had drained from his face and he was gnawing on his bottom lip. Estelle looked wobbly. And out of my peripheral vision, I could see Steve and Bill staring directly at me. I couldn't stall any longer.

"Uh, I did, Rodney."

"You really wrote this crap?"

I didn't answer right away. I thought maybe he was kidding.

"Umm, not sure I would categorize it as, uh, crap," I stammered.

"Oh, it's crap all right," he assured me.

"But, Rodney, just a few days ago in New York you said you loved them. Estelle told me you laughed out loud."

"I ain't laughin' now," Rodney shot back.

Estelle tried to jump in, but Rodney cut her off.

"How long da ya think I've been doin' this?" he asked, glaring at me.

He waited for my answer.

"I'm not really sure," I finally answered, not liking to be put on the spot like that.

"Forty fuckin' years! That's how long. You think I'm gonna let you fuck up my life after all these damn years? No fuckin' way, big guy."

"I wasn't trying to," I answered respectfully, feeling my blood starting to boil. Wasn't he supposed to be intimidated by writers?

Creative people learn to live with rejection. It comes with the territory. What I didn't like was the public humiliation.

As disappointingly as the events had unfolded, they were about to get worse. Rodney methodically ripped the scripts into tiny pieces and hurled them right at me. The flurry of paper flew into my chest and fell to the floor. If anyone in the room had been confused as to who the target of Rodney's fury was, it was now crystal fucking clear.

At this point in his tirade he paused. Something or someone had apparently caught his eye.

"Hey, common ova here, doll face." He motioned to one of the young girls hanging around. "Not you, Pinocchio," he barked at one of the star-struck teenage boys approaching him.

A pretty, blond, inebriated college student, looking like she was fresh off a farm in Kansas, sashayed over to him and bounced up on his lap. He put his arm around her tiny waist.

Steve Keeney tried to direct him back to the disaster at hand. "Rodney, I'm sorry for this, but I have your signature on those scripts. You approved them. You said you liked them. Estelle said you liked them. We have a contract. And, incidentally, we start shooting at 6 a.m."

"If I'm not there, start without me. Heh, heh," Rodney fired back. "Just give me a jingle and let me know how things turned out."

Steve, a nervous guy to begin with, started to tremble.

Rodney gulped down another Miller Lite and made eye contact with another one of his admirers. "Comova here, you adorable little thing." A petite girl with teased, heavy metal hair, wearing a skin-tight, super-short, hot pink dress approached. "Not you, gorgeous," he said to her, raising his eyebrows. "You," he clarified, pointing with his pinky to a young guy nearby. "Don't cry, little lady, you'll get your chance with Uncle Rodney."

As Rodney was flirting around, I gathered up the scripts. A mix of emotions surged through me, first and foremost, rage. Sure, he was Rodney Dangerfield, but I knew the scripts were funny. Bill thought they were funny. Steve thought they were funny. Estelle thought they were funny. Shit, Rodney thought they were funny just a few days ago.

As we were standing there, I kept mentally replaying what Estelle had told me: "Rodney approved the scripts. He even laughed out loud. And he never does that." Either she'd been hallucinating or Rodney had. But it didn't matter. It was close to 2 a.m., and Steve was already in for the entire cost of the production…Rodney or no Rodney.

"What can we do, Rodney?" Steve pleaded.

"I don't have a fuckin' clue what you're gonna do. But I know what I'm going to do, and that's not read this shit. I'm going to party."

Rodney and his boyfriend got up and went over to the creepy crowd at a makeshift bar. Starfuckers of all ages were tossing back shots and inhaling copious amounts of white powder.

"Ya see?" he announced to his clan. "I don't get no respect, I tell ya. No respect at all. Not even from these nudnick ad guys." They went wild with ass-kissing laughter.

Fuck him, I thought. Bill Dear could see I was about to lose it and pulled me aside.

"Don't get too worked up, Steve," he whispered in my ear. "I've been in this spot a million times with characters like this. If we can decipher what his damn problem is, you and I can hit a bar and rewrite the scripts. We'll stay up all night if we have to. Trust me, it won't be that difficult."

"Well, this is a fucking first for me," I told Bill. "I thought I'd seen everything by now."

His reassurances helped. I slipped the suicide note back into my shirt pocket.

We motioned Steve over and told him our plan, but before we headed out I had to know why Rodney had double-crossed us and what specifically freaked him out. After all, some of my lines were lifted directly from his material. Regaining some of my confidence, I made my way through a pot cloud and found Rodney at the other end. There's only way to handle a bully. He had landed the first punch. I was about to land the second.

"Rodney, Bill and I are prepared to stay up all night and rewrite the scripts, but——"

"It's your funeral, heh, heh."

"Right, but I need to know specifically what you found so objectionable, why you changed your mind. Don't worry about hurting my feelings."

My sarcasm was lost on everyone but Bill, who turned away stifling a laugh. Estelle came rushing over and broke into our summit meeting fearing the worst. "Guys, let me have a few minutes with Rodney."

Bill and I slowly backed away and took in the wild scene in front of us. Rodney's entourage was stoned and sloshed out of their minds. They were dancing on the bar, making out and then passing out. And that was just the guys. After about ten minutes, Estelle came back, pulled us aside and gave us her best take on the situation. Part of it, she explained, was that he was just flat-out exhausted from his shows and wasn't thinking clearly. "He's not a well man," she reminded us. As if we needed reminding. She didn't have a clue as to the rest of the equation. He changed his mind? He's temperamental? He's a prima donna? Take your pick.

Rodney was indeed a comedic genius, but he was also a nut job who was fucking up my commercials. I glanced over at Steve, who was leaning against a wall with one shoulder. He was white as a ghost. I really felt bad for him—he didn't deserve this crap. No matter what happened, it was still my responsibility to deliver the campaign. *Fuck this lunatic,* I thought. *If I'm going to stay up all night rewriting these spots, the least this asshole could do is tell me why he tore them up. That much, he owes me.* I interrupted Rodney again, who by this time had a giant bong in one hand and a crotch in the other.

I looked him straight in the eye. "Sorry, Rodney," I broke in, "but I have to rewrite these scripts, and if I'm gonna get them right, I need to understand exactly what you find so objectionable."

He cocked his head to the side and let out an exaggerated sigh. He wanted me to go away, but he could tell I wasn't doing anything of the sort. I started pumping him with questions about the boards and, after a few minutes, he finally gave me a sense of what he was after. I pushed back at him several times, catching him in contradictions. When we finished our little tête-à-tête, I came to the conclusion that my original scripts weren't that far off. I also got the impression that he was forming a begrudging respect for me. Maybe it was my probing or that I'd stood up to him, but my antenna picked up a change in his demeanor. He didn't love me, but he definitely hated me less.

On our way out of the dressing room, I stopped to talk with Steve.

"Steve, please don't worry about this. I'll figure it out. I promise. It's my job to win over Rodney, and I will. Go home and get some sleep. I'll see you in the morning."

"It is morning," he reminded me.

Bill and I drove downtown, where we found a funky local hangout. We ordered three pitchers of Coors and stayed up most of the night rewriting the spots. Naturally, I was upset about the whole thing, but that quickly dissipated with our first pitcher of beer. Beer or no beer, though, I knew that when it was time to dig down deep within myself, I could always come up with a solution.

Thanks to my last-minute chat with King Rodney, the rewrites weren't that painful. I figured out that the key to the whole imbroglio was to make sure that he was front and center in each spot. In the final analysis, his issues were less about the copy and more about the size of his penis.

Early the next morning, Bill and I went to see Rodney in his trailer. We knocked on the door and received the first good news of the day. He was there.

"Here you go, Rodney. I think these will work for you," I said pseudo-cheerfully, my head pounding, as I handed him the revised scripts.

"I'll be the judge of that," he retorted, picking up where he'd left off a few hours ago. He quickly glanced over the rewrites. We held our breath.

"Not too shitty," he declared. "They need work, but they're not half bad. Who wrote this?" he asked, looking directly at me.

"We did," I answered, glancing over at Bill.

"Nah, had to be you with the big schnoz," he said, his bloodshot eyes zeroing in on me. He turned to Bill.

"You're too ugly to have written these. Heh, heh." He saw an opening. "Ya know, you're so ugly, if you opened the front door on Halloween, kids would give you candy."

*He might be an asshole,* I thought, *but he's a damn funny asshole.*

"Come in here, big fella. We'll punch these up."

My prayers had been answered. Rodney was on board. I knew something had connected between us last night. He trusted me. Bill and I stepped toward the door.

"Not you," he told Bill. "Just this one with the ostrich beak." I followed Rodney inside his trailer, feeling a little bad for Bill but glad we were on course. We sat down at a small, cramped kitchen table.

"These are a lot better, Numbnuts," he said. "But they're still not funny enough. Got a pencil? Let's take out some of this crap." He crossed out some of my lines and began writing new ones. "What do you think?" he asked, turning the scripts toward me.

"They're both funny," I said apprehensively. I couldn't believe he was asking for my opinion.

"Wrong," he countered. "This one may be okay. But this one sucks. Where did you learn to write? On a prison wall? How about this?"

"That's definitely funny."

"Ya think so?"

"Yeah, definitely funnier than my line."

"That's not exactly a death-defying feat, Bonerhead. What about this?"

"Uh, not really," I said, gaining confidence. "Doesn't really go with that scene." I was becoming increasingly more comfortable working with him, and he was enjoying the back and forth. I was struck by how open he was to my suggestions. Who would have thought? And he wasn't the least bit defensive.

"I have an idea, Rodney."

"Well, blow me over with a feather," he said, pointing his pinky at me.

"When you're sitting at the diner counter waiting for your coffee, you should try to pick up the attractive girl next to you."

He thought for a second. "Yeah, that'll work. How 'bout if I ask her, 'Do you live alone?' and she blows me off?" He paused for a second. "Then I turn to the camera and say, 'I don't need her. But I do. I need her, I need her,' and start whimpering like a lonely old man?"

"I like it. And you don't even have to act the 'lonely old man' part."

He shot me a look. Truth be told, everything out of this guy's mouth was hysterical. But the most remarkable part was that here I sat, mano-a-mano, working with one of the greatest comedians who ever lived…and he was asking me what was funny.

He wrote down another line.

"Whadaya think?"

"Yeah, absolutely."

"Wrong, Numbnuts. You suck. Again."

"Okay, what do you think of this? In the elevator spot, when you're standing next to the lady listening on her portable radio with that big, dumb antenna, you ask her, 'Can you get Mars from here?'"

"That's not half bad. Write that down, but make it in English this time."

He tossed out another line that I wasn't 100% percent sure about it. "I think I like it, but I dunno. You're the big schtarka here."

"Well, you're also a comedian."

I sat there soaking in his compliment. He took a long, thoughtful pause.

"Yeah," he finally went on. "Every time I see your face, I crack up."

Rodney Dangerfield starring in Steve Penchina Inc.'s TV spot for KIMN Radio. (1980s)

I should have known.

By this time, the assistant director was kicking down the trailer door. "We gotta start shooting, you two. We're way behind schedule. They're funny enough."

Rodney and I walked out of his trailer the best of buddies. He approved all five commercials. Steve, who was hovering around like a vulture on lunch break, started breathing again. He had aged ten years overnight.

Our plan was to shoot three spots the first day and two the second. But we had to move fast. Rodney and I continued working together all morning. Some of the lines that were funny in the trailer didn't come off on the set, so in between scenes we were constantly making adjustments. He also liked changing things on the fly. He had a great ear for what worked and what didn't.

As impossible as he had been the night before, he was the consummate professional when the camera was rolling. He delivered his lines perfectly each and every time. He didn't deviate a fraction of a second from one take to another, and each was hysterical. The cadence and "melody" of his delivery were impeccable. It was like he had a metronome built into his head.

Rodney and I collaborating for KIMN Radio commercial.

Pity the poor actor who threw off his timing. If they couldn't keep up with him, or kept blowing their lines, he demanded Bill get rid of them on the spot. He couldn't care less about hurting their feelings. We went through four actors by noon.

The first morning went beautifully, but when we broke for lunch, Rodney dropped a bombshell.

"Boys, I'm on a five o'clock plane outta this cow town."

"What?" Bill squealed. "We're only halfway through."

I glanced over at Steve. The blood was draining from his face again. At this rate, I was afraid he wouldn't live long enough to see his campaign break.

"Rodney, we've got three more spots to shoot," Steve said, hysterical and totally fed up. "We have to finish. You can't leave now."

Steve and Estelle took Rodney aside and tried talking some sense into him. All I could hear him say was, "I don't give a rusty fuck. You have me 'til 3 and that's it. I'm gettin' outta this fuckin' cow town!"

I stayed out of the line of fire this time. He and I were getting along well and I didn't want to screw things up. Steve would have to take this blowup on by himself. It was a clear-cut breach of contract. They argued for twenty minutes, but it was futile. Rodney simply didn't give a shit. He was leaving in three hours, contract be damned.

Before their conversation had even ended, Bill and I began scrambling to map out a new shooting strategy. The schedule was tight to begin with, but now we had to pull off somewhat of a miracle to shoot one more 30-second spot and two 10s in three hours.

We immediately concluded that we had to shoot everything in the same location. We didn't have time to move the camera and equipment around, and relight each scene. Bill and I reworked the scripts and ran them by Benedict Arnold Dangerfield. He was okay with the changes.

We came up with a scheme that allowed us to create what appeared to be three seemingly different locations by simply turning the camera in three different directions. We shot one 30-second spot in six takes, which left us with under an hour to shoot the two 10s. We nailed the first in 45 minutes, and were down to the final spot.

Just our luck, the actor playing alongside Rodney kept blowing his lines. Rodney, Bill and I were ready to strangle the poor jerk.

"Hold on a second," Bill suddenly shouted. "I have an idea."

He jumped out from behind the camera, yanked the actor out of the way and took a seat beside Rodney. The assistant director took over the camera. Conferring quickly with his newfound partner, the camera rolling, Rodney ad-libbed a great line.

Rodney Dangerfield and Bill Dear improvise a last-minute scene in a commercial for KIMN.

Rodney (to Bill, staring at his headphones):

"Hey, this is a great city.

I always thought Denver was an omelet."

(Absorbed in the music, Bill doesn't answer.)

"Hey, you? I'm talkin' to ya.

(pause)

"Whaddya comin' in for a landing?"

Announcer v.o.: KIMN Radio 95. The Best Show in Denver.

Amazingly, we got it in two takes.

Rodney was true to his lousy word. Three o'clock sharp, he was in his limo on the way to the airport. Bill, Steve and I collapsed against a production truck and let out a collective sigh. It wasn't relief. It was a death rattle. Rodney had been an F5 tornado tearing through Denver, wiping out everyone and everything in his path.

The next morning, I flew back to New York to finish the spots. Still on a tight timetable, I had to transfer, edit and mix the film, record the announcer voice-over and ship everything to the stations in just two days. The five commercials broke in the Denver metropolitan area that weekend. When they aired, not only were they the talk of Denver, they were the talk of the entire radio industry. Rodney instantly became a cult figure in the radio biz and Steve Keeney, bless his weakened heart, became a cult figure himself for landing such a big star for a local campaign.

Working with Rodney taught me two important things: one, you have to punch a bully right in the face, and two, never panic in a crisis. There's always a way out.

KIMN was the last time Rodney did a commercial for scale. Between our radio spots, his Miller Lite campaign, his New York nightclub Dangerfield's and several new television appearances, Rodney's career was red-hot again.

Things kept moving ahead for me as well. Steve rewarded my KIMN work by giving me another radio station, KYGO Lite FM, and I continued to pick up several more accounts while interviewing nonstop for a business partner.

One quiet Saturday morning at home, my telephone rang.

"Hey, Pinnochio, guess who?"

He has one of the most distinctive voices in the world, but for the life of me I couldn't imagine why Rodney was calling me at home on the weekend.

"I'll play along, who?"

"It's your pal, Rodney."

"Rodney? Rodney who?" I joked.

He ignored me.

"Hey, kiddo, listen. Could ya do me a small favor?"

"For you Rodney, nothing."

"Can you get me a couple of video cassettes of our KIMN radio spots? I want to show them off to a couple of friends of mine."

"No problem," I said. "When do you need them?"

"Right now. I got some people here from outta town."

"Man, you don't make life easy for me, do you?" I answered.

"Stand in line. You're not alone, kiddo. Heh, heh. Pretty please, Mr. Steve-o?"

"I'll see what I can dig up. Where do you live?"

I grabbed a couple of blank cassettes I had lying around, copied the spots and walked them over to his East Side apartment. I rang the bell and the door swung open to reveal the same ole Rodney. His Vegas dice robe was hanging open exposing his boxer shorts, his black socks were pulled up on his skinny scrawny legs and he was wearing the same old leather slippers. Standing behind him in their skivvies were two of the teenage boys who had been with him in the dressing room in Denver.

Rodney took the tapes and politely thanked me.

"Put these in the machine, boys. It's those spots from that cow town in Colorado," he said as he shut the door on me. "They're funny. I'm good, I tell ya. I'm damn good."

"Hey kiddo," I heard him shout to one of the boys as I walked away. "How long's it gonna take for that brewski? We'll have a Jewish president by the time it gets here, heh, heh."

# 23 THE DELICATESSEN BOYS

Even from 30 feet away I liked him. I felt like I was on a blind date that might actually turn out to be good for a change.

I was tucked behind a potted palm in the Oak Room at the Plaza Hotel, going over my notes, when I saw Arty Selkowitz rushing toward me. He was noticeably trying to avoid eye contact with everyone there. I had tried to pick out a restaurant where we wouldn't run into people from the industry. I knew he was paranoid that someone from Benton & Bowles would spot him with me, do the math, and conclude (correctly) that he was looking to make a move.

Arty was shorter than I expected, but he was well built with the broad shoulders of a water skier. He made a solid, serious impression in his Brooks Brothers gray suit and tie with expensive brown, lace up shoes. He had intense, no-nonsense eyes, but his face lit up from beneath his horned-rimmed glasses when he laughed. If I hadn't known he was Jewish, he would have passed for the perfect Darien, Connecticut-bred, WASP account executive.

After 11 years in account management at Benton & Bowles, Arty had risen to Senior VP, Group Account Director on Proctor & Gamble, the crown jewel of the giant, $3 billion agency. He had told me on the phone that he was considering a new challenge and was seriously contemplating a break from his traditional past. He was ready to roll the proverbial dice on an entrepreneurial venture. It was something akin, he told me, to a midlife crisis. He had already bought a new red Firebird but evidently that wasn't enough.

After a few minutes of small talk about family, kids and the people we knew in common, I asked him how he felt about leaving behind a good salary and secure position to essentially start over from scratch.

"Well, I'm here," he said.

After ordering our Tabs, I assiduously laid out my vision for the agency. We discussed what types of accounts we wanted, how big we'd like to get, what our individual roles would be and spoke frankly about our strengths and weaknesses.

Well, he talked frankly anyway. I exaggerated my strengths and totally lied about my weaknesses. I had a clear, simple vision: I would take him on as an equal partner; I would be responsible for all the creative, and he would be responsible for everything else. If we didn't agree on something, the one with more expertise in the area would have the tie-breaking vote. The end.

"If you want to embezzle money from me," I volunteered, "you could become a rich man. I don't ever want to see another balance sheet again."

Arty worked almost exclusively on P&G for big brands like Crest, Scope mouthwash and Pampers. But he was excited about the prospect of working on non-packaged goods accounts, like computers or banks, for a change. As for me, his pedigree marketing background was exactly what I was after. I knew from my own experience with P&G how much they demanded from their account directors. They had to be extremely buttoned-up and knowledgeable in every facet of marketing, media and strategy.

Arty would be the perfect complement to my frenetic, freewheeling ways. He was intelligent, reflective and mature, and despite his reserved disposition, he had a good sense of humor. He would need it working with me. As far as I could tell, he was an honest and decent family man with a wife of 20-something years, Betsey, and their two young children, Adam and Jed.

He bragged that he had never taken off his wedding ring. Debbie and I, on the other hand, had been going in and out of battle every few weeks at this point. But I knew better than to let him in on the family drama so soon; I certainly didn't want to scare him off. Plus, his role as my personal psychotherapist was something I planned to spring on him after he accepted the position.

We talked for an hour or so, but just twenty minutes into our meeting my gut was screaming, "Don't let this one get away!" I left lunch feeling optimistic for the first time since my interview marathon had started a year and a half ago.

But before diving in head first, there was still one crucial piece of the puzzle that had to be in place: Arty had to see my reel. And even more, he had to like it. We arranged for him to come by my office in a couple days so he could take a look at it.

By this time I had moved out of my in-law's Germanic apartment and into one of those communal, temporary office spaces on Madison Avenue where small companies shared the reception area, conference rooms, word processing and telephone operators. The rent was reasonable, so it was an ideal setup for a startup like mine.

For our meeting, I borrowed a TV and VCR from a nice guy down the hall, Doug, who worked for Affinity Broadcasting. Arty and I talked more at length about business strategy and financial matters. Although we had only met in person that one time at the Oak Room, we were both enthusiastic about the prospect of a partnership.

"So, want to see my reel?" I asked, somewhat apprehensively.

"That would be good," he replied.

He sat through the reel fairly expressionless.

*Uh oh,* I thought. *Why isn't this guy laughing? I know he's kind of straight, but, give me a freakin' break here.*

At long last there was an optimistic sign: he cracked a grin after watching "The Monk."

Then the million-dollar question: "What do you think? Do you like it?"

Just as he was about to open his mouth, the receptionist interrupted us with an urgent call from Arty's secretary: A client needed to talk to him right away about some important business.

"Let's talk tomorrow," he shouted to me as he ran out.

*Now what?,* I thought. He hadn't mentioned anything about the work. I was no closer to knowing what he liked, or if he related to my brand of creativity, which was kind of important since it was the product he would be selling. I lost sleep that night, worried that after all this time of dead-end meetings I had lost my one good prospect—over my reel, of all things.

The next day, rings under my eyes, I called Arty.

"So, you never said what you thought about my reel?"

"Oh, I'm very enthusiastic," he declared in the same tone he might have used to tell me his dog had been run over by a Allied moving van.

*Good enough,* I thought. *I'll take it.*


We didn't date very long. We didn't have to. It was love at first sight. I didn't make a single reference call about him, other than once bumping into an old art director friend of mine who'd been working at Benton & Bowles for years. I casually brought up Arty's name.

"I would die to work with him," he told me. "There isn't a person in the creative department who wouldn't. He's a great guy. Very smart."

"Everyone says he's such a great guy. Isn't there anything negative about this guy?" I asked, hoping I wasn't tipping my hand.

He thought for a moment. "Yeah, he's short."

Four weeks later, Arty and I were married. And we kept our own last names. To be candid, I would have preferred his last name to be Higgins or Smith. It would have balanced out the ticket better. But I quickly embraced the mouthful that was Penchina, Selkowitz Inc.

# 24 THE TYPEWRITERS, NOT THE SCARVES

Our first capital expenditure was a used IBM Selectric typewriter Arty bought for $40 from the super generous human resource department at Benton & Bowles. He lugged it back to our office, tucked under his arm to save the cab fare. I loved the man's frugality.

The two of us were the veritable odd couple. Arty was totally left-brained, meticulously organized and compulsively neat. He was the only person I knew who kept a can of Pledge and a dust cloth in his top desk drawer. I was the anti-Arty: overly sensitive, mildly hysterical and hopelessly messy. By the end of the workday, he couldn't wait for me to go home so he could clean up.

Our partnership was true to my original vision: I would continue doing all the creative work and he would do everything else. For now that left me working on a new batch of TV spots for Steve Keeney's FM radio station, KYGO-Denver, along with writing several new print ads for DEC and a new Attorneys Professional Association ad for Garlick.

Arty sent out a terrific announcement letter to every friend, relative, colleague and client he knew. He began the letter talking about the Xerox "Monk," our biggest claim to fame. Then he outlined his impressive Proctor & Gamble background, described our creative philosophy and all the awards I had won. He closed by explaining the virtues of working with a small agency whose owners had been big-agency big shots. He seemed to enjoy every minute of his new life, and I was thrilled to have another person around who I could kvetch to all day.

In the midst of the 1981 recession, I created our first announcement brochure.

# Good advertising is a luxury you can no longer afford.

In times like these, good advertising isn't good enough.

Advertising in the 1980's must be brilliant.

It must be able to cut through the competitive clutter and capture the consumer's imagination.

And it must be grounded in sharp strategic thinking.

Penchina, Selkowitz Inc. is a unique combination of brilliant creative execution and smart strategic thinking that you rarely find at even the largest agencies.

Steven Penchina has created some of the most successful advertising campaigns in the country. His work has won over 100 awards including *Advertising Age's* "Best Commercials in the Last 50 Years," and the Clio Advertising Hall of Fame.

Arthur Selkowitz has earned an outstanding marketing reputation at top advertising agencies for successfully introducing new products and repositioning declining brands for the biggest packaged-goods companies in the world.

We believe Penchina, Selkowitz Inc. can help build your business even in difficult times like these.

How do we expect to accomplish this?

Simple. We'll never settle for good advertising.

The announcement brochure for Penchina, Selkowitz Inc. 1981

PENCHINA, SELKOWITZ INC.
575 Madison Avenue, New York, N.Y. 10022 (212) 486-1462
For more information, contact Arthur Selkowitz, President

The new promotion piece paid off almost instantly. The president of Hermes, a small 100-year-old, high-quality Swiss electronic typewriter company, called and invited us out to his New Jersey headquarters to pitch his account. Our first presentation together went flawlessly, as if we had been doing this our whole lives. Incredibly, they hired us on the spot. Sure, we had only been in business five weeks but we were batting a thousand. If this were Major League Baseball, we'd be on our way to Rookie of the Year.

Excited about our first win, we got on the phone and called everyone we knew about our new Hermes account. Arty called Betsey with the good news.

"Oh, that's wonderful, honey. When can I get some new scarves?"

"They're not scarves," Arty chided. "They're typewriters."

I called Debbie to tell her the same, but after finding out they weren't on Madison Avenue, she just sighed, "gotta go," and hung up. (Or maybe that's just how I remember it happening.)

"I have so many of their beautiful things, Stevie," my mother told me when I called home to Great Neck.

"Ma, it's not Hermès from France. It's Hermes typewriters from Switzerland."

"Oh?" she said. "I've got pea soup on the stove. Talk to you later."

My sister asked when we were going to France.

"They're not in… They're a typewriter…."

"Wait, why do you want the typewriter division when you could be advertising all those beautiful clothes?" she interrupted. "Ask them if you could have their clothing business instead."

Even the trade press got it wrong. But at least they spelled Penchina, Selkowith correctly.

# 25 THE CHAIRMAN

Near the top of our new business target list was Burroughs Computers, whose CEO and Chairman was the former Secretary of the Treasury, W. Michael Blumenthal. Before we even had the chance to follow up on our first letter, Arty received a call from Burroughs' marketing director, a wonderful man and straight shooter named Bill Beckham.

In our letter we had preemptively addressed any concerns about our work with DEC representing a conflict of interest. Technically, it should have, but we made it clear we were only doing project work for them at this point. Apparently Burroughs wasn't fazed.

Bill asked if we would fly out to Detroit for a chat. Before Arty had even hung up the phone, I had the airline tickets in hand. Arty immediately grabbed his Advertising Red Book (a thick, heavy book that listed virtually every possible brand and business and how much they were currently spending on advertising). We found out that in the previous year, Burroughs had spent $8 million on advertising in the U.S. with Campbell-Ewald, a $200 million, conservative Detroit shop. It would be a real David-and-Goliath feat if we could knock them (and the other agencies they were considering) out of contention.

We arrived in Detroit and meandered through the back streets of the decaying inner city to get downtown to Burroughs' worldwide headquarters. Once there, we headed directly into a series of meetings with Bill Beckham. We found him to be the salt of the earth. The three of us hit it off beautifully. He loved our reel and the case studies we presented but, more importantly, he understood us. He related to Arty's seriousness of purpose and marketing smarts, and seemed to get a big kick out of my personality and sense of humor. I liked that he instinctively understood my need for the freedom to think unconventionally. He told me that my innovative approach to advertising was something Blumenthal was specifically looking for. That said, I could tell Bill was reassured by the fact that Arty watched my every move and made certain everything ran smoothly. "You're a good tandem," he told us.

"Our business is complex," he went on. "And the politics around here are nasty. If we wind up going with a smaller shop, you guys are going to need a lot more staff."

It was obvious he was concerned about our size.

"That won't be a problem," Arty answered.

It ran against our grain, but we had no choice but to tell Bill a giant white lie about our size. We said that Penchina, Selkowitz was billing in the $20 million range and had a staff of 25. We knew we could do the work and were willing to go head to head with any shop on creative and strategy, so we didn't want mere details like these to stand in our way.

Despite our size, Bill thought Arty and I would be a good fit for Blumenthal. "He likes sharp, quick, creative thinkers. He has no patience for big, bureaucratic operations. We soon discovered that Bill had been Assistant Director of Transportation in the Carter administration, which was where he and Blumenthal had met.

Over our next few trips to Detroit, our conversations went well beyond advertising. We spent hours talking politics, sports and race relations (Bill was African-American and deeply involved in Detroit's black community).

We especially bonded over tennis. I was a strong tennis player, and it turned out that Bill was just getting into the game in a serious, obsessive way. He was constantly asking me for pointers, and even suggested that if I could turn him into an A-player, we would be his agency of choice. Obviously, I thought he was kidding, but 'til this day I have a sneaking suspicion that maybe he wasn't.

Blumenthal asked Bill to interview several shops and get back to him with three or four recommendations. About a month later, Bill called us to announce that we'd made the first cut. The next step was to set up a meeting with The Chairman in New York. (Bill only referred to Blumenthal as "The Chairman." It was never "Mike," never "Mr. Blumenthal," never "The CEO." It was always "The Chairman", as in Mao.)

Selected as one of three finalists, Arty and I felt we had a decent shot at the business. Bill had also let on a number of times that he was pulling for us behind the scenes. (Not coincidentally, his tennis was improving.) There was only one problem with meeting The Chairman at our offices. We didn't have offices. We also didn't have a secretary, an account team, creative staff, media or research departments, a traffic coordinator, or TV and print production people… The list goes on. What we did have was communal space that we shared with about 175 other people.

Not having our own offices hadn't posed a problem for us before. Our current clients were small and couldn't have cared less. Besides, we always went to their offices. But this would never stand with an account the size of Burroughs. With revenues of $10 billion, they were the second-largest computer company in the world behind IBM. We had to find a way to convince Bill and The Chairman that we were about 25 times bigger than we were. And we only had six days to do it.

The first thing we did was reserve the largest conference room. We went to work making it "ours." I took all the print ads out of my beautiful portfolio case, spray-mounted them on Styrofoam boards and hung them around the room. I also hung them up in the reception area and throughout all the hallways giving the impression we owned the entire floor. Then, I called my buddy Doug from down the hall to see if I could borrow his TV and VCR. He came right over and set up all the equipment for us in the conference room.

"I've made everything idiot-proof, you guys. All you have to do is hit 'play'."

We didn't have an agency sign, so I blew up the logo from our stationery, cut it down to size, and mounted it on a big sheet of white Styrofoam. The morning of our presentation, I taped the sign to the wall, centering it directly across from the elevators. Had there been any confusion prior, visitors would now know exactly where they'd arrived: the worldwide headquarters of Penchina, Selkowitz Inc., the biggest, most powerful ad agency on the planet.

But the coup de grâce of The Great Deception was bringing in live bodies to fill up all the empty offices on our side of the floor. Between friends, employees of friends and former coworkers, I brought in more than twenty people, and stuffed them into every spare office there was. I doled out layout pads, markers, copy paper, computer printouts, books, magazines, legal pads…basically all the ingredients they needed for "work." I even supplied them with tchotchkes and family pictures of the Schwartzes lying on the beach at the Jersey Shore to line their windowsills.

When the day of reckoning finally arrived, the Chairman's secretary, an old battle-ax, and former personal assistant to J. Edgar Hoover, called to warn us that we had exactly one hour with The Chairman and not a minute more. She also strongly recommended that we have lunch, either roast beef or turkey on whole-wheat toast and a Diet Coke, waiting for him. Arty quickly ran out and happily took care of the culinary chores, picking up some fresh-baked brownies on his way back.

Afraid to put our shared receptionist's acting skills to the test, Arty and I waited for our guests nervously at the elevator bank. We made sure not to block our sign, which, to be fair, not even an eight-axel truck could have accomplished.

As luck would have it, the entire floor was undergoing major renovation at the time. Electrical wires dangled from the ceiling, stacks of plasterboard lined the walls, and thick electrical cables "secured" by duct tape ran the length of the floor just outside of the elevators. Not a minute late, Bill and The Chairman stepped out of the elevator and, as if on cue, Murphy's Law went into effect. The Chairman tripped over one of the cables and went sprawling to the ground. As I reached out to grab him, I brushed against the Penchina, Selkowitz sign, knocking it loose. I watched it float gently to the floor like a snowflake.

"What's going on here?" The Chairman growled, wiping plaster dust off of his suit. We'd managed to piss him off in less than 15 seconds.

"Pardon the mess," Arty answered. "We're expanding."

"Temporary sign," I added.

"Would you like a quick tour of the agency?" Arty suggested quickly, trying to take their minds off the construction.

"Why not?" Bill replied.

We showed the two of them "our offices" and introduced them to our impressive staff, which, as it turned out, wasn't a moment too soon—several of them were stepping out to lunch (method acting, apparently). I held my breath when Bill asked one of my "senior art directors" how much the photography cost on a particular ad. But my friend Barry, who I'd known since Hebrew school, managed to come up with a plausible number on the spot. And with that, our 25-person-strong agency had survived its first test.

"Shall we get down to business, gentlemen? Our main conference room is just down the hall," Arty announced proudly, relishing his presidential skills.

It didn't take but two minutes for me to conclude that Blumenthal was the shrewdest, smartest, coldest, most intimidating person I had ever met. He was scary smart—a Carl Sagan-Stephen Hawking-Henry Kissinger-George Will-Frankenstein of sorts. He knew about things he couldn't have known about.

He probed and dug and bored into us on every conceivable area of advertising, mentally noting each answer. Then, having gathered enough information on the subject, he would trip us up with our own expertise. He wasn't being churlish; it was just the way he worked. His mind was frighteningly facile. It was exhausting trying to keep up with him but, in an odd way, our exchanges were somehow scintillating. The pressure of the moment acted to heighten my concentration. He fired questions at us like a Gatling gun:

"Tell me about your other accounts," he asked.

"How did you get them?"

"What is their marketing and advertising strategy?"

"How big is their ad budget?"

"How did you arrive at that figure?"

"What are their short- and long-term objectives?"

"Other than advertising, what else do you do for them?"

"Do you do any market research?"

"How much validity do you give it?"

"Do you think it's a waste of money?"

"Does it help in the creation of your advertising?"

"Do you buy your own media or use an outside source?"

"Is one better than the other?"

"How do you decide the split between TV and print?"

"Do you handle public relations?"

"Why not?"

Fortunately, Arty and I were on top of our game. We gave smart, snappy answers to each and every question.

I glanced at my watch and noticed we were already running late. I quickly went to our reel. I shoved the cassette into the VCR and hit PLAY. Nothing. I fooled around with all the buttons. Still nothing. Panicked, I grabbed the phone and called Doug. *Be in, be in,* I prayed. He finally answered and rushed over.

"This is Doug, our tech guy," Arty announced with great flair.

"He can fix anything," I added.

I always had to add something (think George Lois).

Doug took a quick look at the equipment. Playing his role to the hilt, even including that smirk techies love to make when they've been called in to fix something elemental, he flashed us a knowing smile when he discovered the problem. "Why, bless your heart," he said. He then bent over and plugged the TV cord into a working outlet.

"Thanks, Doug," Arty and I said sheepishly.

Anticipating that The Chairman wouldn't have the patience to sit through a long reel, I had edited it down to 10 spots, exactly three and a half minutes. As usual, we led with "The Monk." For the first time since he came in, I saw The Chairman smile. He actually laughed out loud when The Monk looked up toward Heaven in the last frame. If nothing else, it broke the tension in the room. Our tension.

He asked me to pause the reel, and he began peppering us with more questions.

"What did the commercial accomplish for Xerox?"

"Did it sell copiers? How many?"

"How much did the machines cost?"

"How much did the commercial cost?"

"How often did it run?"

"What did it do for Xerox's overall image?"

"Who was their target audience?"

"How long did it take you to come up with the idea?"

"Is that fast or slow?"

This was all leading up to one humdinger of a question:

"How do I know you can do something like that for me? How do I know the 'Monk' wasn't a fluke?"

Arty and I looked at each other and responded virtually in unison: "Look at the rest of the reel. You tell us if it was a fluke."

I hit the play button again, and Arty and I sat back confidently as The Chairman watched the rest of the reel. Despite his being such a serious person, I got the distinct impression that the more outrageous the concept, the more he liked it. He might have been born in Berlin like my mother-in-law, but he did, in fact, have a sense of humor.

Arty and I had prepared a well thought-out marketing and advertising analysis of Burroughs. Going in, we had decided we weren't going to pull any punches. We figured we had just one make-or-break shot with the boss and we didn't want to sugarcoat it. For sure, we weren't going to beat out the competition with our worldwide network of offices.

Based on our empirical observations and some limited research Bill had shared with the agencies, we made some judgments about Burroughs' public perception. The news was not good.

Those who knew of the company perceived it as old and stodgy. Most didn't even know what business Burroughs was in despite the fact it was a $10 billion, Fortune 500 Company. Incredibly, a significant number of people thought they still made those old-fashioned adding machines, a business they had abandoned decades ago. Some even confused Burroughs with Burry's, the cookie company. And if all of that wasn't depressing enough, there was virtually zero awareness of their advertising…despite an $8 million national advertising budget.

Anticipating Blumenthal might want to commit hara-kiri at this point, we offered him specific, comprehensive recommendations on how we would solve each of these problems. Near the end of our presentation, I noticed The Chairman glance at his watch again and then look to Bill.

"Well, I'm sorry, gentleman," Bill announced as he got up, "we have another meeting to get to. A well-done presentation, though. Thanks for all your hard work, and thanks for lunch. Those brownies were a big hit." (I could tell that last comment made Arty's day.)

As The Chairman pushed back from the table, he asked us one final question: "Do you guys wear three-piece suits?"

"Huh? Umm, no," Arty answered, perplexed.

"I don't even own a suit," I went along, not knowing where this was going but feeling obligated to add something. "As a matter of fact, this one is rented and I have to get it back by 2:30."

The Chairman cracked a smile.

"The agency we have now," he went on, "they have ten account executives assigned to us, and they march into my office, all in a line, dressed identically in three-piece suits, white shirts and ties. I can't stand that. And I don't need ten people in a meeting all saying the same thing and yes-ing me to death. The two of you would be quite sufficient," he said pointedly.

"That wouldn't be a problem for us," Arty replied, making the greatest understatement of all time.

"I'm paying for your expertise," The Chairman continued. "I don't like sycophants. I want original thinking like that 'Monk' idea. And Alka-Seltzer. And that Joyce Brothers's mother commercial. They were clever. I'm not saying we have to be funny in our ads, but I don't want some rehashed idea I've seen a million times. I want to be surprised. I want you to push the boundaries. Also, I don't want you to show 'the box' in our ads. Every computer company has a box, and they all look the same. It's not necessary to show the machine. Can you do that?" he asked, his eyes focusing directly on me.

"Guaranteed," I answered.

Just then, the "receptionist" barged in to say Blumenthal's secretary was on the phone. Bill took the call. The Chairman grabbed a brownie for the road, and we escorted him, carefully, to the elevator.

After making certain that Bill and The Chairman were safely in the elevator, we shook their hands and off they went. Arty and I went back to the conference room for the post-game analysis.

"The Chairman played it close to the vest," Arty said, "But I think we did well on the substantive questions."

"He definitely liked the reel," I added.

What we didn't know were the intangibles: personal chemistry, the size issue, whether he was on to us and, of course, how we stacked up against the other finalists. But overall we both had a good feeling.


Several weeks later, late one Friday afternoon, the phone rang in Arty's office. It was Bill. Nervously, we picked up the call on speaker.

"Well, fellas, I just left The Chairman's office, where we reviewed all the agencies."

"Uh huh," Arty said, squinting his eyes and holding his elbows close to his body like a prizefighter.

"He told me he wants to go with 'the two guys from New York.' I wasn't certain which 'two guys' he was referring to."

Ba bump, ba bump. My heart was in my throat.

"But then he said, 'You know, the delicatessen boys—the ones whose names sound like a Jewish/Italian deli.' For the life of him, he couldn't remember the name of your company." He was laughing.

"Congratulations to both of you. You beat out two much bigger agencies. Now don't disappoint."

Arty and I beamed at each other and gave a silent high five. I knew what Bill had said, but I couldn't process it. The three of us talked a while longer. Bill had a laundry list of projects that needed attention, and each one (naturally) had to be completed yesterday. He asked that we fly out Monday morning so he could introduce us to the rest of his marketing staff and begin setting up meetings with key executives.

We couldn't thank him enough for guiding us through the process. I would be giving him tennis lessons into the next century.

(Years later, The Chairman was honored as the United Jewish Appeal "Man of the Year," and he graciously invited us to attend. During the cocktail hour, he confessed that he hadn't fallen for any of our stunts that first day. They had already done their due diligence and, frankly, he couldn't have cared less that we were a startup. On the contrary, I think he actually relished the notion that he put us on the map.)

After hanging up with Bill, Arty and I jumped to our feet and hugged. We were stunned. It was almost incomprehensible what we had just pulled off. Just five months after opening our doors, we had struck gold, oil and buried treasure. We always had confidence in ourselves, but to beat out the two other finalists, one of which was a $350-million agency with enough resources to drown us, was simply mind-blowing.

We had done it. On our own terms. In our own way. With nothing more than our instincts…and a couple of teeny-weeny lies.

After coming down from our initial high, the two of us sat in our small office, frozen to our chairs, grinning ear to ear. We fully understood what this meant: we would now be able to hire real staff, get a real office with a real conference room, buy our own real equipment (sorry, Doug) and give ourselves a real salary. But best of all, we'd be able to buy a real Penchina, Selkowitz Inc. sign.

Suddenly, Arty twitched and blinked, startling himself out of his celebratory daze.

"Holy fuck, Steve. Now whadda we do?!"

# 26 THE QUESTION ISN'T WHO'S BIGGER? IT'S WHO'S BETTER?

I'd been stuck before, but never like this. And never with so much riding on it.

I was having a late working dinner at O'Neil's on West 57th with Jim Handloser, my first creative hire at the agency. I'd stolen him from Jerry Della Femina's place, promising him fame and riches. He was a droll but intelligent, and an exquisitely tasteful art director. Despite his Herculean efforts to appear super cool at all times, he often came across as a loveable Don Knotts.

We were scheduled to present our first campaign to Burroughs in just two days, but after more than a month of pure agony, we hadn't even come up with one decent idea, much less a good one. It was almost midnight and we were on our fourth venue of the day. We had started out early at the office, worked over lunch at the Brasserie and sweated out an unproductive afternoon on a bench in Central Park.

After landing Burroughs, everything had changed dramatically for Arty and me. We moved into new offices at 840 Third Avenue, hired about 15 people (which got us close to the number we told Bill), hung up all my ads (now professionally framed), leased a Xerox machine and mounted a beautiful, brushed-chrome Penchina, Selkowitz Inc. sign alongside our front door—this time with shiny screws (not shiny duct tape).

Arty and I were spending a significant amount of time in Detroit learning the computer business. The Chairman had given us explicit marching orders: sell the Burroughs B20, their new, technologically-advanced office desktop computer, while simultaneously delivering a strong, compelling corporate message. Burroughs was treating us to a comprehensive crash course on all of their computers, advanced software and operating systems, as well as virtually every aspect of their marketing, manufacturing, management, sales and R&D efforts.

We were working fast and furiously to get up to speed—not only on Burroughs, but also on the industry in general. And if all of that wasn't enough, The Chairman had us on a ridiculous timetable. We had to develop the campaign, get his approval, sell it to the senior management and sales force, bid it out for production and have it on network television and in print media *in less than three months*. Like every client I'd ever had, they were late to announce their new product, which meant Jim and I had to work around the clock to help them compensate.

The all-day orientation meetings had left me cross-eyed.

"Did you understand any of that?" I asked Arty as we left a particularly grueling session on the B20's operating system.

"Not a damn thing," he confessed. "You need a PhD in computer engineering to understand that crap. What about you?"

"You're joking, right? I was biting the inside of my cheek so I wouldn't fall asleep. That was way worse than college. But you picked up something, no?" I asked in a panic.

"Not really," he answered.

"But, you asked all those smart questions!"

"Goes to show how good account guys are at faking it."

"I'll tell Betsey that."

He shot me a look.

The more difficult part of The Chairman's two-pronged approach was the corporate message. I understood the general capabilities of the B20, which were rather straightforward: a lot of storage, great speed and a large, graphic computer screen. But we had to find a way to position Burroughs in the world of big computer companies. Plus, we had to separate them from the so-called "seven sisters"; Sperry, NEC, Hewlett-Packard, DEC, IBM, Data General and Control Data. But what turned our already-difficult dilemma into a total clusterfuck was the fact that we were advertising a company that had effectively no awareness in the marketplace.

Arty developed a very smart strategy that pitted Burroughs directly against IBM, the gold standard in the industry. The intent was to sell the public on the idea that when faced with choosing a computer company, there was IBM, Burroughs, then the seven sisters. It shrewdly placed Burroughs into the IBM sphere, despite the fact that IBM was ten times their size and, frankly, a better computer company overall. Arty had devised a brilliant strategy. Now I had to come up with equally brilliant advertising.

"So, Jim. Where are we?" I asked, after the waitress took our order.

"Same fuckin' place," he answered.

"Ya know, maybe we're going about this the wrong way."

"Huh?"

"We've been concentrating on selling the B20, right?"

"Yeah?"

"Well, maybe we should make the IBM-Burroughs comparison first, then figure a way to work in the B20 story."

"Uh huh."

"Uh huh? All you've got is 'Uh huh?' Give me a freakin' idea, Jim. We're gonna get our nuts chopped off, and you won't have a job anymore. And believe me, Della Femina won't take you back when I get through with you."

"Anyone ever tell you're easily riled?"

I was so riled I couldn't respond.

"All right," he said, finally summoning some energy. "We've got IBM, Burroughs, then everyone else, right? And IBM is bigger and better in almost every way, right? So, how in the fuck can we compare ourselves to them?"

"Aha!" I exclaimed, pointing my finger in the air like Ralph Kramden hatching one of his cockamamie, get-rich-quick schemes with Ed Norton. "Because there are some things we do better than IBM."

"Oh?"

"Yeah. Service, for one. Not to mention, some highly advanced software, storage capacity and reliability. Shit, our B20 is rated higher than their Datamaster… Whoa, wait a minute. Wait a minute. I think I've got something."

"I'm all ears."

"Lemme run to the bathroom first."

I got up, then sat down.

"IBM is much bigger than us, right? But there are some things we do better."

"Yeah?"

"So, maybe we point out the things we do better and make the case that just because IBM is bigger than us, doesn't necessarily make them better. We'll do an underdog thing."

"I like it," Jim said, sipping his wine.

Forgetting about my bathroom run, I grabbed a linen napkin and jotted down a line (I know it's a cliché, but it actually happened): "Just because you're bigger, doesn't necessarily make you better."

We stared at it. It was close. I could feel a surge of energy rushing through my body. I loved this part. I knew I had it; it was only a matter of time until the perfect line bubbled to the surface. All I had to do was get out of my own way and let it happen.

"Ya know, maybe we should pose it as a question." I suggested.

The waitress arrived with our food. I shoved both plates aside, slapping Jim's hand as he tried to snag a fry.

"I got it. I fuckin' got it! Gimme another napkin."

As he reached for the napkin, he knocked over his wine. Attempting to corral the glass, he dumped his entire plate of food onto his lap. The cheap wine glass splintered into a million pieces and flew across the restaurant. Everyone around us looked up. Jim, totally embarrassed, looked around sheepishly for another napkin.

"No napkins!" Don Knotts announced to the entire restaurant.

"Gimme your felt-tip," I snapped, worried I'd forget the line (which, in the end, I never do). I scribbled the words onto my crisply ironed, white linen napkin: "The question isn't who's bigger. It's who's better."

I held it up to Jim, who was preoccupied with his crotch—or, maybe more specifically, the hamburger, ketchup and french fry concoction on top of it.

"Whaddya think?" I asked.

He glanced up for a second. In the midst of his personal anguish, relief flushed over his face.

"That's it, I like it, we're done. Let's go home. I gotta take a shower."

Feeling triumphant, I pulled my dinner plate toward me and began eating while Jim ordered a replacement burger. It was the best damn cold hamburger and fries I'd ever eaten.

The next morning I ran the idea by Arty.

"It's great," he said, with his usual ebullience. "So what've you got for TV?"

"What, the line isn't good enough for you? You want TV, too?"

"Yes, and also print. We're on a 7:15 tomorrow from LaGuardia. We're meeting with Bill first, and then with The Chairman later in the afternoon."

He went back to his legal pad, meticulously brushing off his erasures.

I still had a lot of work ahead of me but the hard part was over. The tagline was killer and I was 100% confident that it would be right up Blumenthal's alley.

Still tired from the day before, Jim and I immediately went to work on the TV and print. We stared blankly at each other until noon—an increasingly familiar experience.

Jim suddenly stood up.

"Where you goin'?"

"Lunch."

"No lunch. We gotta work hungry. Keeps you sharp."

Jim slumped back into his chair.

"You're gonna need the whole afternoon to pull the presentation together, ya know?"

"We're fucked," Jim said reassuringly.

We had easily tossed around 25 new ideas, but nothing quite came together. Every half-decent approach felt like it had already been done, and visually we just couldn't escape from showing the computer box. Exactly what Blumenthal had said not to do. The more we dug into the box issue, the more I realized how prescient The Chairman was. It's not really about the hardware; it's about the benefit of the hardware plus the software, and the increased productivity computers bring to businesses.

Arty poked his head into the office. "You guys are beginning to look a little green. Can I order some sandwiches?" Jim blew him a kiss, nodding his head vigorously. "And would it help to see any of my notes?"

"I guess it couldn't hurt." I replied.

He was back in a second with a pile of legal pads and papers. "Don't wrinkle anything," he warned.

Flipping through his perfectly organized and legible annotations triggered an observation I'd made weeks earlier in Detroit.

"Ya know, Jim, when The Chairman came over from Bendix, he raided IBM's senior management. Virtually every senior executive I met there previously worked at IBM."

"That's interesting," Jim said, his stomach growling.

"I think so, too, but I don't know what to do with it."

"Maybe we could use those executives," Jim mused.

"Like how? Testimonials?" I grumbled. "You know what I think about those."

"No, these could be different."

He took out his layout pad and drew the outline of a person sitting at his desk in a business suit in front of the B20. Underneath his rough illustration he wrote, "Joe Schmo, Executive Vice-President, Sales, Burroughs Corporation."

We stared at the pad a few moments. Then we stared at each other.

"I guess you're looking for a headline at this point?" I asked.

"Yes, that would be nice, if it's not too much trouble."

I sat back in my chair, thinking. I felt my blood percolating again. After a couple of minutes, I grabbed Jim's marker out of his hand. I wrote down the first sentence that popped into my head: "A testimonial for Burroughs computers from someone who spent ten years at IBM."

"Bullseye," Jim shouted.


The spot was fresh, smart, bold and original. No computer company had ever done anything like it. And because the person telling the story was so unusual and unexpected, it didn't feel like your run-of-the-mill testimonial campaign. In fact, it felt really smart.

I ran everything by Arty later that afternoon. Amazingly, he loved all of it. But, true to his account guy upbringing, he had some concerns.

"What if IBM sues? Do we have to use those three letters? Would the campaign work without referencing IBM so explicitly?"

"In two letters: no," I answered.

"Look, I agree that The Chairman will probably like the strong, competitive stance, but what if he doesn't have the cajones to go along with it? What if his lawyers won't let him? Do you have backup?"

Do? You? Have? Backup? These are the four words creative people hate most. My head started spinning.

"It was all I could do to come up with this. It's dead on your strategy."

"It is, but we've gotta have something in the bag just in case."

"You're a cruel man, Selkowitz."

I grunted and headed back to my office.

In my gut I knew Arty was right. He's always fucking right.

"I'll show you something at the airport," I shouted back to him, totally disgusted.

By the time I made it to the gate in the morning, Arty had been sitting there for an hour going over his presentation. On the plane I took him through all the creative. He had a couple of nits, mostly legal, but he was otherwise pleased.

**A TESTIMONIAL FOR THE BURROUGHS B20 FROM SOMEONE WHO SPENT 17 YEARS AT IBM.**

Most people think that because IBM is bigger than Burroughs, that makes them better than Burroughs.

After putting in so many years at IBM, I can tell you that bigger doesn't necessarily mean better.

Take small business computers: The Burroughs B20 and IBM's Datamaster.

Incredibly, the Burroughs B20 series can offer up to five times more memory capacity, can store twice as much data, can have more work stations (this networking capability is especially important for large businesses), offers more kinds of printers, and, in order to get more information on the display screen, the B20 screen is 25% larger.

To operate, all you do is open the carton, plug it in, choose one of our many business software programs (payroll, accounts receivable, inventory control, etc.) tilt the screen to your desired height, and you're off. (Our step-by-step training manuals are so easy to use, even a corporate vice-president can be doing sales projections in a matter of hours.)

And if any questions come up, just pick up the phone and call our hot line. (90% of all questions are answered in the first call.) Furthermore, we have service depots in 19 major cities throughout the U.S.

So you see, when it comes to choosing between IBM and Burroughs, take it from someone who knows both.

The question isn't who's bigger. It's who's better.

**Burroughs**

THE QUESTION ISN'T WHO'S BIGGER
IT'S WHO'S BETTER

Borroughs first print ad ran in business publications like *Forbes, Fortune* and *The Wall Street Journal* (1982)

**DR. W. LEE SHEVEL**
SENIOR VICE PRESIDENT, CORPORATE OPERATIONS
BURROUGHS CORPORATION

Our first 30-second TV spot for Burroughs (1982)

"Holy crap, Mikey likes it!" I declared loudly enough that half the plane heard it.

In the short time we'd been together, I had learned that Arty was an accurate barometer of the creative. He had the same sensibility and mind-set of a client, always scanning for problems. All good account people do this; it's their job. But I hated it. Early in my career, I thought account guys were simply taking potshots at my work, and I fought them with everything I had. Arty, however, saved my ass countless times by anticipating problems I didn't foresee. I totally trusted his judgment.

Arriving in Detroit, we grabbed one of the city's banged-up cabs and made our way to Burroughs' headquarters. We went directly to Bill's office and took him through our presentation. He liked it, but as Arty had predicted, he was more than a little concerned.

"It'll certainly get The Chairman's attention, I'll tell ya that," Bill said with a nervous chuckle. "I'm not sure how he'll respond to citing IBM so explicitly. Do you have to show their logo?"

Arty looked at me.

"Yeah, Bill, we talked about that, but that's what makes it so powerful. It's a punch in IBM's solar plexus."

"It certainly is," Bill replied with a grimace. "I'm with ya. Just a little nervous, that's all. It's definitely a far cry from what we're used to around here."

"Don't worry, Bill. I'll sell it. It's exactly what The Chairman's been pushing for."

"I hope so…for all of our sakes," he said, leaning back in his chair, laughing to himself. He liked it. He was just scared shitless of it.

This was a high-stakes meeting. If it went well, Penchina, Selkowitz Inc. would likely become a prominent new player on Madison Avenue. If we tanked, Arty, Bill and I would most certainly be filing for unemployment. The Chairman wasn't one for second chances.

By now, it was nearly four o'clock, and the three of us had been waiting outside Blumenthal's office for more than two hours. Arty sat patiently, reading one of those unbearable trade publications. I was running back and forth from the men's room.

Finally, we heard the intercom buzz. Battle-ax growled that we could go in. Walking into his large corner office, we were enveloped by the undeniable aroma of a Havana cigar. I loved it. Bill and Arty instantly became nauseated. Blumenthal was finishing up some paperwork behind his massive desk, which was adorned with mementos and photographs from his past life as a cabinet member.

"Hello, fellas," he greeted us, semi-warmly, not lifting his eyes off his papers. "Take a seat on the sofa. I'll be right with you."

*Not too bad of a mood,* I thought.

The three of us sat down and collected our thoughts, not saying a word to one another. The nerves were picking up.

The moment The Chairman pulled up his chair, Bill jumped straight into the presentation. He delivered a succinct review of why we were there, who in senior management we had met with (politically, this was very important to Blumenthal), which divisions we had visited and a top-line assessment of what we had learned over the past couple of months. There wasn't a scintilla of small talk. Bill then handed the floor over to Arty, who took The Chairman through our marketing and creative strategy. As usual, he asked a couple of pointed questions that Arty parried easily.

Arty then looked over at me. I was on.

I was anxious, but confident considering the eerie silence that always comes over the room right before the creative is presented. Everything boiled down to this moment. It's why the client had chosen our agency to begin with, and where they'd be investing millions of their dollars. We were asking them to bet the company's bank account and future on what we showed them over the next few minutes. No pressure, of course.

I started with a quick preamble of the thinking behind the campaign and, without tipping him off about the idea, explained why a strong, competitive approach was what Burroughs needed. The Chairman's eyes told me he was with me. I held up the first storyboard with Dr. Shevel and read the script.

"When it comes to computers, most people think of IBM before Burroughs. After all, they are bigger.

"I worked for IBM for seventeen years, and I can assure you, bigger doesn't necessarily mean better.

"Take small-business computers. The Burroughs B20 has five times more memory capacity, storage and power than IBM's Datamaster.

"And our screen is twenty-five percent larger.

"So you see, when it comes to choosing between IBM and Burroughs, take it from someone who knows both."

When I got to the tagline, I dropped the storyboard at my feet and held up a second board with the Burroughs logo and our tagline. I read it with flair:

"The question isn't who's bigger. It's who's better."

I gave him just two seconds to absorb it and then moved quickly to the other storyboards and print. I wanted him to digest it, but not over think it.

He got it. He loved it. He didn't need time to think about it. He was going with it. In less than five minutes, it was all over. His beaming face said it all. He looked outside to the reception area, searching for someone to share his exuberance with. There was no one around. He asked Bill a few technical and legal questions, and seemed satisfied with the answers.

Arty then launched into his media presentation. I totally tuned out. I was elated. As far as I was concerned, I was back in New York having a beer with my friends at the Red Blazer on 81st, right around the corner from my studio apartment.

After Arty finished up, Blumenthal picked up his phone and called an impromptu meeting with all the management heavyweights on the floor. They walked in, one by one. He grabbed the storyboards and personally presented our entire pitch. He wasn't asking them what they thought; he was offering them a sneak preview of their new ad campaign.

Most of them liked the campaign's aggressive tone. Naturally, there were questions.

"Is it legal to mention IBM by name?"

"Yes," I said.

"Is it okay for ex-IBM executives to be in a Burroughs ad?"

"Yes."

"Does it have to be the actual person or could we use actors?"

"Only the real person will work."

"What if he can't act?"

"I'll make him."

Burroughs' chief counsel asked Blumenthal how he felt about the possibility of IBM bringing a lawsuit.

"That would be the best possible outcome," he answered. "It would call attention to us, which is exactly what I want. It would also suggest that we're making them nervous, playing right into our strategy of pushing the remaining six sisters off a cliff. I hope Katzenbach (IBM's chief counsel and Blumenthal's friend on the Business Roundtable) does call me. Then I'll know I've hurt them. If it winds up in *The Wall Street Journal,* all the better."

As we packed up to leave, The Chairman noticed something sticking out of the portfolio.

"What's that?" he asked.

"Oh, it's nothing," I said, keeping my head down and continuing to zip.

"What is it? Another idea?" he pressed on.

I hesitated for a second.

"Well, if you really want to know," I conceded, "it's your chickenshit campaign."

"Meaning?"

I hesitated again. "If you were too chickenshit to go with our recommendation, I would have shown you this. But it's not even close to what we're going with."

"Can I see it?" he asked.

"Yeah. No. I don't think so," I said.

"Why not? I'm curious."

"You'd lose respect for us," I said flatly.

The Chairman leaned back in his chair and howled. The tension in the room instantly evaporated. Everyone was laughing and smiling. I got the distinct impression people didn't usually say no to him. Arty pressed in between us and quickly zipped up the portfolio.

"Gentlemen, thank you for your time," Arty announced, pushing me out the door.

The two of us smiled all the way back to New York. After a weekend of celebration, Jim and I immediately went to work on the production. We chose Henry Sandbank to direct all of our Burroughs' spots. He was a brilliant man and a brilliant director. We were up against an impossible deadline, working day and night for two months to film, edit and complete the television and produce all of the print for newspapers and magazines, simultaneously.

On Christmas Eve, just two days before the first commercials were to break, Arty and I flew to Detroit to get The Chairman's final approval on the TV. As was too often the case, we had spent the afternoon waiting for him. Now, six o'clock in the evening and everyone gone for the holidays, his door flung open. With briefcase in tow, he moved rapidly toward the elevators, presumably on his way to St. Bart's or wherever CEOs go for Christmas. He noticed the two of us waiting in the empty reception area.

"Are you boys waiting for me?" he asked, genuinely puzzled.

"All afternoon," Arty replied, respectfully ticked off.

"What do you need?" He asked quickly.

"Your approval on the finished commercials," I said. "They're breaking this weekend."

"Well, I'm catching a plane. What do we have to do?"

"If I can use your VCR for a second, I'll shove in the cassette and you can be on your way in exactly one minute."

"Okay, but I don't have a lot of time."

In two minutes (he watched the spots twice), he approved everything, wished us a happy holiday and, like Santa, took off into the night.

Merry Christmas to all, and to all a good night.

What a fantastic present Arty and I had received.

About a year later, The Chairman increased our ad budget and gave us the entire international business as well. He loved our tagline so much he used it on everything from newsletters, in-house correspondence and press releases to trade shows and computer conferences all over the world.

As TWA once said in its famous airline campaign, we were "Up, up and away."

# 27 MIGHTIER THAN THE SWORD

Although we received several phone calls from the press, we hadn't officially announced our big, new account. With Burroughs safely on course, I finally called Phil Dougherty, my good friend at *The Times*. As I was beginning my spiel, he interrupted. Oh, no. I thought.

"Where's your office?" he barked.

"850 Third Avenue," I answered nervously.

"Where's that?"

"50th Street."

"I'll be there at eight o'clock sharp tomorrow morning. I don't drink coffee. Have hot tea with milk, no lemon."

I hung up with Phil and looked over at Arty. He was already dusting.

The next morning Phil walked in precisely at eight. For the first time, we were face to face with the iconoclastic columnist. He was exactly as I had pictured: a rumpled, irascible Irish beat reporter with an improbable twinkle in his eye. We gave him a quick tour of the agency and then sat down in Arty's office. Against my partner's strident protestations, Phil would not take off his tan McGregor raincoat—a man after my own heart.

He seemed to have taken a liking to us from the start (or maybe it was the prune Danish Arty had picked up for him). Arty was officially two for two on pastries.

After a quick tour of the office, Phil flipped open his little reporter's notepad and interviewed us for over an hour. He started with the usual questions: size, accounts, staff, backgrounds, starting date and so on. He went into more depth on a series of questions related to Burroughs and the computer industry in general. But then he threw us a curve ball.

"What makes you think you can keep an account of this size?" he asked. "You know, all the big boys will be coming after you."

Again with the big boys!

I took a deep breath to stall. "We'll continue to do great work, service their asses off and keep pleasing The Chairman." C+ answer, *I thought*.

"You know, Phil," Arty interjected, "We already beat out the big boys." A+.

"Who were they?" Phil probed.

"Campbell-Ewald, the incumbent, Jerry Della Femina, Benton & Bowles, and several others," Arty answered.

"Impressive," Phil acknowledged.

I got the impression that Phil liked our entrepreneurial spirit. He liked that we picked up such a large account on our own with no connections, no inside deals and no mergers.

Phil was professional and delightful, although Arty and I were petrified that we were going to stumble somewhere and have it wind up in print the next day. He was notorious for that. As soon as he finished his tea, he thanked us for our time and left abruptly. We had survived.

Arty and I waited on pins and needles for the story to break. The next day, no story. The day after, no story. The day after that, still no story. We must have blown it, I thought. Every night around midnight, I raced down to *The New York Times* building on West 42nd street to buy the first issue of the day, hot off the press.

# The New York Times

Copyright © 1982 The New York Times      NEW YORK, FRIDAY, SEPTEMBER 24, 1982

## Advertising | Philip H. Dougherty

## Penchina's Direct Way

**T**HE story of how Penchina/Selkowitz Inc. won the advertising assignment for the Burroughs Corporation's B-20 small-business computer system is interesting in its simplicity.

Arthur Selkowitz, the new agency president, simply wrote a letter and asked for it.

That's right, just the way it's supposed to be done. No friends-of friends stuff. Certainly not bowling over the client with flashy office space or even with promises of tremendous in-depth service.

It's only a six-person shop and when last August the prospective client visited in the form of its chairman, W. Michael Blumenthal, former Secretary of the Treasury, workmen were pounding it into shape.

"The other agencies were ready with prepared presentations and we came in with just our brains," said Steven Penchina, chairman and creative director.

He did not know it, but, according to William J. Beckman, vice president for corporate communications at Burroughs's Detroit headquarters, the others were Della Femina, Travisano & Partners and TBWA Advertising in New York; Clinton E. Frank Advertising and the Creative Works in Chicago, and Campbell-Ewald, the Detroit-based incumbent that continues with the corporate advertising assignment.

The account, Mr. Beckman said, is billing $4 million this year and will be bigger next year.

Mr. Penchina, a 37-year-old copywriter who with Allen Kay, an art director, created the Xerox monk campaign at Needham, Harper & Steers, began the Steve Penchina Agency more than a year ago, and then, after an extensive search for a marketing partner, added Mr. Selkowitz, 39, last June.

One of the first things the partners did was to analyze their own fairly extensive advertising experience and get up a potential client hit list in both the business-to-business and consumer areas. There were about 110 letters sent out.

Mr. Selkowitz is not about to share the details of anything so powerful to possible competitors, but he did say that the missives included the agency philosophy, which in part is that "the most motivating influence in advertising is a brilliant creative idea that is grounded in a strong strategic premise."

"Clients need more than good advertising," Mr. Penchina interjected. "They need brilliant advertising. You have to do something that's bold." And since he learned to write body copy at Carl Ally Inc., and TV spots at Wells, Rich, Greene, he should be able to deliver that.

Mr. Selkowitz's letters were directed to chief executives and were followed by personal phone calls.

Burroughs was not the first reward for persistance. Hermes Products previously assigned the shop its electric typewriters — a $1 million account. And just recently and not previously announced, Pfizer came in with a special assignment in its Leeming/Pacquin division, and the Mitel Corporation, a worldwide Ottawa-based maker of telecommunications equipment, came aboard.

**Steven Penchina, left, and Arthur Selkowitz**

"If you break your back and work hard, you will get all the business you want to get," Mr. Penchina said. "Inevitably, it will come in. Show that you're young, aggressive, hungry and you can steal business from almost anybody."

We're famous.
*The New York Times* article announcing our new Burroughs account (1982)

Finally, after nearly a week of disappointing trips I grabbed a fresh paper out of the lobby vending machine and turned to the Media section.

There it was.

I skimmed the article, and then ran across the street to a pay phone to call Arty in Connecticut. He had just fallen asleep. I read him the entire story word for word. He was ecstatic. The only thing he didn't like was that his name wasn't in the headline. But we loved that Phil included a photo of us.

Penchina, Selkowitz Inc. had put its stamp on Madison Avenue.

If I never did anything else in my life, the feeling of unbridled joy, pride, accomplishment and relief I felt opening up *The New York Times* that night would sustain me forever.

Maybe even longer.

# 28 IMUS AND STERN: THE WAR AT NBC RADIO

"You must be fucking kidding me!" the man with the mustache screamed into the phone. "Who was it this time? Both? Well. That. Just. Makes. My. Fucking. Day!"

I was sitting comfortably in an overstuffed leather chair in a spacious Art Deco office at 30 Rockefeller Center when the general manager of WNBC Radio, Randy Bongarten, took a call from one of NBC's in-house attorneys. Once again, the station was being sued.

I felt awkward sitting there overhearing the conversation, but Randy motioned me not to leave. Maybe he wanted me to get the full flavor of what it was like at the station. Each day brought another raging wildfire Randy had to put out, ignited by some over-the-top gag, insane indiscretion or slanderous remark made on air by one of his two shock jocks, Don Imus and Howard Stern.

Penchina, Selkowitz had just beaten out a dozen creative shops for the coveted account. WNBC had a celebrated track record of producing outrageous, award-winning advertising, and this win would more than likely solidify our reputation as a hot creative shop. Plus, an account like this has a certain cachet about it. And that never hurts. Now that Stern had joined the station, I could only imagine the outlandish TV and PR value the new account would bring us.

Imus had been at the station for more than a decade and was an iconic figure in the New York scene. He virtually invented shock-jock radio and had an enormous following. He spurred hundreds of copycat DJs across the country, but only "the I-man" was Imus. His *Imus in the Morning* show dominated a.m. drive time with its cynical, biting, irreverent, provocative, sleazy, pithy, controversial, hostile, uncensored, cerebral humor.

Imus lived on the edge and the closer he got to it the more titillating he became. With his legions of fans he could do no wrong. He made a lot of money for NBC by just being his nasty ol' self. His life was an open book. He would talk candidly on his show about his alcohol and cocaine addictions, his marriage, his brother Fred, his ranch in New Mexico, politics, pussies, wimps, fakes and phonies, his open contempt for NBC management, everyone on the station's staff, his boss Randy, the new parent company General Electric, corporate America, commies, gays, blacks, Russians, WASPs, Latinos, Jews, Italians, Arabs and Mexicans. Nothing and no one was safe from the man.

He was the quintessential New York wise-ass. His razor-sharp, acerbic wit was made for this town. I met him for the first time later that morning in Randy's office. He often jaunted in after his show under the guise of just hanging out with the boss. But I think he was really there seeking approval. He preached that he couldn't give two shits about what anyone thought. But he did. He was a complex man.

"Who is this?" he asked Randy, pointing at me as he walked in. He sounded annoyed.

"He's our new ad maven," Randy answered. "He and his partner, Arthur Selkowitz, are creating a new campaign with you and Howard."

"Howard? Who's Howard?" he mocked.

"Steve Penchina," Randy continued, ignoring Imus's dig. "This is the infamous Don Imus."

I stuck out my hand and he begrudgingly shook it. I remember being surprised by his soft grip and wondered if that indicated he wasn't quite the tough guy he projected and that his macho, eat-shit demeanor was more of an act than reality.

He glared at me.

"What happened to the other guy, Della…Della Femina?" he asked Randy, continuing his menacing gaze.

"Jerry's great. But we decided to make a change. Penchina, Selkowitz Inc. has a good handle on how we should brand ourselves now that Howard's on board."

"Howard?"

"Don't knock him," Randy cautioned. "His ratings are skyrocketing."

"Yeah, well, let me tell ya, if Stern beats me, I'll eat a dog's penis."

He turned to me again.

"So, which one are you? Penchina or the Jew?"

"Both, Penchina *and* the Jew," I retorted, delighted with my pithy answer. He wouldn't give me the pleasure of a half-cracked smile.

"So, don't tell me this Howard guy's gonna be in our ads?" he asked Randy, flipping through the day's *Times.*

"You're both in the ads. Howard needs support in the afternoon. And you, you're like an 80-year-old grandmother with saggy tits. You always need support."

"You're a riot, Alice, a real riot," Imus shot back. "Don't quit your day job."

"I want Steve to spend some time with the two of you," Randy continued. "He needs to get to know you guys. God help him, I want him to start with you, Don. By the way, what the hell did you say on air today? The lawyers are all over me."

"Fuck the lawyers. They're all pussies. Don't you know that by now? If I listened to those candy-asses, this station wouldn't have a dime. The only reason you have your shitty-ass job is because of me."

I felt bad for Randy. He was a terrific guy: bright, affable, and despite his onerous corporate responsibilities, in possession of a wonderful sense of humor with a contagious, high-pitched laugh tucked behind his Tom Selleck–Magnum P.I. mustache.

The next week I began interviewing Imus. Heretofore, my fondest memory of him was the time when he stole the Soviet flag from the Rockefeller Center skating rink to protest the 1980 Olympics. He hated the Russians and wanted the U.S. to boycott the games, which they eventually did. It was the only good thing President Carter ever did.

What immediately struck me about him was his distinctive celebrity persona. I had seen this many times before with actors or big-time celebrities, the common thread being that they all had the same detached gaze. Imus virtually never looked me squarely in the eye. It was a dismissive thing, as if what I had to say didn't matter. He was well aware of how intimidating he could be and used it opportunistically to keep people off balance, ensuring he was always in the dominant position.

But I had my job to do and I needed to find out where his head was, what thoughts he had about his show and what ideas, if any, he had about the advertising. Basically, I needed to understand what made him tick.

I interviewed him on and off for a couple of weeks. As he got to know me better, he was generally respectful, although I think it unnerved him to be nice. While Imus made his living talking to hundreds of thousands of people every day, he was rather uncomfortable one-on-one. He was often flanked by an entourage of guys from his studio, including Artie Rosenberg, his news man Chuck McCord, a producer and a writer or two. They were his security blanket.

Imus was relentless in his criticism of people. He could be vicious and he enjoyed it. I'm not even sure he could help it. It was like the tale of the scorpion stinging the frog: As the frog carries the scorpion across a river, the scorpion suddenly delivers a fatal sting.

"Why did you do that?" the frog asks before it dies. "Now we will both die."

The scorpion shrugs. "Because I'm a scorpion, and that's what I do."

Yet Imus had this other side to him. I won't call it nice, but it certainly wasn't mean. "You want something to eat?" he would ask me out of the blue. "What about some water? I've got cases stacked over there."

After spending a fair amount of time with him, I realized the two of us had a lot in common. For instance, he was always testing, watching and making sure I was "with him."

After asking me something he would tilt his head ever so slightly, watching my reaction. I check out people the same way. It gives me a solid head start.

We both also had severe trust issues. We probed and doubted and questioned until we felt safe; we shared the same dark insecurities. I don't know where his came from, but I had a father to thank for mine. As a young boy, I would pass him on the way out of the house, and out of nowhere he'd slap me on the back of the head.

"What's that for?" I asked.

"That's for nothing."

"Huh?"

"That's for later. Maybe you haven't done anything bad yet, but I'm sure you will later and I may not be around."

Imus was most definitely an intellectual. He was extremely well-read and had a restless, curious mind. He could go mano-a-mano with any politician, businessman, news pundit, sportswriter or celebrity who walked into his studio.

His personal problems, including his drinking and drug addictions, occasionally wreaked havoc on the station. Once, years earlier, he went on a bender and disappeared for a month. Nobody knew where he was. Eventually, the station tracked him down out West somewhere and, after considerable negotiation, let him return to the show on the condition he attend AA meetings every day. Back on the air he talked candidly about the whole episode. One of Randy's unpleasant responsibilities was making sure Imus attended all his meetings and was sober and ready to go every day.

Imus and Randy were always butting heads. Randy would frequently bolt into Imus's studio to squelch a particular line of conversation or set the record straight about something. Imus simply refused to censor himself (as did Stern). Noticing Randy, Imus would sometimes go ballistic, live on the air. His tumultuous relationship with Randy became a big draw for the show. Randy found himself in a catch-22: He recognized that his acrimonious relationship with Imus was good for ratings, but at the same time he couldn't risk losing advertisers or exposing the station to more lawsuits and public criticism. Plus, it all took an emotional toll on Randy.

I wasn't yet sure how, where or when I would use Imus's interviews in the advertising, but gathering information on the "product" is always a vital step in the creative process.

Finishing up with the I-man, I turned my attention to Stern.

Whereas Imus had a holier-than-thou, I'll-kick-your-ass-if-you-fuck-with-me personality off air, Howard was the antitheses of his on-air personality. He was reflective, soft-spoken, and a truly decent guy. And although he was fast becoming a megastar, he remained humble and down-to-earth.

From day one Stern had a mammoth following in his afternoon time slot, which had historically garnered low ratings. Thanks to his new show, WNBC now had a powerful one-two punch, the radio equivalent of Mantle and Maris.

Howard had come to New York from a station in Washington, DC. He'd been summarily fired when he pulled a sick, albeit morbidly funny, gag immediately following a horrific Air Florida jet crash in the winter of 1982. While the plane was still smoldering, with hundreds of bodies floating in the frozen Potomac River and survivors clinging to life on chunks of mangled fuselage, Stern, live on air, called Air

Florida's flight reservations desk and asked for a one-way ticket to the 14th Street Bridge—the exact location where the plane had just gone down. "Are you planning on making regular stops there?" he queried.

Minutes later, he was out of a job.

WNBC couldn't resist his insane, whacked-out humor and soon offered him a contract. He was an instant star. Their management team and sales force were absolutely giddy over Howard's surge in the ratings. New advertisers couldn't sign up fast enough. He wasn't just successful—he was a phenomenon. Although delighted, Randy and WNBC management were puzzled. Where was Howard's audience coming from? To more precisely target advertisers, the station needed more data on his listeners. They elected to conduct a large-scale market research study. The assumption going in was that Howard's audience was made up mostly of male teens who couldn't get enough of his deviant, juvenile, tits-and-ass humor. The research results surprised everyone.

It turned out that the bulk of Howard's listeners were actually middle-aged housewives from the suburbs of New York, New Jersey, and Connecticut, who, while their husbands and kids were off at work and school, had their ears glued to The Howard Stern Show. This audience became known as Howard's "closet listeners" because, when asked directly by pollsters if they listened to Howard's show, they would reply with such answers as "Not in a million years would I turn on that sick, filthy trash." Truth of the matter was, the sicker and filthier he was, the more they listened. *The Howard Stern Show* was their dirty little secret.

His male audience was a different story. It was cool to tell your buddies around the water cooler at work that you listened to "that sick bastard" while driving home from work.

The research provided another fascinating fact that applied to both Howard and Imus: a large part of their audience was hoping to be listening, live, when either one of them was yanked off the air for some heinous remark.

Approaching Howard's office, I spotted the 6'5" DJ, eyes closed, peacefully perched atop his office chair in the lotus position. His long, lanky frame filled up the tiny, windowless room, reminding me of the scene from *Alice in Wonderland* where she eats the cake.

"Are you the agency guy?" he called out, sensing me at the door.

"I'm half of 'em, anyway. Steve Penchina. Nice to meet you."

"Welcome to my palatial palace," he said, stretching out his long arms, almost touching the walls and gesturing for me to pull up a metal folding chair.

The vibe was 180 degrees from his morning counterpart. There was no intimidation factor, no bullying, no dripping sarcasm, no sizing me up and no grumbling.

"I see you're into meditation?" I asked.

"Yeah. It relaxes me. Puts me in the right frame of mind for the show. Makes me focus better."

An hour from now, this introspective, mild-mannered man would turn into a raving, perverted lunatic. Who would believe it?

The first thing that struck me was his voice. It was loud and booming, but paradoxically soothing.

His hair was short back then, and he had a dorky mustache that went perfectly with his Jordache jeans and white sneakers, a far cry from the cool dude he is today. (Shortly after, he would get a makeover from a professional stylist.)

Before we got into the advertising, we spent some time chitchatting. He was obsessed with his health, took karate lessons and, like me, had painful lower back problems. I turned him on to Dr. John Sarno at NYU, who apparently helped him considering Howard later dedicated his bestselling book Private Parts to him. (It should have been me!)

Howard was not the intellectual Imus was, but he was incredibly quick-witted, street-smart and savvy. He had an incisive, split-second response for everything I asked him. Our interviews went fast. I didn't have to chip through ten inches of solid granite to find out what was on his mind. He was candid and direct and a delight to work with. He made big chunks of his time available to me, and thanks to his genial personality, we got through our interviews quickly. As I had with Imus, I filed everything I learned from Howard in the back of my mind, never sure what I might use.

While I was interviewing Imus and Howard, Arty was interviewing other key people that kept the station running, like the program, promotion and music directors. Arty and I shared and digested all of our notes and, satisfied that we had everything we needed, we set up a meeting at 30 Rock to take Randy and his promotion director through our findings.

"All sounds good," Randy said after the presentation. "How soon can I see the creative? You know, we need to be on the air by sweeps period." (This is the time each fall when all radio and TV shows establish their ratings for advertisers.)

*Why should it be any other way?* I thought.

Arty quickly came up with the strategy. The idea was to capitalize on all the craziness Stern and Imus brought to the market and, despite the two jocks' vastly different personalities and shows, communicate the common denominator of WNBC: sick, sharp, outrageous, entertaining urban radio.

I went right to work on the creative, asking one of my Young Turks, Sal DeVito, to work with me. Sal was short, about 5'5", but he was a giant of an art director.

Our main task was to figure out how to meld the two radio personalities into one unifying concept. In reality, they were worlds apart but in a larger sense they were similar: twisted, witty, New York wise-asses.

As was often the case, I initially didn't think the assignment would be difficult. We had amazing subjects to work with, after all. As was also often the case, it was far more challenging than I expected.

I took Sal through all of my interview notes, hoping a good idea would come to at least one of us. We thought we had the campaign a half-dozen times, but in the end nothing really panned out. It was frustrating as all hell. Three weeks later, we were lying on my office floor with our tongues hanging out.

One morning, Sal hesitantly walked into my office holding a sheet of paper.

"Whatcha got there?" I asked, finishing up my coffee and donut.

"I dunno," he said sheepishly. "Not really sure. It may be a germ of an idea, maybe not. Seems more like a print ad than a commercial, though. Maybe you can turn it into something, Boss?"

"Let's have a look," I said.

It was a simple list of about 20 names. But I didn't have to read past the first two to see where it was going. It was a roll call of apologies to people and institutions Imus and Stern had offended on their shows.

"Sal, you sonofabitch, this is genius!"

He beamed.

"Now, how do we turn this fucker into a TV spot?" I mused.

"That's where you come in, Boss."

As I had done with Jim, we stared at each other for hours. I got up and gazed out onto Third Avenue. Heavy traffic, big trucks, lots of honking. Ever so slowly, something began formulating in my head.

"I think I may have something, Sal. Hand me one of those legal pads, will ya?"

I sat down at my desk. With Sal hovering over me, I sketched a picture of a conference table and drew a crude likeness of Stern and Imus sitting at opposite ends. In between them sat Randy, like a school principal that had to split up his two class troublemakers.

"All we have to do is get Randy to read off the list in a serious, businesslike fashion."

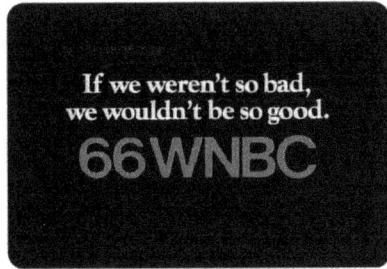

A billboard from the
"If we weren't so bad, we wouldn't be so good"
campaign for Stern and Imus.

"Bingo," Sal said. "I'll draw up the board."

My only concern was getting Randy to agree to act in the commercial. Something told me he wouldn't be excited about this.

"Wait, Sal," I yelled out as he was leaving. "We need a tagline."

"You're the best in the business, Boss," he yelled back, running down the hall.

# 29 I'D RATHER HAVE THE PLAGUE

Going after new business is like exercise. You have to do a little each day; otherwise, you wind up in bad shape.

From the start Arty and I lived by certain rules: We would only conduct our business in a forthright and ethical manner. There would be no kickbacks, no shady deals and no hiring sleaze-os with invisible hip-pocket accounts (clients that leave the agency when they do). We diligently built our agency with first-rate, trustworthy, blue chip clients like Burroughs, Citibank, *Newsweek*, NBC, *The New York Times*, Squibb, Kraft Foods, Jefferson-Pilot Insurance, McGraw-Hill, Mitel and others. We were very proud of that.

When we took on new accounts, there was always a trade-off between how much money we could make and whether or not we'd be able to showcase the advertising on our reel or in the press, providing us with important exposure. It also depended on our financial state at the time. If we were rolling in cash, we would pass on borderline-creative accounts. If the opposite were true, we'd be a whole lot less finicky. Arty and I estimated that we pitched an average of 30-35 accounts a year–large, small and everything in between. And a story came with each and every one of them.

## Meineke Muffler Shops

Meineke was a large franchise chain of transmission and muffler dealerships with a sizable ad budget, almost entirely in television. Print-dominated accounts were more labor-intensive and thus less profitable. With TV, on the other hand, we could produce three or four spots, run the hell out of them, and make a good profit on the media commission.

We presented to Meineke and, considering that our hearts and Jewish upbringing weren't into automobile transmissions, did surprisingly well. The client said they'd get back to us after completing the rest of their agency reviews. Sure enough, a couple of weeks later we received a call from their corporate headquarters telling us we were their first choice. They asked us to pull together a compensation proposal. In order to do that, we had a number of conversations not only with their headquarters but with their large dealer group as well.

Arty spent a lot of time going back and forth between the two groups, trying to learn how their business operated. Often in a setup like this, the franchisees are pitted against headquarters on almost every issue, including—and especially—advertising. We had to be careful to structure the deal equitably lest we lose money on the business.

Dealer groups, like fast food chains and car dealerships, are notoriously difficult to manage. There are too many cross-purposes and conflicting interests. We eventually worked out a fair compensation package, but as we were finalizing our proposal, both Arty and I began to have second thoughts about the business.

The money was fine, but we began picking up early signals that there was considerable friction between the dealers and their headquarters. The last thing we needed was to get caught in the middle of two warring factions. If this were McDonalds, it would be a different story; we'd cry all the way to the bank. But we knew from asking around about the account and looking at their past advertising that we weren't going to get a whole lot of creative mileage out of their mufflers. Plus—and we couldn't put our finger on it exactly—there was something about the account that made us feel uneasy.

"I don't know, Arty," I said one afternoon, returning from a photo shoot. "I've been thinking about this group and I'm not sure Meineke is our kind of client."

"Funny you should say that," Arty replied. "I just got off the phone with the head of the franchise group. It was a very unsettling conversation, to say the least."

"Oh?"

"The guy told me in no uncertain terms, 'If we give you our business and I find out that you listened to headquarters and went and did something against our interests, you and your partner will find yourselves in the East River, wearing cement shoes.'"

I laughed.

"They weren't joking," Arty said.

"No fuckin' way."

"Steve, do I make stuff like this up?"

"Holy shit," I said. "We better find a delicate way of getting out of this."

Arty immediately grabbed the phone and dialed the head of the franchise group.

"Good afternoon. This is Arty Selkowitz…Oh, yes, I'm fine, thank you. Yes, he's fine, too. So, after agonizing over this decision, Steve and I have decided that we're going to pass on your account…Oh no, that's not it. We were quite interested. I'm afraid we're just a bit overloaded right now…But we want you to know that we deeply appreciate your consideration and wish you all the luck with your new agency, whoever should be so fortunate. Yeah. We're sorry, too…Okay, well, thank you very much for being so understanding. Perhaps we'll talk again in the future."

## First Albany Corporation

Fortunately, not all companies were so menacing. A headhunter had given us a lead on a prosperous, old-line investment-banking firm in Albany, New York, called First Albany Corporation. We looked into them and found out that First Albany was a family-owned business that had made a small fortune issuing New York State municipal bonds and successfully spotting trends in the stock market with shrewd proprietary research techniques.

One of their top analysts, Hugh Johnson, appeared on a popular 15-minute radio show several times a week, where he offered astute investment advice and spotted market trends that were often picked up by other big Wall Street firms. We were skeptical, however, that they had an advertising budget that was large enough to break through the clutter in this highly competitive industry. They were up against all the big names (and big budgets) on Wall Street: Merrill Lynch, Smith Barney, E.F. Hutton, Loeb, Rhoades and so on.

Lots of clients will tell you they're willing to spend whatever it takes to make an impact, but when it's time to open their wallets, their story suddenly changes. *Our business is a little soft right now. We need to wait 'til the fourth quarter. We didn't realize how expensive television cost. Couldn't we get by with a couple of radio spots?*

This happens frequently with smaller, inexperienced clients who are not familiar with creative and media costs. The P&Gs, Budweisers and General Motors of the world know exactly what they need to spend to drive their businesses, right down to the penny. Despite our reservations we made the three-hour drive upstate.

On our way up on a dark and overcast day, Arty devised an escape plan in the event this became a huge waste of time.

"If either of us looks out the window and says, 'It looks like rain,' that means we're not interested and should cut the meeting off. On the other hand, if one of us says, 'It looks like it's clearing up,' that means it might be promising and we should stay and pursue it. How does that sound?" Arty asked.

"Simple. Got it."

"You sure? I don't want you getting mixed up."

"I. Got. It. Arty."

Our meeting got off to an inauspicious start. The firm's two major owners had to cancel at the last minute, leaving us with their two sons and five of the dullest bankers to ever write a check. The discussions crept along ad nauseam for more than two hours. I didn't need to have a Ph.D. in business to understand that there was no way in the world these people were to going to spend a dime on advertising. When we told them it would take several million dollars to make even the smallest dent in the marketplace, the blood drained from their faces. I looked over at Arty. He was still going strong. Maybe he saw something I didn't.

Arty offhandedly asked a simple question to one of the owners' twenty-something sons. Up to this point, the guy hadn't uttered a word, but Arty wanted to include him in the conversation. As son #1 started to answer the question, he began sweating profusely, clicking his ballpoint pen so furiously it looked like it was beginning to smoke. While trying to spit out the answer, the poor guy began hyperventilating. He started wheezing and gasping for air, all the while trying to spit out a couple of words.

"Forget about it," I shouted out to him. "It's really not that important."

He turned blue and looked like he was about to pass out. I glanced around the room. No one seemed particularly concerned. Finally, one of the young assistants got up.

"I need to get him a paper bag to breathe into," she said as she scurried out of the conference room.

She quickly returned and shoved a brown bag onto his face, which by now had gone from blue to emergency-room green.

"Not to worry," she said. "This happens all the time."

He breathed into the bag for a few moments and soon regained his composure. He tried to answer Arty's question again, but we frantically waved him off. "That's not necessary. We'll circle back to that later," Arty told him in his most compassionate voice.

*This happens all the time?!* I thought to myself.

This seemed as good a time as any to end the meeting. I got up and walked toward the window.

"Hmm," I said, casually, "Looks like it's going to rain out there."

I turned to Arty to see his reaction. He was in the middle of a side conversation with two of the bankers and didn't even blink. Maybe he hadn't heard me. I looked out the window again and repeated, louder this time, "My heavens, it looks like it's going to rain out there!"

"Oh, that's too bad," said the other son, utterly unfazed by his brother's near-death experience. "I was planning on playing golf this afternoon."

My astute partner continued babbling away, totally oblivious to the code. *Okay,* I thought, *Arty must want to consider these nuts.*

Once the owner's son regained his composure, the meeting went on as if nothing happened. Several minutes later, Arty looked toward the window and announced, "It looks like it's going to clear up."

"Who's on third?" I wanted to scream.

"Well, maybe I'll get my golf in after all," Ben Hogan chimed in.

I seriously considered launching myself out the window, but we were on the ground floor and it wouldn't have done much harm. It then occurred to me: maybe the golf bit was their code!

"Time for a bathroom break," I announced to the room.

I checked the bathroom stalls to make sure we were alone.

"What the hell is going on here?" I asked Arty. "You want to keep going with these guys?"

"On the contrary," he said.

"So why are you saying 'It looks like it's clearing up?'"

"Huh? Uh, maybe I got it mixed up," he confessed.

"Okay, if I say 'It's about to rain,' do we want to stay or leave?" I asked him. Dead silence. "Are you fucking kidding me, Arty? You're the one who made up the goddamn code! And by the way," I continued, lowering my voice, "this poor guy he's fucking choking to death and these people aren't even remotely concerned about him? Have they never heard the word pul-mon-ol-ogist?!"

Arty was laughing so hard tears were rolling down his cheeks.

"Let's get the hell out of here and go home," I told him. "They don't have a budget anyway. Besides, that guy's gonna leave soon to play golf. In a fucking hurricane."

We went back to the conference room and made up some lame excuse to put an end to the circus. On the highway, speeding back to New York, we did, in fact, run into a gigantic thunderstorm.

"Just so I'm clear," Arty asked. "Would this mean we wanted to stay or leave?"

**International House of Pancakes**

At long last Arty and I were able to use a personal connection to help us win a piece of business. We never had the good fortune before. My friend Garlick, of Attorneys Professional Associates, had arranged for us to meet his cousin Harvey in Miami. Harvey owned 35 International House of Pancake franchises throughout the state, a huge operation. We were ambivalent about pursuing a retail account, but IHOP was a well-known brand that advertised heavily on TV. We could make money on this. Also, my family from Great Neck had a lifelong relationship with these pancake people through Garlick. It was worth a shot.

Arty and I flew down to Miami to present to Harvey. I had met him on a number of occasions when he visited the Garlicks next door to us in Great Neck.

We hadn't expected the offices of a pancake house franchise group to look like a Frank Gehry design, but we weren't anticipating that their offices would resemble a World War II rations warehouse, either. In we walked.

Stepping into the dank, grungy lobby, we noticed an ancient black telephone hanging on the wall where most companies have a delightful receptionist. Taped next to the phone were directions on how to dial the staff. I picked up the receiver and dialed 1, for Harvey.

"So glad we came," Arty said. "Classy operation." He was sulking again.

A few minutes later, a hulking figure appeared before us, sporting a belly that said, "There aren't enough pancakes in the universe to satisfy me."

"Come on back, gentlemen," Cousin Harvey bellowed, barely making eye contact with us.

He led us down a dark hallway and into a messy, musty office. Piles of dust-covered 50-pound sacks of pancake mix were stacked halfway up the window, blocking the daylight. He sat down behind his desk, which was covered with syrup samples and jelly jars the way most executives' desks are decorated by photos of family ski trips to Aspen.

"Well," Harvey opened, pointing at Arty. "I know one of you is a Penchina, and I'm quite certain it's not you. Way too short for a Penchina."

*Great. Thanks for the help, Harvey.*

"Mr. P, how have you been? Last time I saw you, you were a little, bitty boy. So, what can I do for you gentlemen?"

Arty remained silent. This was far too lowbrow for his faux-WASP Connecticut sensibilities, and he wanted to make sure I understood that.

"Well," I began, already psyched out. "Mike told me you might be looking for a new agency. We both have a lot of experience in the food industry: Arty worked on a number of Kraft products for many years, and I created campaigns for Borden's—Wise potato chips and Drakes

Cakes—Mueller's macaroni and also Pringles at Proctor & Gamble. We know how to advertise food."

No response.

This kind of pitch is the hardest of the hard. It's like talking to yourself. The only thing you can do with a client like this is to keep moving ahead. If you wait for a reaction you're finished.

I took out a cassette from our portfolio.

"I'd like to show you our reel and take you through some case studies. Do you have a VCR?"

"We do."

I scanned the room.

"Uh, where is it?" I asked.

"It's broken."

"Aha, okay. Can I take you through some print, then?"

"It's your show."

I grabbed half as many ads as we had rehearsed and began presenting: the marketing problem, the creative strategy, our execution and the result. Halfway through the second ad, we were interrupted by an elderly woman at the door. I recognized Harvey's mother.

"Oh, you're a Penchina, all right. You've got the nose. How're your father and mother?"

"Oh, they're great, thank you. This is my partner, Arty Selkowitz."

"Nice to meet you, Aaron."

"No, it's…Forget it…Nice to see you. I'll send regards home."

She plopped down a giant, greasy meatball Parmesan hero on Harvey's desk. "Here you go, dear, enjoy."

"Excuse me," Harvey said, taking a massive bite out of his hero sandwich. "I'm famished."

"Excuse me," was the nicest thing he said to us all day.

Thoroughly demoralized and now starving to death, I zipped through the rest of our print.

No response. Not a single word. Not even one disingenuous question. I gave a sideways glance at Arty. He was glaring at me.

Finally, in between mouthfuls of meatballs, Harvey mumbled, "Tell me, what would a new TV spot cost me?"

"Well, that would depend on the concept," I answered.

"Oh, just give me a ballpark figure," he insisted, wiping tomato sauce off his face. "I won't hold you to it."

Either because he didn't want to spend another miserable second there, or because he was beginning to feel guilty that he hadn't opened his mouth yet, Arty chimed in.

"According to the American Association of Advertising Agencies, the average production price of a commercial is around $75,000. Our commercials range from about $50,000 for our smaller clients, up to $350,000.

"You must be joking," Harvey snorted. "I have a nephew who shoots all of our spots for two Gs each."

*Bullshit,* I thought. *Film stock cost more than that.*

(It's amazing how these types of clients all have this nephew— he's a communal nephew charging a nominal fee to shoot any commercial they can dream up, no questions asked.)

While still thinking about a response to Harvey's bullshit nephew assertion, Arty tried out an approach my father had been begging him to consider:

"Ahem. So, Harvey," he broke in, "Let's cut to the chase. What will it take to get your business?"

Harvey leaned over sideways, nearly tipping over in his chair, lifted up one of his huge ass cheeks and slapped his back pocket where his wallet was bulging out. "That's what it'll take, gentlemen. Put it right here."

We were nonplussed for a second. But as soon as Arty and I made eye contact, it clicked. Harvey wanted a kickback on our commission from the media buy.

We we weren't that kind of agency.

"Well, thanks for your time, Harvey," I said with all the genuineness of a rejection letter. "Say hi to Mike."

We gathered up our stuff, zigzagged around the big pancake sacks and made our way to the door. Arty couldn't even muster a solitary "so-long."

Harvey shrugged and went back to his hero.

As we drove back to the hotel, Arty silently scolded me with another of his telltale looks, the "this-was-all-your-fault-and-a-big-waste-of-time" one.

When we got back to the hotel, I went up to my room and took a long, hot shower to wash off the smell of artificial maple syrup, pancake mix and greasy Parmesan cheese.

"Put it right here, boys" rang in my ears between the water drops.

## Goody Products Inc.

The worst part of the new business process is the speculative pitch. Agencies spend enormous amounts of time, money and manpower to create advertising at no cost to a prospective client in hopes that the client will be so bowled over by the agency's superlative work that they will happily reward them with their business.

I don't know of any other profession that gives away its services so willingly, and at such magnitude. I can't imagine my dentist being very enthusiastic if I tried this approach on him.

*Dr. Levine, I'd like you to do an implant on this molar for free, okay? Be aware, I've got an appointment tomorrow with a dentist up the street on another tooth, and a third one on my canine at another dentist on Park Avenue. Whoever does the best job will surely get my whole mouth. I'm planning on getting a lot of work done over the next couple of years, so it could be quite lucrative for you.*

Goody Products, the leading manufacturer of hair and beauty products in America, contacted us about handling their advertising. The marketing director, new to his position, candidly asked us what would be an appropriate fee to pay the five final agencies for a speculative campaign. We suggested a stipend of $5,000 to cover out-of-pocket expenses. He responded that that sounded reasonable.

Twenty-four hours later, he called to inform us that he ran the stipend idea by the other agencies and decided he wasn't going forward with the fee. Baffled, we asked what had changed his mind.

"Well, fellas," he said, "two of the agencies insisted they would gladly do the work for free and the other two simply went along."

Put on the spot, we had to quickly decide whether to stick to our guns, thereby taking ourselves out of the running, or to go along with the other agencies, do the work for zilch and take our chances that our creative would beat out the competition. We told him we needed a day to think it over.

While Arty and I were going back and forth on our decision, we got a call from Goody. They'd decided not to advertise.

### Newsweek

Out of the blue one morning, we received a call from Bill Bergman, *Newsweek* magazine's director of marketing. He told us he was familiar with our work and was interested in talking to us about his account. He asked to come to our office but emphatically instructed us not to do anything in preparation for his visit. He just wanted to meet us and chat for about an hour.

Which was exactly what happened.

The only thing we did was show him our reel and a few print ads that were hanging in the conference room. The three of us hit it off from the get-go. Bill was a smart, affable, self-deprecating, no-bullshit kind of guy, and the neurotic son of a prominent New Orleans rabbi. Except for the rabbi part, the three of us were quite similar. After the hour was up, he said he'd be back to us in six weeks. I didn't hold my breath.

Exactly six weeks later, almost to the day, Bill called to tell us we were *Newsweek's* new ad agency. He turned out to be one of our best clients— and a friend. Sometimes, though not often, things turn out exactly the way they're supposed to. Not only did we get the account without a speculative pitch and without spending a dime, but the advertising we created for Bill over the years was some of the best our agency ever did.

We created a branding campaign for him that competed directly against their main rival, *TIME*. We positioned *Newsweek* as the weekly news magazine that wasn't afraid to take on the big controversial issues of the day: AIDS, the Middle East conflict, drugs, alcohol addiction, homelessness, religion and politics, to name a few. The interesting thing about the campaign was that we only used photographs taken by *Newsweek's* award-winning photojournalists. I would sit with the magazine's photo editor for hours upon hours, choosing just the right shot for our ads.

Our first two ads for *Newsweek* (1985)

There were times when I'd be called into *Newsweek's* offices late Sunday night for meetings with their editor in chief when there were fast-breaking stories or an international crisis. It was a tremendously exciting and rewarding account. And all we had to do to get it was answer the telephone.

## Nynex

For many months, Nynex (the old AT&T in New York) had been conducting an extensive search for a new agency. Every well-known shop in the business wanted in on this multimillion-dollar, iconic brand. By this time Penchina, Selkowitz was on a roll. We were billing about $30 million (honestly), had about 25 talented employees, and were being invited to pitch the best accounts in the business.

Nynex Corp. had gotten a hold of Arty and invited us to make a credentials presentation for their sizeable business. We showed them our reel and took them through several case histories relevant to their business. We still didn't enjoy it, but we'd been getting this new business process down. Soon, we received a call from their marketing director informing us that we'd been chosen as one of six finalists. They held one big orientation meeting for all the agencies, which was always a bit awkward, but it gave the participants an opportunity to catch up with one another. We were told they wanted the agencies to present a strategic recommendation.

This was somewhat unusual. Most clients want to see agencies' creative approach and are less concerned up front with their strategic thinking. Nynex was smart, though. They knew they had a significant strategic problem on their hands and reasoned that if they couldn't solve that first, it wouldn't matter how creative the creative was.

The problem was complex. Their Yellow Pages phone books, a gigantic moneymaker, were perceived by consumers as a single, powerful brand throughout the United States. But years earlier, the company had decentralized their business into multiple regions, each with its own separate marketing director, budget and advertising campaign.

This had created confusion in the public's mind. Moreover, a slew of competitive "yellow" directories had since flooded the market, effectively taking away Nynex's commanding Yellow Book leadership position in the industry.

Nynex sought an agency that could look at their entire business model and develop a comprehensive marketing and advertising strategy. The shop with the best strategic recommendation would automatically pick up the creative assignment...and the $20-30 million ad budget that came with it.

It was a significant opportunity for us. Nynex advertised heavily on TV, which would give us invaluable exposure, not to mention cash. Since the assignment was exclusively about marketing, Arty bore most of the responsibility this time.

With his marketing acumen, this project was right up his alley. He enjoyed the challenge of complex marketing and management problems. After toiling away for weeks, I heard a scream from his office, "Steve, I got it! I figured the whole thing out!"

I ran down the hall to his office. "That's great, Arty. Do you have print?"

In our presentation, he boldly recommended they do away with their individual regions and funnel all their marketing and advertising dollars into one centralized entity, under one marketing director. The consolidation would allow Nynex to run a single, cohesive brand campaign serving the needs of all the regions. Arty's proposal and detailed timeline provided Nynex with the specific steps each region would have to undertake over the next twelve months. The client's enthusiastic feedback in the meeting told us Arty had nailed it.

Late one Friday afternoon (evidently, the only time clients call with news), we received a phone call from Nynex's marketing director telling us they had been "blown away" by our presentation and were awarding us their account. As with Burroughs this was a transformative moment for Penchina, Selkowitz. It doubled our size overnight. We called an agency meeting and gave everyone the good news and an early start for the weekend.

On Monday morning we arrived at our office to find a phone message from Nynex, presumably about setting up orientation meetings. Arty called right back.

There was a funny hesitancy in the marketing director's voice. He stammered around for a few moments but finally got his words out.

"I don't know how to say this, so I'm just going to come right out. We've decided we're going with another agency."

"You're not serious," Arty answered.

"I'm really sorry, but I'm afraid I am."

"How. Is. That. Possible?" Arty fumed. "What could have possibly changed over the weekend to make you renege on your decision?"

"Well, let's just say there were politics involved."

"What politics?" Arty shouted.

"I'm very sorry," he answered. "That's all I can say."

We thought we had seen it all, but this was beyond the pale. We asked around and eventually found out that one of the finalists, a shop with a superb creative reputation and a famous owner, had gotten hold of Nynex's management over the weekend and somehow convinced them that Penchina, Selkowitz was simply too small to handle such a big, complicated account. And just like that we were out.

All's fair in love and advertising.

# 30 MUD, BLOOD AND A FRENCH ACCOUNT

Arty and I had just landed at Charles de Gaulle airport in Paris the Fall after we lost Burroughs. We tossed our bags into the trunk of a Hertz Ford Escort and were on our way to the small town of Arques, about two and a half hours north of Paris, to pitch Cristal d'Arques, a billion-dollar, family-owned, genuine crystal glass company.

Cristal d'Arques had a fascinating history. Right after World War II, the family had gotten hold of some leftover GI machinery. After combining it with a unique kind of fine sand found only in this area of France, they began manufacturing inexpensive lead crystal glass and stemware. It was a runaway success and to this day their products can be found in virtually every department store everywhere in the world.

Arriving in Paris at seven a.m., we planned to check into the Intercontinental Hotel and get a few hours sleep before the long drive north. We'd been up all night and I was nursing a cold. When we tried to check in, the hotel insisted we would need to pay for the previous day.

"That's a total rip-off," Arty told the reception clerk. He turned to me. "You know what, Steve? We should just skip the hotel. A thousand bucks for a few hours of sleep is lunacy."

"I'm cool with that Arty, but I won't be able to drive," I said. "I'm zonked on all this cold medicine."

"No problem," he said. "I'm totally awake. I actually feel invigorated."

"You sure?"

"100%."

An hour later, I was awakened by the sound of lacerating metal, breaking glass and the thud of my head hitting the roof of the car, upside down. The scenery before me was spinning around as the car tumbled over and over, eventually landing in a wet ravine just off the highway.

*What the fuck?! Am I dreaming?*

My first sensation was feeling cold blood on my face, which I took as a good sign. I was alive. Arty was dangling above me, his seatbelt the only thing holding him up. His horn-rimmed glasses were crushed into his face and scalp; his blood was dripping all over me. My wrist felt like it was broken.

"Arty, what the fuck happened?"

"I dunno. I must have fallen asleep. I don't remember a thing."

"So much for your being 'invigorated.' How fast were you going?"

"I'm not sure, but you know me. I was moving. So what do we do now?" he asked sheepishly.

"For starters, we gotta get the fuck out of this car." I wiped my face. "Is this your blood or mine?"

"Does it matter?"

"Fuckin' A, it matters. It matters a whole damn lot. Are you all right?" I asked, more seriously.

"I dunno. I think so."

"You don't look so fuckin' all right, I can tell you that."

I could see small shards of glass stuck into the side of his face and top of his head. It was definitely his blood.

Smelling gas, I reached over and turned off the engine. (Funny, how you think of these things, without ever thinking of these things).

"What do we do now?" Arty asked again.

Arty didn't usually ask a lot of dumb questions. He was clearly in shock. I unhooked my seatbelt and crawled through the opening where the windshield had been ten minutes before.

I yelled to Arty to crawl out. He said, okay, but didn't move.

"Arty, you gonna get out of there or what?!"

He didn't so much as move a finger, so I wriggled back into the car and unbuckled his seat belt. He fell on top of me. I was pinned to the seat again. Eventually, I wiggled out from under him and pulled him out of the Escort.

"Sit here on this rock," I told him. "I'll run up the hill and flag down a car. Don't go anywhere." He looked very pale and was shivering; I was concerned he was going into major shock.

I stood on the side of the highway for what seemed like an eternity. Car after car sped right by me.

"You French, fucking frog!" I yelled out. "You can't see I'm covered with blood here and what's left of my goddamned car is smoking in the ditch down there?"

Finally, a big 14-wheeler came to a screeching stop right in front of me. The truck driver didn't speak any English, but one look at me and he immediately radioed ahead for an ambulance.

I ran back down the wet embankment, skidding on my ass, almost slamming into Arty sitting on the rock. "There's an ambulance coming to take us to a hospital."

"Is it on our way?" he asked.

"On our way where?"

"On our way to Arques."

"I have no fucking clue. Does it matter? What the hell are you talking about?"

"We have a presentation to make," Arty proclaimed.

"You're joking?"

"No, I'm not," he said with an attitude that suggested I was the irrational one.

"Arty, we almost bought the ranch a minute ago. We're not making any presentations to anyone."

"But all the work is done," he argued.

"Are you fuckin' hallucinating? The second we're out of the hospital we're going home. You're bleeding all over France for Chrissake. It's not besherit, Arty. We're out of here."

"Tell you what," he said, squinting at me. "I'll make you a deal." He couldn't see two feet in front of him without his glasses. "If the storyboards are intact, we'll continue to Arques. If they're crumpled or dirty or destroyed or whatever, we'll fly home tonight. Fair enough?"

"You're negotiating?!"

No response.

We stared at each other for a few moments.

"Fine," I finally acquiesced. They couldn't possibly be in one piece.

I would have agreed to anything to end this ridiculous conversation. The Ford was fucking totaled.

I walked around to the back of the car and noticed the trunk had popped open. I looked around for the portfolio and spotted it lying in a patch of mucky grass. Aside from being covered with mud, it appeared to be in good condition. Incredulous, I zipped open the case and looked in. The storyboards were pristine. The entire presentation was like new.

The ambulance arrived and took us to a small village hospital where almost no one spoke English. The X-rays of my wrist wee negative. It was just a bad sprain. But the doctors and nurses spent the next four hours painstakingly tweezing minute shards of glass and metal from Arty's scalp, neck and ears. Miraculously, he didn't even need stitches—just around fifty little Band-Aids.

We each called our respective wives and gave them heart attacks. They were both hysterical, having called the hotel a million times and hearing that we hadn't checked in yet. Both wives gave us crap about our driving. Betsy, because of Arty's reputation for speeding, and Debbie, because I should never have trusted him behind the wheel. (She knew how bad a driver he was.) I was a little taken aback. Debbie seemed genuinely worried about me. Could there be a break in the clouds?

I called Hertz and told them we totaled their Ford Escort and needed a new one. After an hour or so, I finally pulled up in the new car and we continued on to Arques. I drove.

When we finally arrived at the hotel some four to five hours late, Madame Durand, the owner of the billion-dollar family business, was waiting anxiously for us in the lobby. She had heard about our wreck on the local news and was worried sick.

Her eyes went wide with disbelief as we limped in, our suits and raincoats covered with a mixture of blood, mud and grass stains. During the many phone conversations we'd had with her throughout the process, she had proven to be a rather cold, tough businesswoman. But now she couldn't do enough for us. She led Arty and me into the dining room, ordered us soupe à l'oignon, croissants and hot tea. She then stayed with us until she was assured that we would make it to our rooms alive.

I soaked in a hot bath for half the night and, after taking every controlled substance I had with me, I eventually got to sleep. Arty was up most of the night washing all the stains off his clothing. He couldn't go to sleep knowing there was filth nearby.

The next morning, every bone and muscle in our bodies ached. The headquarters for Cristal d'Arques was about a quarter of a mile down the road. It hurt just to breathe, much less walk.

The Durand family and other senior executives were waiting for us in their conference room. When we hobbled in, everyone stood up and burst into applause. *We can definitely play the sympathy card,* I thought.

Arty delivered the best opening line in advertising history. "In the States, there's a saying that 'an agency would die for an account like this.' Well, never have two people come so close."

Another ovation.

We had put a lot of work into our presentation. Our research told us the single biggest barrier to the purchase of crystal glassware was that, due to its high cost, consumers were reluctant to use their crystal for fear of breakage. Most families, after receiving their obligatory wedding crystal, stashed it away in their dining room cupboard where it collected dust until Thanksgiving or their kid's communion. Based on this one point, I developed a TV campaign around a young couple hyper-terrified of breaking their expensive crystal.

Our first Cristal d'Arques TV commercial, "Crystal you won't be afraid to use."

Three days after returning to the good ol' US of A, Madame Durand called.

"Oh, merci beaucoup, Madame," I overheard Arty say. "Oh, yes. I'm très better, merci." After several painful minutes of mangling the French language, he hung up and dashed into my office.

"We got it, Steve."

"I heard. Isn't that great?" I answered. "I bet we got the sympathy vote."

"Impossible," Arty retorted. "They're French. They must have really liked the storyboards."

# 31 YOU WIN SOME, YOU LOSE SOME AND SOME CUT YOUR HEART OUT

"Steve," Arty called out the second I walked into the office one rainy morning in the summer of 1985. "Take a look at this."

He thrust a trade paper at me before I had a chance to take off my raincoat.

I glanced at the headline: *Burroughs-Sperry Merger Talks Fail.*

We had heard rumblings about a merger, but it seemed so far in the distance that we hadn't given it much thought. I skimmed the article.

"Well, at least it failed," I said.

"Yeah, for now, but it looks like it's definitely going to happen. It's only a matter of time," Arty answered, staring out the window.

"So?"

"So, if Burroughs ends up acquiring Sperry, it might turn out well for us. But if it's the other way around, anything can happen."

I sat down on Arty's sofa, staring at the headline.

"No way in hell The Chairman would do a deal where he didn't come out on top," I said. "We should be in good shape, no? What's your assessment? You're always right about this kind of stuff."

"I only see two, make that three, potential problems," he began cautiously. "One, you're dripping on my sofa. Would you mind not doing that?"

I got up and tossed my wet coat on the other end. He didn't notice.

"Two," he continued, still staring out onto Third Avenue, "after completing the merger, the Burroughs/Sperry entity would be twice as big as it is now, which leaves us vulnerable to the whole size issue. We don't have enough staff, no worldwide network, all of that crap.

"And three," he said, "is the problem of Bill's lovely replacement."

A year earlier, our good friend and protector Bill Beckham had been inexplicably—at least to us—transferred off our account and replaced by a lovely young lady we affectionately called the Wicked Witch of Detroit. We knew right from the get-go that she was trouble: we didn't particularly like her, and she felt the same way about us.

"She's a pain in the butt," Arty went on, "and I don't trust her as far as I can throw our conference table. She'll be a real wildcard in all this."

"You realize," I added, "if it were up to her, we'd be dead and buried by now." I paused for a moment. "You think anyone would visit our gravesites?"

"You're getting morbid," Arty replied, annoyed. "I don't know. Maybe our kids."

"I told you, the minute Bill was taken off the account it spelled trouble for us."

Burroughs represented about half of our business, which cut two ways: It was tremendously profitable for us, but it also left us vulnerable. If anything were to happen to Burroughs, we'd be in big shit. We found ourselves in a Catch-22. Burroughs was so big that it required almost all of our time. If we took our eye off the ball even for a second on our biggest account we would leave ourselves exposed. Some giant shop might swoop in and steal it away from us.

Arty and I were well aware of the possibility and were constantly working to bring in more accounts to balance out the shop. And we were successful. We had added Citibank Private Bank, Squibb, NBC,

Jefferson-Pilot Insurance, *The New York Times, Newsweek,* and others—all solid accounts—but none was the size of Burroughs (another reason the Nynex fiasco hurt so much.)

Blumenthal had always stood by us but the Wicked Witch of Detroit had really sunk her nails into the advertising, and, unfortunately, he gave her a lot of freedom. She fancied herself a creative maven but her instincts were atrocious. She wanted total control over the advertising, but we wouldn't let her push us around. She hated us for that.

"Remember the first time she came to our office, and Brookstein (the senior Burroughs account executive from our team) offered her a cup of tea because we told him she didn't drink coffee?" I said.

"Yeah, who could forget," Arty replied. "She barked, 'What do you think this is, a tea party?!'"

"If that weren't so fucking hostile, it would have been hilarious," I replied. "Who in the hell says that to someone?"

Arty was pensively staring out the window again.

"I've always told you that change is usually for the worse..."

"That's wonderful, Arty. That'll help me sleep at night." I got up from the sofa. "So, where do we go from here?"

"Well, we'll just have to see how it all plays out."

I grabbed my raincoat. "You know, it could go the other way too, God forbid."

"Whadaya mean?" Arty asked.

"They could consolidate all the advertising with Sperry's agency. I'm pretty sure it's Young & Rubicam. They're huge and they have a million damn offices. They'll kiss her ass all over the globe."

Arty heaved a heavy sigh.

We had little choice but to keep going about our business; as usual, we were busy as hell. Sooner or later, there'd be an opportunity for us to speak with The Chairman and get the lowdown directly from the kingmaker.

Several weeks later Arty was able to talk with Blumenthal. It was indeed a takeover by Burroughs, but The Chairman was spinning it as an equal merger and swore us to secrecy. He said he would soon need us to develop a full-page announcement ad to run in the *Times* and *Journal*, and possibly a TV spot. He also told us that he would be changing their name and logo, and wanted our input on that as well. It sounded like business as usual.

We were reassured that The Chairman was calling the shots. Arty took the opportunity to ask him directly where we stood vis-à-vis the merger, explaining that we didn't want to be caught off guard with any major changes.

"Just keep doing what you've been doing," The Chairman replied. "You guys have nothing to worry about."

That was indeed true—until the Wicked Witch pulled a fast one and convinced him to let her conduct a small agency review that included the two incumbent shops. We went ballistic over this, but had no choice but to participate. In any event, based on our last conversation with The Chairman, we were confident all would turn out fine.

We began working on all the projects Blumenthal had outlined; the agency was humming. A few months went by and all was quiet on the merger front. We continued pitching business, and had recently picked up a lucrative blue chip account, Squibb Pharmaceuticals. There wasn't a whole lot of glamour in the advertising of adult diapers, but the account had the potential of dwarfing Burroughs in size—possibly as big as $30 to $40 million dollars in billings. The aging of America was profitable business.

We drove out to Squibb's New Jersey headquarters with our first creative presentation. The line of thinking that informed the creative strategy was that Squibb was revolutionizing the way America looks at incontinence. We were on a nice roll when a secretary barged into the conference room and announced that Arty was needed on an urgent phone call. My stomach told me that whatever this was, it wasn't going to be good. We rushed out of the meeting, and the young lady escorted us to a vacant office down the hall.

Arty took the call. I was unable to listen in, so my eyes were glued to his face. His countenance suddenly turned ashen.

"Uh, huh. Who got the business?" he asked, stone cold. "Uh, huh. Doesn't surprise me… How long do we have? Uh, huh… Well, I'll have to look at our contract… That doesn't seem fair. You owe us a considerable amount of money… I'll need to get back to you."

He slammed down the receiver. He was shaking with the rage he refused to reveal on the phone.

"So, we're out?" I said, more as a statement than a question.

He nodded.

"And she's trying to screw us on our severance."

He nodded again.

"She enjoyed making that call," he finally spoke up, beside himself with rage. "I could hear it in that annoying, screechy voice of hers."

He slumped back in his chair. He looked like a birthday balloon the day after the party.

"How the hell do we go back in there?" I asked.

No response again.

The two of us sat there motionless in the dark, nondescript vacant office, not saying a word, staring out at the wet, nondescript lawn of this lousy, nondescript New Jersey office building. I was a far more emotional person than Arty. By this point, we'd been together five plus years, and he was always steadfast and calm as hell. (Look how he acted during our car crash!) So much so that I had begun to rely on him to keep me grounded when I came unglued over a client remark or a piece of creative that didn't turn out the way I expected. But this he took personally. He was crushed.

After some time we finally gathered ourselves and rejoined the meeting. Somehow, someway we managed to finish the presentation; we were both on autopilot. The consolation prize of the day was that the client approved our entire campaign.

Arty and I were not naïve; we were well aware of the vicissitudes of the business. As Carl Ally once said, "You begin losing an account the day you get it." Besides the obvious loss of income, what weighed heaviest on us was the feeling of betrayal by the man who had given us our start.

It reminded me of the Kol Nidre prayer on Yom Kippur, where promises made over the past year are deemed null and void. Of course, the difference is that on Yom Kippur you atone for your sins and get a clean slate for the next year. There was no clean slate here. They never even gave us the money they owed us.

I thought back to a time years earlier, when I received an emergency phone call just as Arty and I were to present the 1983 advertising at Burroughs' worldwide retreat in Orlando, Florida. My mother-in-law was dying. The Chairman heard about it and offered me his corporate jet to fly back to New York in the middle of the night.

I remembered vividly the time when Arty, Bill and I sat with him in his office late one Christmas Eve smoking Havana cigars and drinking 18 year-old Chivas Regal scotch while he poignantly told us remarkable stories of how, at the age of thirteen, his family slipped him out of Nazi Germany on a ship to Shanghai, China, where he went to escape the Holocaust an survived by scavenging for food out of strewn garbage on the streets.

I also remembered when The Chairman had personally invited us to attend his "UJA Man of the Year" dinner a few years prior. During his acceptance speech in front of 1500 people in the Grand Ballroom of the Waldorf-Astoria, he actually took the time to mention us, his "creative ad agency in New York."

Penchina, Selkowitz had an amazing run with Burroughs—and we had him to thank for it. But our hearts were broken that such a personal and rewarding relationship ended the way it did.

The Chairman gaveth, and taketh away.

We didn't hear from him again until about a year later when we received a handwritten letter. He wrote that he'd been quite shaken when he heard the news about our car crash. Unbelievably, he went on to say, "I feel terrible about your accident, and only hope that your near-death experience was not the result of losing the Burroughs account. If it was, I truly apologize."

Arty and I thought about the letter for a long time. We honestly couldn't decide whether we were happy, angry, sad or still depressed over it. Arty's initial reaction was, "Skip the letter and give us the money you owe us." (The money, incidentally, went to Burroughs's new agency, the $3 billion Young & Rubicam, presumably at the direction of the Witch).

But in the end, in a surprising and profound way, The Chairman's letter meant more to me than the cash.

# 32 SUZUKIS ARE FOREVER

Less than a year after losing Burroughs, Squibb announced they were selling their incontinence division to Johnson & Johnson, and we lost that as well, millions of dollars of lost income in just a few months. We had no choice but to significantly cut back our staff, some of whom had been with us from the start.

Not only was my agency slipping away, so was my marriage.

Debbie had landed a job producing a soap opera in Germany and was spending more and more time there. Things had gotten increasingly worse between us. The distance didn't help. Arik, Ditty and Daniel were away at college, so they were spared some of the fireworks. I was doing my best to hold the marriage together until Josh graduated high school; he was in his senior year. But it wasn't to be. On a trip back home from Cologne, Germany, I convinced Debbie to see a prominent new marriage counselor with me. It was a Hail Mary pass.

On a freezing winter day in February, we met at the psychologist's office on Park Avenue. Neither of us was speaking to the other. After giving the therapist some background on our relationship (or non-relationship), he asked us a simple question:

"So, why are you two here?"

Debbie answered first. "Because I want you to convince my husband that I'm through with him."

I turned to Debbie. "Really? I said. "That's seriously why you came here?"

"Yep," She answered.

I paused for a moment, thinking.

"Well, then," I said. "I guess there's no reason for me to be here."

I got up, put on my coat and scarf and left.

After 20 long years the ballgame was over.

I soon learned that breaking up was the easy part. Getting a divorce was a whole new can of worms. I wanted to make sure I obtained a "Get," or Jewish divorce, from her so that if I ever wanted to get married again, I would be able to get married by a rabbi. Debbie decided to thwart this.

Since a Justice of the Peace had married us, obtaining a Get wasn't a simple matter. If she wasn't going to give it to me, I had to find some other way of obtaining one, not an easy task.

My Get journey started out with an elderly orthodox Rabbi in Brooklyn who was an expert on the subject of Jewish divorces. He told me to contact a group of Rabbis who would convene a Rabbinical Court, and would help me obtain a Get in New York. Under Jewish law it would require some Talmudic creativity and a little tzdaka (charity), but in the end I would get my Get.

A meeting of ten orthodox rabbis with pais (long side curls), black hats and coats was convened at my synagogue on 68th Street in the city. The Rabbis had me sign a bunch of paperwork—in English and then in Hebrew (I didn't understand a word). Because Debbie wasn't present, everything had to be strictly kosher.

I signed all the documents. They then held a small service, at the end of which I received a legal document. All I could make out were the names of the rabbis, the name of the rabbinical court and the names

Steve and Debbie Penchina. I was asked to hold up the document and pass it to one of the other rabbis, who passed it to another, who passed it to a third. The ceremony was complete.

All that was left now was the tzdaka, or charity, which went down more like a payoff. I had a fistful of $100 bills that I walked around the room with.

"Here's something for you, rabbi."

"One for you, Moishe."

"One for you, thank you."

"This is for you."

"One for you, Schlomo."

"A $100 for you, thank you very much."

"Some tzdaka for you, rabbi, thank you for joining us."

And so on, until my fist was empty. I then gave the head rabbi $500 for the divorce certificate, officially certified.

Now came the interesting part.

One of the rabbis took a copy of the Get and told me that since Debbie didn't appear, he would hold onto it until she sees the wisdom of picking it up. Until such time, it would be held for her in a safe in Brooklyn. In the meantime, since I was there in person, I was now officially divorced under Talmudic law. Isn't the Jewish religion wonderful?

Arty and I were loath to admit it, but we found ourselves in a deep depression over the loss of Burroughs and to a lesser extent, Squibb. It lasted months, and it's tough to bring in new business when you're in a funk like that.

With a lot of hard work and focus we made a healthy comeback; we never, however, reached the heights of our Burroughs days. We were pitching nonstop but it was becoming very costly. We were up against much larger shops that threw gobs of money at business development, even for tiny accounts. For big accounts it wasn't unheard of for agencies to drop $50,000 to $250,000, or even more, on speculative presentations. The giant agencies sometimes presented finished commercials totally on spec.

Boutiques like ours simply did not have the resources to effectively compete with them. We would have to come up with another strategy: we needed a sugar daddy.

We began having merger-and-acquisition talks with a number of good, solid agencies. If we were acquired, our strategy was to remain an independent, autonomous shop within the framework of a much bigger agency. This would give us the deep financial pockets we sought but also allow us to run our business as we saw fit. Neither of us was overjoyed with this new direction. Rightly or wrongly, we both felt that we had failed in some way.

On the upside, however, Madison Avenue was full of agencies that merged after having difficulty gaining traction following the loss of their linchpin account. In point of fact, they often wound up much better off after combining shops. During the late eighties, giant advertising holding companies like Interpublic and WPP were buying up smaller agencies the way Imelda Marcos bought shoes.

Over a ten-month period, we entered into serious discussions with a half-dozen shops, four of which ultimately made us bankable offers: TBWA (which later acquired the iconic Chiat/Day of Venice, California), Keye/Donna/Pearlstein, also from L.A., W.B. Doner from Baltimore and Detroit, and DMB&B, Arty's old agency, the former Benton & Bowles.

There are many things that come into play in a merger, and both Arty and I felt the offer from Doner was perhaps our most advantageous. We both very much liked and respected the owner, Brud Doner, who was getting on in age and preparing for his succession. We matched up well with their management and their president, Herb Fried. Our two agencies were equally enthusiastic about the merger prospects, and our vision of the new entity was identical. Over and above their lucrative offer for our agency, they wanted us for the right reasons: Arty for his marketing and management expertise, and me for my creativity and good looks.

After negotiating for several long months, we scheduled a final handshake with their management committee in a Washington, DC hotel room. Everyone was enthusiastic. The Doner folks had ordered up champagne, and now the only thing left to do was sign a term sheet. But, at the very last minute—literally, Brud casually tossed out a final request. "You wouldn't mind if my son, Fred, joined the agency as president, would you, boys?" He asked.

Besides the fact that this came out of the blue (and that his son's only real agency experience was doing who-knows-what in his dad's media department in Detroit), he wasn't even at the fuckin' meeting!

The timing of the demand, on top of the fact that I had spent the last 7½ years under the distinct impression that Arty was president of Penchina, Selkowitz, threw us for a total loop.

Brud turned to Arty. "You wouldn't have a problem with that, would you, Arty?"

The elevator couldn't come fast enough.

We soon connected with Keye/Donna/Pearlstein, a wonderfully creative midsize shop out of Los Angeles that handled the big Suzuki car and truck business. After several positive phone conversations with Len Pearlstein, the majority owner, we flew to the West Coast to meet with them. The first meeting we had was with Paul Keye, partner and creative director. He was older than us and had a gentle, professorial demeanor. He was a superbly talented writer. One of his big claims to fame was the public service commercial he wrote for the Ad Council's "Just say no to drugs" campaign.

This simple, 15-second spot set the gold standard for pro bono advertising for years to come.

The commercial opens on a sizzling hot frying pan. The announcer says: "This is your brain."

A broken egg drops into the sizzling frying pan.

"This is your brain on drugs."

"Any questions?"

We spent several pleasant hours talking with Paul and screened their impressive reel.

Arty and I then spent the next two days with Len Pearlstein, a sharp, plump, hyper-confident man with a quick laugh and a generous lust for life, which, on that night, included a fine Cuban cigar and a bottle of Robert Mondavi Reserve. I ignored his bow tie and suspenders for the time being. (I had this thing that I never trusted a man who wore bow ties and suspenders. Maybe it was a lawyer thing.)

We had an enjoyable and productive time with Pearlstein, and we all agreed to take the next step: Lenny would come to New York and see our operation. If things went well, we would meet with our attorneys and, hopefully, hammer out a deal. We were a good fit for one another. Pearlstein wanted a toehold in New York with a top creative shop, and we wanted more critical mass and access to greater resources.

But a funny thing happened on the way to the merger… The sunny, funny man we met in California was not the guy who showed up in New York.

After meeting at my place for drinks, we all went out to dinner at the Four Seasons. For some reason Pearlstein was a nervous wreck, sweating through his shirt, under-tipping the taxi driver, over-tipping the maître d' (we still got a lousy table) and creating such a racket over who picked up the dinner check that the entire restaurant stopped and gawked. If that weren't embarrassing enough, the poor guy's Black American Express card was declined. Twice.

By the next morning, Arty and I were beginning to have just a smidgeon of reservation about the pairing. But we chalked up the night's semi-hysterical behavior to the simple nervousness of a man trying way too hard to impress in someone else's backyard. We gave him the benefit of the doubt on the declined American Express card, too. He said it was a bank error. Besides, even if he was a bit of a schmuck, the fact remained that he would be 3,000 miles away most of the time. For me, the bottom line was still the creative, and there was no denying the quality of their work.

Later that morning we all sat down with our attorney, Phil Reiss. Phil was considered the brightest lawyer on Madison Avenue and was an expert on agency acquisitions and mergers (Martin Sorrell of WPP, the world's largest advertising holding company, didn't make a move without Phil's approval). He was also a wonderful, fun and witty guy—if he liked you.

Phil got right down to business. I don't know if it was Len's arrogant demeanor, his L.A. persona, or even his bow tie for that matter, but I could tell immediately that Phil took an instant dislike to him. Phil spread out Pearlstein's financials in front of him, and the two immediately locked horns.

"The value of your agency is fundamentally based on one big account, Suzuki. What happens if you lose it?" Phil questioned.

"I'll never lose Suzuki," Pearlstein declared emphatically. "They're like family."

"Burroughs was family to them," Phil countered, peering over his bifocals at us. "And look what happened. Their biggest account did a merger and my guys were out—overnight."

"Thanks for reminding us, Phil," I joked, trying to cool the rising tension in the room.

Pearlstein countered, "Well, that's not going to happen here," he said, with the smugness of Ross Perot.

"Oh, and why not? You have a long-term contract with these guys?"

"No, but they love me. They don't make a move without me.

WHO WROTE THIS SH*T?!

They were at my son's bar mitzvah."

"That's very sweet," Phil said. "But the valuation of your shop is essentially based on Suzuki, and despite all the tender moments you've shared with them, there's still no guarantee they won't pull up stakes and take their cars and trucks elsewhere. You know this business."

"Oh, yes, I do," Pearlstein answered. "I've been doing this for over 20 highly-successful years. I can read my clients like a book. I know these people. They will never leave me. You know the line 'Diamonds are forever'?" Pearlstein asked.

"Yeah?" Phil answered.

"Substitute Suzuki for diamonds."

That's how it went for most of the morning, back and forth on this one issue. Everyone was getting frustrated. Mercifully, Arty called for a bathroom break. While Pearlstein made some calls to back to LA, Arty, Phil and I visited the men's room.

"Tell me," Phil said as soon as the door slammed behind him. "Why do you guys want to go into business with this schmuck? He loses Suzuki, the whole agency goes under just like what happened to you. Okay, maybe not overnight—he's got a few other nice accounts—but soon enough. And then you'll be stuck with him."

"Don't hold back, Phil," I said. "Tell us how you really feel."

"Look guys, no matter how he spins it, it's a one-account shop." Phil smoothed his prodigious black hair in the mirror. "And that's dangerous," he went on. "The Japanese walk, the ballgame's over."

Arty and I were perplexed. When we visited Pearlstein in L.A., he couldn't have been more impressive. His bubbly personality and sure-fire confidence had really pulled us in. Who was this obnoxious guy fighting with Phil?

Arty hadn't said anything for a long time; I knew he wasn't happy. He finally spoke up. "Well, let's go back in and see what develops. What do you think, Steve?"

"I dunno… I guess so. Can't figure this guy out. Maybe Len sent his goofy twin brother here instead?"

Arty reached for the door. "Okay, round two, men."

Back in the conference room Phil was losing his patience and cornered Pearlstein.

"Look Len, this X factor has to be taken into consideration on the overall price of the merger," he demanded. "I realize my guys have to buy into your agency, your shop being bigger and all, but I can't let my guys do this unless the price of your agency stock declines dramatically. As of now, it's just too damn pricey. It will take them forever to get their investment back."

"I can't do that," Pearlstein answered flatly.

Phil leaned back in his chair, crossed his hands behind his neck and heaved a big sigh. He was making one last push.

"You really think these Japanese love you so much?"

"Definitively," Pearlstein said.

"Why? They're so enamored with smart, Jewish agency owners? Let me tell ya, the auto business goes south—and there are indications that it might—you're history like any one of the thirty-five agencies we represent here."

"Len, we'd like to do this," Arty broke in. "We like you and your agency, but this merger has to be equitable for both of us, and right now it isn't. Your price is way too high. We'd be paying you off well into the next century."

Pearlstein wouldn't give one penny on his price. As much as I was looking forward to a new partnership and getting involved with a big car account, it wasn't to be. I didn't even have to look at Arty to know where he was netting out. The fact that he hadn't said very much in the last couple of hours told me all I needed to know.

"Well, we're very disappointed, Len," Arty said. "We really wanted this to work out. We felt we were a great fit. But you're asking too much for us to buy in. In the long term, I'm certain everything would work out. It's the short term we're concerned about, Len. We don't want to go into heavy debt before we even begin."

"Well, I'm sorry, too," Len replied.

And that's where it ended.

Pearlstein got up, put on his sports jacket, adjusted his goofy bowtie and stormed out of the office in a huff, calling Phil a deal-breaker among other unsavory things. In a puff of cigar smoke, Lenny and our merger were gone.

A year later, almost to the day, I picked up the current issue of *Advertising Age* and a headline stopped me cold:

"Suzuki Puts Ad Account up for Grabs"

# 33 OUR $3 BILLION SUGAR DADDY

The Keye/Donna/Pearlstein merger now in the history books, we continued to talk to several more candidates.

Almost from the day Arty and I had gone into business, Roy Bostock, Arty's old boss and now CEO of D'Arcy Masius Benton & Bowles (DMB&B), had kept in touch with us. Over the occasional lunch he always maintained it would be difficult to hold on to big accounts with a small platform like ours. In fact, during the Burroughs/Sperry merger he called Arty to suggest we join forces with his $3 billion shop to buffer ourselves against a large multinational agency swooping in and picking off our biggest account. With the perfect vision of hindsight, that probably would have kept us from losing Burroughs to Young & Rubicam, almost the same size of DMB&B.

Year after year, Arty respectfully declined Roy's advances. I, on the other hand, was gradually coming to the conclusion that merging with a giant shop would be a smart move. As our finances got tighter, I kept gently prodding Arty to at least have another lunch with Roy. I'd gotten to know him over the years and I liked him. He was direct, very sharp, enamored with our reel (he couldn't believe how far we had come in eight years), was a jock like me and, most importantly, laughed at all my jokes. I felt confident he would agree to our terms and not nickel and dime us on our price. My persistent nagging eventually wore Arty down, and he reluctantly agreed to sit down with his old mentor.

Slowly but surely, Arty began to cave. We had several very positive meetings and lunches with Roy; eventually we were joined by Craig Brown, their affable CFO, and we negotiated a very good deal. Penchina, Selkowitz Inc. would become an autonomous, independent subsidiary of DMB&B and operate as a stand-alone creative boutique. Importantly, we would have access to their worldwide resources and deep pockets. They offered us a more-than-attractive price for our agency, bought our assets, gave us a generous amount of DMB&B stock and signed us to a lucrative multi-year contract. Roy promised that DMB&B would funnel any small accounts that came their way; in turn we would help them creatively on an as-needed basis. It was a win-win.

The new partnership took off nicely. We tapped into DMB&B's impressive research, media and strategic planning departments, working closely with their public relations agency to help each other garner new business. Thanks to DMB&B's prominent reputation and worldwide ranking, we were able to compete for much bigger accounts, while they helped us fund pitches.

But over time it became evident that eliciting their help wasn't as simple as just asking for it. If we needed to make a big media presentation, for example, we often ran into difficulty getting their top media director. DMB&B's interests always came first. When we attempted to use their vast strategic planning library, we discovered they only had useful databanks and case histories for mega-industries like automobiles and beer—not exactly the kinds of accounts we could realistically go after.

After several years of frustration, it became apparent that the disconnect between our two shops was simply too great. This was most striking in our approaches to new business. DMB&B's presentations were laden with mind-numbing research and esoteric media analysis that wasn't particularly useful to the clients we were targeting.

# The New York Times

THE NEW YORK TIMES, MONDAY, JANUARY 9, 1989

**THE MEDIA BUSINESS**

## Advertising | Randall Rothenberg

### D.M.B.&B. Acquires Penchina

PENCHINA, SELKOWITZ INC., a tiny New York agency known for its work for Burroughs computers, was acquired on Friday by D'Arcy Masius Benton & Bowles, the $2.5 billion advertising giant. Executives of the agency will receive an undisclosed amount of cash and stock in D.M.B.&B., and a percentage of their agency's profits.

This is the second merger in recent weeks of a small, creative shop into a large advertising company. Last month Tracy-Locke, a division of the Omnicom Group, acquired Altschiller Reitzfeld, a $60 million agency whose founders are perennials on advertising's award circuit.

The willingness of these agencies to sell their independence illustrates the growing difficulty small shops are having in an increasingly competitive advertising and marketing environment. As American corporations battle for larger shares of existing markets, they are turning to established agencies that can provide them with services beyond good creative work. For their part, large ad agencies that once eschewed low-paying accounts are now eagerly pursuing them, squeezing smaller ad companies with fewer resources out of new-business presentations.

"The conventional wisdom is that the small, talented agency will have a great future in this business. Frankly and empirically, we don't accept it," said Steven M. Penchina, the chairman and creative director of Penchina, Selkowitz. "For all the talk of big clients going to small agencies, to them 'small' means a $150 million agency."

Penchina, Selkowitz has $20 million in media billings, but the road to that figure has taken the two founders up mountains and down rocky valleys, literally as well as figuratively. The agency was founded in 1982 by Mr. Penchina, who is 43 years old and is best known as the writer of Xerox's "merry monk" ad campaign when he was at Needham, Harper & Steers, and Arthur Selkowitz, who is 45 and was a senior vice president at Benton & Bowles, where he helped manage the Procter & Gamble account. In 1983, the agency landed the Burroughs Corporation account, which tripled in size, to $12 million, in only three years and accounted for more than half the agency's billings.

When Burroughs merged with the Sperry Corporation, the new company, Unisys, wanted an agency with an international presence. "We were 97 offices short," said Mr. Penchina, so they were dismissed.

The partners laid off three-quarters of their staff and went on a search for new business, an activity to which they were unaccustomed.

"When you have one central account of that size, it becomes difficult to broaden your base," explained Mr. Selkowitz, the agency's president. "That client almost becomes a parasite to the agency."

At one point, their search took them to France in pursuit of J. G. Durand, a large manufacturer of glassware. Mr. Selkowitz fell asleep at the wheel of their car and the vehicle tumbled off a mountain road. The men were injured, but won the account.

Still, their difficulties have continued. Recently, the agency lost some Thomas J. Lipton Company assignments to Young & Rubicam — the same agency that took the Burroughs account from them. That competition, and the desire to play on a larger stage — "It's been a while since I've done a network TV ad," Mr. Penchina said — led the agency to seek a buyer.

During the last year, Penchina, Selkowitz was courted by several large agencies, including Keye/Donna/Pearlstein and Roux, Seguela, Cayzac & Goudard. The merger with D.M.B.&B. came about in part because of Mr. Selkowitz's 11 years there and his long friendship with Roy Bostock, president of D.M.B.&B.

Penchina, Selkowitz will keep its name and operate as an independent unit within D.M.B.&B., but Mr. Bostock said he would "aggressively review all prospects and current clients to find opportunities" for it. He said its presence within D.M.B.&B. would help draw business-to-business advertising, a Penchina specialty, to D.M.B.&B., and that its creative reputation would enhance the stature of D.M.B.&B.

"In this business, perception is, in many ways, reality," he said. "Given the perception of these guys, it will help us achieve recognition for our superior creative product."

---

A good example of this came during preparations for a joint pitch for the $100 million Prudential Insurance account. The client mentioned their desire for a less formal, more approachable agency. DMB&B took them quite literally and overreacted. They ran out and rented several sofas, club chairs, floor lamps and a few oriental rugs. They then yanked out all of their beautiful conference room furnishings (including, unbelievably, the conference table), and replaced everything with the "homey" furniture.

When the client arrived, they had trouble understanding where they were. Was this a business or someone's living room? No one, including our own people, knew where to sit. Total confusion ensued until Roy took each client by the hand and led them to their respective seats. But there was no clear hierarchy in the seating arrangement (not so easy without a conference table), which made it impossible for both client and agency to distinguish the president from the promotion assistant.

As the presentation droned on everybody became listless, lounging on their cushy sofas like Roman senators. A conference room without a conference table doth not a conference room maketh.

What's more, DMB&B insisted on presenting a total of six different campaigns in addition to the one Arty and I had created. That meant the poor client was subjected to roughly 25 storyboards, 35 print ads, and God knows how many promotional pieces and brochures, sending the message: "We're not sure what we've got here, so we're going to show you every damn thing we did." It was the polar opposite of our creative philosophy, which was to present one dynamite idea and live or die by it.

When Arty and I finally got up to present, we looked out over the room and quietly burst into laughter. Everyone had tuned out. Some were even leafing through the old *LIFE* magazines the agency had sprinkled around to give the room that extra "Home Sweet Home" atmosphere. Arty and I muddled through our presentation, but nobody cared. At long last, the meeting came to an end.

We didn't get the business.

We trudged on for two more years, but we eventually agreed that the merger wasn't what we all had hoped for. Roy asked us to fold our business into the DMB&B tent. Arty would become worldwide account director on Proctor & Gamble, reporting directly to Roy—precisely what he had originally wanted to avoid. I would share creative director responsibilities. Unfortunately, whereas P&G was a natural fit for Arty, I couldn't bear the thought of working for "the quicker picker-upper" for a minute, much less the rest of my career.

Arty and I found ourselves in an awkward position. Neither of us wanted to stand in the other's way after all of our years together. We spent weeks discussing the pros and cons of Roy's offer. Although earlier Arty had wanted no part of his old agency, this deal would work for him now. He liked P&G, and his new position would require a lot of international travel, providing him loads of autonomy and distance from the office politics he loathed.

Loyal to the end, he said if I didn't want him to take Roy's offer, he wouldn't. But I knew it was the right move for him. And I would never stand in his way. I gave him my blessings and a framed collection of 32 Penchina, Selkowitz Inc. logos.

I passed on Roy's offer, deciding to continue with Penchina, Selkowitz sans Selkowitz. Arty moved up to the management floor and immediately threw himself into his new position. We were only separated by four floors, but it felt like four continents. Arty seemed to adjust as easily to his new/old job as he did when he first joined me eight years earlier—maybe a bit too easily. I had trouble understanding how he could make the jump from wild and crazy creative boutique to giant, conservative, global holding company so easily. Hadn't I taught him anything? I couldn't help but feel cheated in some way. Arty's future was set; mine was anything but.

The first six to eight months after our separation I fell into a deep depression. I was alone again and missed my partner. Even though the past few years had been a bumpy ride for us, at least there was an "us." I always knew that when I walked in every morning, Arty would be there sitting at his desk, head down, a glass of Diet Coke (it was Tab when we started) by his side, frantically scribbling away on his yellow legal pad with one of his perfectly sharpened pencils, while continuously blowing away his erasures. Without passing "Go," I went directly to his office where I enjoyed my coffee and jelly donut while my partner nervously monitored my every movement, terrified that the jelly and powdered sugar would wind up all over his papers. We would shoot the shit for a while until he threw me out, saying, "If you don't leave me alone, we'll never make any money."

Although we spoke often on the phone and would have lunch together whenever he was in town, it took me a long time to get over the loss. But I was determined to see the agency through. I succeeded without him when I started nine years ago, and I would do it again. Roy had generously offered me several new account directors to replace Arty. I picked up some business, including the Eurostar train, French Tourism and Computer Associates, but it was tough sledding. Not only because I didn't have Arty, but also because the economy was going through another rough period. Once again, agencies big and small were chasing after the same accounts.

During the economic downturn of 1991, I finally tossed in the towel. It was not a happy day, to say the least. I spoke to each one of my employees separately. Naturally, I was miserable, but I hadn't realized how unhappy they would all be. It was flattering in the saddest of ways. The one consolation for me personally was that everyone who worked with me went on to have long and successful careers which is something I remain very proud of.

Jim Handloser, my first, very suave hire, became creative director at a top creative shop, as did my first copywriter Rochelle Klein. Bob Needleman, who designed my first 150 Penchina, Selkowitz Inc. logos and worked with me on virtually everything—from my first big assignment for DEC to *Newsweek*, NBC, Citibank and others—opened his own successful agency. So did my trusty, feisty art director Sal Divito, who worked with me on WNBC Radio and Burroughs. His highly creative and award-winning shop, Divito, Verdi is still going strong today.

After ten years, a million laughs, a few tears, an office full of awards and a litany of satisfied clients, Penchina, Selkowitz was now a treasure trove of fond memories. Sad as it was to close my doors, I felt no shame.

I was the head of my agency for more than twice as long as I ever lasted at any other shop, proving once and for all that I was my own best boss and that if you just left me alone I could achieve greatness.

I was responsible for helping our clients make a lot of money.

I had made a close, eternal friend in Arty. (As a matter of fact, he just called me to make sure I described something accurately in the book. Twenty years later and he's still busting my ass.)

My bank account was brimming with cash.

And Penchina, Selkowitz had earned (and still has) the reputation as one of the foremost creative shops on Madison Avenue.

To think it all began with a hamburger at the Plaza and a Swiss typewriter everyone wished was a French scarf.

# 34  GO KNOW

I was jogging through the maze of hallways at Memorial Hospital in Hollywood, Florida, searching for room E115. I had just flown in from New York for what I feared would be my last visit with my dad. My brother and sister couldn't get away this time. We had all been taking turns visiting him so I made this trip alone. By this point my poor mother was exhausted from caring for him.

When I finally reached his room, the doctor was just walking out. I pulled him aside and asked how my dad was doing. He told me that, as always, my father was in decent spirits but it wouldn't be long. I tried to fully digest what he had just said. I knew my father was dying, but hearing those words so directly rocked me back on my heels.

"I'm soon to geev heem an injection. It weel make heem more comfortable," he told me in a thick Israeli accent.

I thought to myself how fitting it was that an Israeli doctor, wearing a yarmulke, was with my Zionist father at the end. It raised my spirits momentarily.

He put his hand gently on my shoulder. "This weel make for a goot time to say your goot-byes," he said in a low, compassionate voice.

My stomach sank. I waited a few moments trying to regain my composure before walking into his room.

"Hey, Dad," I said in my best, perkiest Kathie Lee Gifford voice. "How're you doin'?"

"Oh, Steve?" he replied, recognizing my voice, his eyes still shut. "When did you get down?"

"Just got in, Pops. Flew into West Palm."

"Where's Mother?" he asked, opening his eyes and suddenly looking worried.

"I just passed her in the hall. She's going to the cafeteria for coffee. Not to worry, Dad, she's okay. Are you all right with that tube in your throat?"

"Do I have a choice?" he shrugged. "What can I tell you? It's a pain in the neck."

"Hey, that's funny, Dad."

He wasn't laughing.

"So what else is new?" I asked feebly.

It was always a little disconcerting talking to my dad. There was always this distance between us. It wasn't just me; it was true for everyone, including my mother. I endured his silence my entire life—the same silence I had to sit through on the Long Island Rail Road when we commuted to New York together back in my NYU days.

One of nine children, Max, or Meyer as everyone called him in Yiddish, had grown up in the early 1900s on Cannon Street, in the heart of the Lower East Side's Jewish immigrant population. He lived in a five-story cold-water tenement with a single cast-iron coal stove in the living room that was used to boil water for the one bathtub. When the tub was covered over with a sheet of tin, it doubled as the dining room table. He shared a bed with his three younger brothers adjacent to the bed that held his five sisters, separated only by a hanging sheet. Everyone slept tzum fesence, which in Yiddish means, "head-to-feet."

As the eldest, my dad had to go out to make money for the family at a very young age. Chasing after the live-chicken trucks barreling down Orchard Street, he scooped up loose feathers and sold them for pennies to be made into pillows. With the leftover pillow profits, he eventually opened Penchina Textiles & Company and took in all my uncles, essentially providing for the entire Penchina brood—some 50 people, including my mother's side of the family.

He shrugged his bony shoulders and closed his eyes again. He was much frailer than the last time I visited him. I sat down at the end of his bed trying to think of something to say. Business, the stock market, the current state of Israel—those had always been easy topics for us to connect over, especially years ago when he was robust. He loved hearing about my agency and was always offering me and Arty advice from the keen perspective of someone who started with nothing and made it to a big house in Great Neck with two, sometimes three, cars in the driveway, summer camps, college for all of his kids and monthly vacations with my mom (and often all of us) to everywhere from Rome to Vegas to Ixtapa, Mexico.

Growing up on the Lower East Side, he learned most of life's lessons the hard way. Despite the hard lumps, he was a generous man in both money and spirit, and couldn't do enough to help people. He was always giving me advice about work and life:

"In business, you need to have a little larceny in you. Tell Arty he needs to bend the rules every now and then."

"Don't screw around with the IRS. But if you do, you might as well do it big. Otherwise, it's not worth the trouble."

When we were going through our merger talks he cautioned, "Ten percent of something is better than 100% of nothing."

"Remember, A&P made a fortune with a markup of just pennies."

I was always kvetching to him about this or that. "The competition out there is murderous, Dad."

"Build a better mousetrap," he'd answer, "and the world will beat a path to your door." It sounded trite, but it was so true.

Whenever I worried about family stuff, he always put me at ease. "I have confidence in you," he would tell me reassuringly. "I know you'll figure it out. You're my genius."

And when I was hopelessly down in the dumps with money concerns, he told me, "Don't worry, Gott helfen (God provides)."

Sitting alone with him, I searched for something profound or loving to say, but I simply froze. The only thing running through my mind was what the doctor had just told me, and I was afraid I would slip up and tip him off that this would be our last time together. What a thought. The words were incomprehensible. My stomach was swirling around like the waves crashing to shore at Hollywood beach a half-mile away. Naturally, I had to go to the bathroom, but I was afraid something would happen…

My mother returned with her coffee. She seemed to be holding up a lot better than I was. But then, she had a lot more experience with this kind of thing: she'd lost her mother, father, three brothers, three sisters and countless other family members. Getting old sucks.

"So, Dad," I finally blurted out. "Any last…" I quickly corrected myself. "Any, uh, words of wisdom for your number two son?"

Silence. His eyes were closed, but I could tell he was thinking.

"Pops?" I asked again, a little louder this time. I was determined not to lose this opportunity. "Some words of wisdom for me?"

All my life he had told me long fish tales and biblical parables to make a point. But now I could see he had nothing left in him. He tried to turn his head to look at me, and then said with a raspy voice, "Go know. I always thought it would be different. I would be eating gourmet kosher meals at a fancy hotel and people would be waiting on me hand and foot like they used to years ago when Mother and I went to Vegas all the time."

He stopped to catch his breath.

"Go know…," he repeated, his voice trailing off.

I understood exactly what he meant. "Go know" is a direct translation from the Yiddish, Gey vissen. It basically means "Go and try to figure everything out. With all the vicissitudes of life, you can't. Life is about fate and faith, and at the end of the day we have little control over how things turn out. Only God knows."

He raised his head slightly to try and eat the hospital's crummy chocolate pudding. I wished he had a bowl of the warm Hershey's chocolate pudding with crushed almonds my mother used to cook for him. He loved that.

"Now, I'm eating all this dreck hospital food. I thought we'd have someone looking after your mother so I wouldn't have to worry about her. And you'd be flying in to visit us on your private jet. My genius."

"I did fly down on a jet, Pop. I just had to share it with 150 other people."

He didn't laugh. I'm not even sure he heard me.

"Go know...," he said again softly.

I leaned over and kissed him on the forehead. I don't ever remember having ever done that before; there really hadn't been any need to. In my entire life, I don't recall ever seeing him sick or helpless or weak. Only once did I witness him out of control. It was at my friend Garlick's older sister's wedding in the backyard of their home in Great Neck, which abutted our house at 23 Old Pond Road, where we lived for over 50 years.

My father and Garlick's father, close friends since moving to Great Neck together in 1944, got so drunk at the reception that my dad couldn't make it home——all of 100 feet away.

My brother eventually guided him back to our house, inch by inch. Before he got to the door, however, he grabbed hold of my mother's prized, rose-covered gazebo and wouldn't let go. It took my brother and two exceedingly strong friends to pry my dad's hands loose. After he threw up several times (also something I had never seen before), my mom finally got him tucked safely into bed where he slept for 24 hours straight. Except for a couple of blizzards in the late 40s and 50s, that was the only time I saw him miss work. That's six days a week for 44 years, less Jewish holidays of course.

In any event, I didn't kiss him often. Nor did Michael. Diane did, but she was a woman and that was cool. Men kissing men was a no-no, even if it was the last time they would ever see each other. But I'm happy I did it. I hope it meant something to him; it meant everything to me.

His forehead felt damp and lifeless. But he was intimidating even in that state. I choked back tears. Without consciously thinking about it, I had been dreading this moment my entire life. Sitting there, I found myself in a quandary. The doctor was waiting to give him an injection to ease his pain, but it would also put an end to his last conscious moments. Maybe I was being selfish, but I wanted those last few moments of clarity with him. I sat there a while longer, then noticed the doctor standing in the doorway with a nurse. This was it.

I leaned over and kissed my dad good-bye again—not just for me, but for Michael and Diane, too. I could see my mother wasn't leaving, so I took her hand and gave her a kiss—I would take her home afterwards. I turned and walked out. I didn't want to see.

In the span of just a few short years I suffered three life-changing events: the end of my marriage and my agency, and now the loss of my dad.

Go know.

# 35 PRADA RULES

I was depressed for more than a year. But after a lot of time and even more therapy, as they say in baseball, I was due for a hit.

On New Year's Eve, 1998, my first night out as a single man after 20 long, painful years of marriage, I met a beautiful young attorney named Dianne who had just moved to New York from Miami.

My friend Kal Liebowitz had insisted I finally "get my ass out the door." It took me a bottle of Bordeaux and two Heinekens with my son, Josh, to get me moving to some cockamamie New Year's Eve party. "I've got a girl for you to take," Kal said. "Call her right away."

"But it's New Year's Eve," I protested.

"Just call her. She's a cool chick. Very attractive and smart. She won't give a shit. Besides, we'll be with a bunch of crazy, drunken people.

"But it's New Year's Eve?" she said when I called.

"Oh, do you have plans?"

"Well, uh, not really? But it's a little last minute, don't you think?"

"Just pretend it's uh, February 9th," I told her. "Forget the New Year's Eve part. We'll have fun," I said, having no clue.

"Well, uh…"

"I'll pick you up at nine. How's that?

"Make it 10:00. I'll need time to get ready. It's New Year's Eve, you know."

I drove over to her apartment with a taxi full of sloshed people; we were heading to a party on the west side. "I'll get in first," I told her when she came out. "You can squeeze in next to me." She proceeded to push one of the girls into the taxi partition. "Excuse me," she politely offered. Practically sitting on me, trying to get comfortable, she crossed her legs and kicked the same young lady in the head. "Sorry," she said again politely.

Swigging from a bottle of Cristal champagne, I looked down at her black, fishnet stocking covered legs. Wow. Her sequenced silk Prada skirt had hiked up to her waist. I loved this girl.

The party on the west side was a disaster: potato chips, Diet Cokes sitting on card tables, Michael Bolton music, that kind of thing. I didn't know her very well, but I got a good sense in the cab.

"How fast do you want to leave this place?" I asked her.

"Not fast enough," She answered.

"Did you have dinner yet?"

"I'm starved."

Not knowing a lot about the West Side, we took a taxi back to the East Side and headed to Serafina on Madison. Perfect restaurant: not too expensive (sends the wrong signal), but not too cheap (definitely sends the wrong signal). We got our table right away, and she excused herself to go to the ladies room. When she came back I was stunned at how sexy and beautiful and tall and what a cool dresser she was. It had been a lifetime since I'd gone out with someone who looked like that. Forget the blondes. Brunette was now officially my favorite color.

We both had pasta and, believe it or not, polished off two bottles of Pinot Grigio and two glasses of champagne, barely making it down the steps of the restaurant out to the curb.

Standing on the corner of 79th and Madison, absolutely hammered and freezing my nuts off in the 20-degree weather, I gazed into her eyes and immediately concluded that I couldn't dare take her home yet. I was antsy to get her on a warm sofa (or bed if I were really lucky enough) but it was way too early in the night for a hot, sophisticated, fun-loving, single chick on New Year's Eve.

I looked around for some place to go. The only bar I knew in the area was Luke's, a sports bar. I looked at Dianne and before I suggested Luke's, I mumbled to her (and myself), "You don't look like a Luke's kind of girl." She had no idea what I was talking about. She was definitely a downtown girl. And I wasn't a downtown guy, yet.

Desperate, I looked down Madison Avenue. It was beginning to snow. I saw the awning of Café Carlyle. Normally this would be way out of my league, but I didn't want to take any chances of losing my hot, shivering Miami chick.

"Would you like to have a drink at the Carlyle?" I asked her like I did this every weekend.

"I'd love to," she politely answered.

We arrived late for the current show. Eartha Kitt was performing. "Oh, I love her," Dianne swooned. "She has the same birthday as me."

For some reason, the maître d' thought I was some kind of a big shot, and gave us a VIP banquet right next to the stage. After tipping him a week's pay, I went even further and ordered a bottle of Cristal champagne. As Eartha was crooning a jazzy, romantic song, I leaned over to Dianne and whispered, "Listen, all I can think about is kissing you, and I won't be able to enjoy any of this until we get it out of the way. I'm too nervous. So, what do you say I kiss you now and get this behind us?"

She didn't answer. I took that as an Arty Selkowitz enthusiastic yes, and leaned over and kissed her soft lips.

I felt it all the way down to my toes and other appropriate places. I leaned back into our banquet, now definitely feeling more relaxed. But something was missing. I called over our waiter. Can I get a pack of cigarettes, please?

"Eeetz against zee law, Monsieur."

"S'il vous plait, Monsieur. It's New Year's Eve." There went the second big tip of the evening.

A minute later he was back with the ceegarettes. Of course, neither of us were smokers. But on thees night I had to. I spent the rest of the evening kissing, smoking and feeling up Dianne's killer legs. We even heard some of Eartha Kitt's music.

It was now 3:00 in the morning, sufficiently late to go home. We walked the four freezing blocks back to Dianne's apartment. Approaching the elevators I stuck close to her as a baby cub would his mother. I didn't ask her if I could come up for fear of her turning me down. I just acted as matter-of-factly as I could.

Inside her apartment Dianne headed for the kitchen to get a bottle of wine. I headed for the sofa. The first kiss safely behind us, we began making out. And making out. And making out. I was torn between just leaving things the way they were—I was loving every second—or trying to be a little more adventurous. I certainly didn't want to fuck things up. This had already been the best three hours of my life.

"So, tell me more about you," Dianne asked. I filled her in on my marriage, the kids, where I worked, what a creative director does, what schools the kids went to, why my marriage had sucked, and so on and so on. "Tell me more," she asked again.

"Well, I'll tell you this, I'm not ever going to get married again."

"Huh? What did you say?"

"After all I've gone through, marriage for me is out of the question. And no more kids. Too expensive. Too difficult."

Dianne suddenly sobered up. She sat up in the couch.

"I think you can leave now."

"What? Huh? Why?"

"If that's really how you feel, I don't want anything to do with you.

I want you to leave now and don't ever call me. Just pick up your shoes and things and leave my apartment."

She went to her room and slammed the door.

*What the fuck?!* I said to myself. *What in the hell just happened?!*

I picked up my things and left.

Walking home I reflected on the best-worst date of my life. *How do I salvage this? I really, really like this girl.*

The next day, against my shrink's advice about staying away from a rebound relationship, I stopped at a phone booth on the way to the Berkshires and called her. I got her answering machine. I hung up.

*Now what do I do?*

*Oh, screw it, I'll leave her a message.* I called back.

"I don't know about you, but I had a great time last night."

It seemed to work.

Three months later, standing in line in Starbucks at 66th and Third, I did the most romantic thing I've ever done in my life.

"Hey, Dianne?" I said.

"Yes."

"Would you like to marry me?"

Everyone in earshot was shocked to hear my proposal. After all, who in their right mind asks someone to marry them standing in line at a Starbucks?

Who gives a fuck? She said yes.

# 36 THE KID IS KING.
# LONG LIVE THE KING.

After playing at this game for nearly four decades, I was long overdue for some much-needed R&R. What began as a two-month holiday turned into a year's sabbatical. It was the first time I hadn't worked since before I'd been put on probation at NYU a lifetime ago and my dad said I had to work for my college tuition.

I enjoyed every minute of my time off. I read, wrote, sculpted, taught copywriting at NYU, got back into serious photography and knocked eight big strokes off my golf handicap. But best of all, I did a lot of daydreaming.

From as early as I can remember I was a world-class daydreamer. I could turn it on and off like a car engine; during school, sermons, standing in line at the passport bureau and during long lectures from parents, bosses or teachers. For creative souls like me, dreaming isn't just a pleasant diversion. It's a necessity. Art directors, copywriters, designers, film directors, photographers, fine artists, musicians and the like need to be able to close their eyes (or not) and let their imagination transport them to a place where up is down, right is left, in is out, round is flat, serious is funny and bad is good, where implausible feats are routine and where, in the privacy of your own mind, you can ask a million "what if" questions without embarrassment.

The "Kid"—that gloriously eager, rambunctious, curious, fearless inner child—in each of us reigns over the part of the brain that's in charge of creative thinking. That is where imagination flourishes.

Your Kid doesn't know the meaning of fear, and refuses to accept the dull and commonplace. He knows that in order to create earth-shattering ideas, conventional rules have to be broken. In point of fact your Kid lives to break the rules. Intuitively, I understood that in order to solve challenging marketing and advertising problems I had to look deep inside, to my Kid. Breaking the rules came as naturally to me as breathing. Most of the time for the good. Sometimes for the bad.

When coming up with a campaign I like to think in threes. If I can create three distinct approaches under one big umbrella concept, then I know I've achieved something.

On the other side of the brain lives the Kid's nemesis: the "Adult." Cautious, logical and oh-so-smugly rational, the last thing the Adult wants is to take risks. He longs for safety and order.

The Adult abhors controversy. He's equipped with a hair-trigger sensor, like a new BMW parked on the street at three a.m., its ear-piercing alarm shattering the night. Bold ideas scare the piss out of the Adult; where your Kid will crush the ball out of the park, your Adult will bunt.

But the Adult's most fatal flaw is his deathly fear of looking silly, the single greatest barrier to creativity. His internal caution switch instinctively shuts down any original thought or action that might bring on the scorn of critics. Scared to look foolish and terrified to say or even think something that's off the wall, the Adult stifles any chance of fresh, innovative thinking.

The problem is that unless we're seriously nuts, the Adult is always present. What we need to do is learn how to corral him (or her), to lock him away somewhere and not let him out until it's too late to do any harm. There's a time and a place for the Adult, but it's not while we're trying to break through creativity's brick walls. It takes an enormous amount of concentration, discipline and commitment to quiet the Adult.

Of course, even a nearly-irrepresible Kid like mine cannot ignore the Adult entirely. Logic and reason play a necessary role in problem solving. Lord knows I needed every bit of my left-brain when working with complex products like computers, software and, ugh, financial services products. But at the end of the day, understanding an issue, no matter how complex, is just the price of admission. The goal is original thought, and the only way to achieve that is to lasso your Adult and cut your Kid loose.

Brilliant thinking requires chutzpah as Bill Bernbach taught us during his Creative Revolution. It also requires unshakeable determination and resilience; there are a million Adults out there licking their chops to give you 27 good reasons to kill your idea.

We have become a risk-averse society; the current state of advertising, like so many other businesses and institutions, is a reflection of that. In this conservative climate, made even more tenuous by the worldwide recession, it is way too easy to kill off intrepid advertising. God help us if a lawyer or network censor has to sign off on a ballsy campaign, because by the time he's finished your idea will be so watered down the paper will be wet. We need to protect our work like it's a priceless Rembrandt.

As onerous as the creative process is, this is only Part I of our job. Part II is selling your brainchild. After all, what good is a dazzling idea if no one gets to see it? (If a tree falls in a forest…) Creativity for creativity's sake is commercially useless. Clients are paying you to be right—and you need to prove that day in and day out. Convincing someone to buy into a bold approach can be almost as challenging as creating it. Business-minded folks often have difficulty connecting to more esoteric, outside-the-lines thinking; you have to help them make the mental leap, which can require being bilingual in Kid and Adult.

I've always found that the best way to get a client on board with your advertising is to first get them on board with the strategy. Strategy is rational, logical and something they're comfortable with. It's their sandbox—and they're used to playing there. So start with that. Grease the skids for your concept.

Bookstores are brimming with "how-to" tomes on selling…but selling is not a science. It's an art. Salesmanship requires finding your own "voice" and shaping your unique style, be it low-key, cerebral or exuberant. I view the art of salesmanship as finding a way to make the other person feel comfortable about that which they're innately uncomfortable. Find something in the work that they can relate to. Draw on a strategic fact. Look for common ground. I often use humor to put a client at ease. No, I don't tell jokes—I just talk about the storyboard, print ad, Internet idea or website in a witty, upbeat way. Humor can go a long way in breaking down barriers.

But no matter what your presentation style, the single most important thing you can do is show unwavering conviction in your idea. Clients are always watching and testing, trying to determine our level of commitment. Show it to them. I never walk into a client meeting without believing that I will soon be walking out with their signature on the "approved" line.

In its purest form, the creative process is no different today than it was when Bernbach, Ally, Wells or Ogilvy roamed the halls. It still requires the stubborn tenacity to dig deep. You have to write, rewrite and rewrite some more, until your concept leaps off the page or screen and grabs the consumer by the scruff of the neck.

But there's one teeny-weeny catch in all this Kid stuff: that adorable little Kid of ours isn't always well behaved. Along with his productive, creative side can lurk an immature, belligerent side that's hell-bent on causing mischief. In my case, the dark side of my Kid was every bit as developed as his productive counterpart. I was stubborn, rebellious, hot-tempered, narcissistic, petulant, sarcastic, impatient, angry, sadistic, intolerant, arrogant, contrary, temperamental, cynical and, every so often, delusional.

The laws of physics also applied. For every great idea I developed, there was an equal and opposite demon that often came with it. My quandary was to figure out how to gain access to my creative side without dredging up my smartass destructive side. Much to my chagrin, my overpaid, overworked team of psychiatrists dealt with this problem for years with unspectacular results. Hard as I tried, my immature self often got in the way. I wasn't happy about this, but I must confess my Kid was utterly thrilled.

I ultimately came to the conclusion that it was more important for me to be insanely creative than sane. And that my therapists, family, coworkers, girlfriends, tennis and golf buddies, teachers and every authority figure I ever came across would just have to deal with it and fuck off. Yes, I could have comported myself with more maturity. I certainly would have saved myself a lot of grief, hair and Pepto-Bismol, not to mention the thousands I spent therapy. But what's the fun in that?

Thinking back over my 40 years in the business, I've come to an important conclusion: the emotional idiosyncrasies that caused me so much trouble during my career were the very same traits that helped me become such a success. Was it worth all the pain I put myself (and others) through? Well, that depends on who's answering the question…My Adult or my Kid?

# 37 SO NOW WHAT?

One of the larger questions we need to ask ourselves is, why was the advertising that came out of the Creative Revolution of the 60s and 70s (and into the 80s) so much more original and powerful than what we see today?

For starters, clients back then were more entrepreneurial and more willing to take risks. The very best CEOs made the big, important advertising decisions by themselves. They innately understood that greatness could not be achieved by committee. It required leadership and vision from the person at the top with no compromises, no watering down daring ideas and no splitting the difference between corporate factions.

These business leaders trusted their gut and refused to be swayed. Indeed if my tagline for Burroughs had to be approved by a committee, it likely would have read, "The question isn't who's bigger. It's who's better in several small areas." My line for WNBC Radio would have turned out something like, "If we weren't so mischievous, we wouldn't be so entertaining."

Additionally, in the 60s and 70s we had training programs for young art directors and copywriters. When they finally learned their craft, they were assigned to a creative group and a hands-on mentor who guided them along, like my Charlie Moss, Carl Ally, Dave Altschiller, Marty Puris, Ralph Ammirati, Howie Cohen, Bob Pasqualina, Lois Korey and, yes, even Allen Kay.

These creative stars set the bar so high it was barely visible from earth. I wore out carpets going back and forth from my office to theirs… until I finally got the ad right. They also did something in their client relationships we seldom see today. They fought ferociously for what they believed in, often standing up to a client at their own or their agency's peril. My God, sometimes they actually told the client, "No."

But the biggest reason for such an overwhelming difference was the time spent collaborating, commiserating and killing each other until they'd emerged with a jewel like Alka-Seltzer's "I can't believe I ate the whole thing." Or Volkswagen's "How does the man who drives the snowplow get to the snowplow?"

Today, the technical and executional capabilities of the computer, stunning as they are, often pass for the idea itself. But as the lady in the old Wendy's commercials used to say, "Where's the beef?"

An entire generation of young talent has grown up not really understanding the difference between a great execution and a great concept. How could they? No one made the effort to teach them.

This is not to say that the new millennium hasn't had its share of exceptional advertising. It has MasterCard's "Priceless," Geico's "So easy a caveman can do it," "Got Milk?" E-Trade's "Baby," the brilliant and enduring "Absolut Vodka" campaign, FedEx's "Relax, It's FedEx," and my personal favorite, Dos Equis' "The most interesting man in the world," to name a few.

It's just that the truly groundbreaking, can't-get-it-out-of-my-head stuff seems to occur less frequently, and doesn't have quite the lasting originality of advertising's golden age.

Creating a luminous piece of advertising from a blank sheet of paper or computer screen is the scariest thing a creative person faces. It takes courage, stamina, tenacity—and one last crucial ingredient. Passion.

It's what keeps you up at night thinking, yet paradoxically has you jumping out of bed early to get to work.

It's what fuels you to slog it out until four a.m. with your editor, photographer, music house or by yourself in a park with your trusty laptop, until you've finally nailed the problem.

It's why you obsess over an edit, a piece of music, a voice-over announcer or an actor who blew his lines and fucked up your award-winning spot.

It's why you tell all the naysayers to buzz off.

It's what gives you the nerve to tell your client who keeps bringing in frightful suggestions from her husband, "Thanks, but no thanks."

It's why something is never quite finished.

Passion enables us, as Apple said, to "think different." Passion compels us to follow in the footsteps of the Energizer bunny and "keep going and going and…" And passion that, when we've been hit with a hellish project and are ready to give up, implores us to stop bitching and, as Nike says, "Just do it."

Fortunately, passion is one thing I have in spades. What I lacked in sanity, I made up in passion. And I thank the same heaven that Brother Dominic was in cahoots with that I found a profession that values— no, demands—it. Because after 40 death-defying years on Madison Avenue, there is one thing I'm absolutely certain of: Neither God, nor the NYC Highways Department, has created another road I would rather have traveled.

www.ingramcontent.com/pod-product-compliance
Lightning Source LLC
LaVergne TN
LVHW041151080426
835511LV00006B/555